Also by Peter H. Michael

Running on Empty: Along an Epic 12,000-Mile Road Trip America Has Its Say on Economic Inequality

eLit Gold Medal in Political and Economic Affairs
eLit Bronze Medal for Travel Essays

Michael on the road listens to Americans better than anyone since Walt Whitman, John Steinbeck, or Bill Moyers.

BOOK CRITIC RONALD PRIMEAU

In his vivid descriptive style, prize-winning author Peter Michael recounts his classic 12,000-mile road trip taking in the expansive variety of people and places of the United States. Michael set out not to fathom the country "in search of America" as Steinbeck, Kerouac and others had but to listen to America tell him what it might. Tell it did.

❦

Remembering John Hanson: A Biography of the First President of the Original United States Government

eLit Silver Medal in Biography
USA Best Book Finalist Award in Biography

The first comprehensive biography of "the most forgotten major figure in American history," reading this volume is enriching. Michael's narrative is a torrent of information in fine detail, a rich trove on a major historical figure.

KIRKUS REVIEWS

Two national book prizes were awarded to what has come to be called the definitive biography of the first president of the original United States government chartered under the Articles of Confederation. Deeply researched, *Remembering John Hanson* chronicles the life of this crucial Revolutionary War figure to whom George Washington reported, and re-illuminates Hanson's two pivotal nation-saving triumphs as the nation struggled to be born.

Palace of Yawns: How the United Nations Failed Poor Nations in the Population Explosion

Independent Publisher Book Award
IPPY Silver Medal in Foreign Affairs

Palace of Yawns is a fast-moving, remarkably adventurous journal of the year Peter Michael spent in Thailand fully engaged in the cultural and historical time and place that Southeast Asia was in 1975 while directing a key multinational United Nations program. Khmer Rouge, Bangkok diplomatic nightlife, tranquil Buddhist monks, Thai princesses, Soviet spies, cave temples, cobras, a Nobel Prize and more fill these pages. In some places, the reader will find it hard to believe that *Palace of Yawns* is nonfiction.

❦

Guide to Freedom: Rediscovering the Underground Railroad In One United States County

An expert compilation of research by the author and others of more than sixty rediscovered Underground Railroad safehouses, routes and personages of Frederick County, Maryland, and nearby, *Guide to Freedom* uses a groundbreaking method for assessing the authenticity of Underground Railroad site claims. *Guide to Freedom* provides detailed entries on several of the nation's most important Underground Railroad sites nearby including the actual Uncle Tom's Cabin, and several highly charged local accounts of Underground Railroad escapes.

❦

All Peter Michael books may be ordered at Amazon.com, peterhmichael.com, or anywhere books are sold. *First Explorer* may be purchased there or at the book's website, FirstExplorer.us.

About the Author

Award-winning author Peter Michael grew up on four continents and worked in a fifth in a career of writing, international advisory roles, and university teaching.

With three of his eight books having won national book prizes, he has appeared on C-SPAN, National Public Radio, ABC News, America Untold, Home & Garden TV, High Noon Entertainment, and in numerous publications.

A graduate of the University of Maryland, Berkeley and Princeton, he has taught at the graduate level in the United States, Japan, Thailand and Costa Rica.

Peter Michael and his wife Vicki, a painter, live on a historic Maryland farm founded in 1768 by the youngest son of the subject of *First Explorer*. The farm is powered entirely by sun and wind.

———— First Explorer ————

First Explorer

A biography of the young Swiss humanitarian who in the early 1700s was first to explore beyond the Atlantic coast, then settled thousands of European refugees to America

Peter H. Michael

FIRST EDITION

Underground Railroad Free Press · 2022

First Explorer

FIRST EXPLORER

Underground Railroad Free Press
2455 Ballenger Creek Pike
Adamstown, Maryland, 21710, USA
info@urrfreepress.com

FIRST EXPLORER

Copyright © 2022 Peter H. Michael

All rights reserved. Except in cases of brief quotations embodied in critical articles or reviews, no part of this book may be used or reproduced in any manner without the express prior permission of the author. Email phm@peterhmichael.com for permission or information.

Book website   FirstExplorer.us
Author website   peterhmichael.com
Author appearances   phm@peterhmichael.com
Editing   WordSpectrum.com

Library of Congress Control Number: 2022902788
Library of Congress Cataloging-in-Publication Data
Michael, Peter H.
First Explorer: A biography of the young Swiss humanitarian who in the early 1700s was first to explore beyond the Atlantic coast, then settled thousands of European refugees to America
Includes bibliographic references and index
   1. Frantz Ludwig Michel (1675-1746?). 2. United States— Explorers. 3. United States—Colonial History. 4. United States— Immigration—1607-1760. 5. United States— Colonial History— Refugees. 6. United States— Maps—1704.

Flesch Reading Ease index:: 43.2
Flesch-Kincaid grade level: early college

ISBN Hardcover   978-1-7923-8574-2
ISBN Paperback   978-1-7923-8573-5
ISBN ebook   978-1-7923-8575-9

The book cover's map was drawn by Swiss explorer and humanitarian Frantz Ludwig Michel during his 1704 exploration of the mid-Atlantic Appalachians, the first by a European beyond the Atlantic seaboard. The exploration and map opened America to settlement beyond the Atlantic into the Appalachians.

First Explorer

FIRST EXPLORER

First Explorer is dedicated to the many generations
of Michels, then Michaels, who have gone before,
to my children, Shanti, Alexandra and Hanson,
and to the family's generations yet to come.

May *First Explorer* bring back to life for
readers everywhere the remarkable
life story of Frantz Ludwig Michel
who became Francis Michael.

First Explorer

First Explorer

On Frantz Ludwig Michel

The most important American traveler of his time. Extraordinary, ingenious, indefatigable America explorer. Michel's idea is that of a humanitarian: establishment of a refuge for people in times of need. His is an uncommon idea, not only for his times.
           Historian Andreas Mielke

❦

On His Humanitarianism

The meaning of life is to find your gift.
The purpose of life is to give it away.
           Pablo Picasso

There is no question that there is more obligation that those who have should give to those who have nothing.
       Audrey Hepburn as UNICEF Goodwill Ambassador

❦

On His Explorations

Exploration is really the essence of the human spirit.
          Astronaut Frank Borman

Exploration is in our nature.
We began as wanderers, and we are wanderers still.
          Astronomer Carl Sagan

❦

On His Vision

Sometimes it falls on a generation to be great.
           Nelson Mandela

Talent hits a target no one else can hit.
Genius hits a target no one else can see.
        Philosopher Arthur Schopenhauer

❦

First Explorer

Contents

I. An Improbable Life
- The Visionary 4
- Nobleman by Birth 6
- Explorer by Nature 11
- Humanitarian by Choice 18

II. Virginia Expedition: Testing a Vision
- Under Way 22
- Life and Death Aboard HMS Nassau 28
- Colony Founded 32
- Colony Vanished 36
- Building Boom 38
- The Naturalist Explores 41
- The Naturalist Records 44
- Native Survival Against All Odds 47

III. Twice Perilous Journey Home
- Chance Encounter? 58
- Fraught Voyage 60
- War, Sentries, Detours and Nerve 65

IV. The Dawn of Refugee Rescue
- Three Humanitarian Families 72
- The Trio's Grand Vision 74
- Michel's Choice 80

V. Maryland Expedition: Bending History
- First Beyond Atlantic Shores 83
- Better Prepared 85
- Where His Sons Would Go 90
- Vanishing Home of the Canoy 92
- Sidetrip Previews the Future 95
- Where German Pioneers Would Settle 97
- Terra Incognita 100

VI. Three Proposals
- Anna Barbara von Lerber 110
- William Penn's Quaker Refuge 115
- The British Lords of Trade and Plantations 119

VII. Second Maryland Expedition
- Proving a Vision 124
- Before Mason and Dixon 126
- Michel's Colonies That Didn't Happen 129
- Pennsylvania Detour 133

Images and Maps 139

VIII. Three Carolina Colonies
The Trying Founding of New Berne 158
Hijacked 164
Imaginary Silver 169
The Rogue 175
Fiasco 176
Last Colonies 180

IX. Searching for Frantz Ludwig Michel
The Case for Returning to Switzerland 186
The Case for Cosmopolitan London 189
Found: Francis Michael, Virginian 190
The Trio Passes On 208

X. The Lasting Sway of Michael's Nemesis
The Curse and Demise of Christoph von Graffenried 214
Graffenried's Ghost 215

XI. Francis Michael Remembered
Refugee Resettlement Bends History 224
Like None Before Him: Francis Michael's Legacy 226

XII. The Family in America
The Sons 234
Lives Refashioned on the 1760s Frontier 240
After the Four Brothers 249

Epilogue
Fates of People 256
Fates of Places 263

Acknowledgements 270

Appendices
Lords of Ralligen to Frantz Ludwig Michel 278
Swiss Social Ranks in the 1600s and 1700s 279
Timeline 1291-2022 280
Michel's 1704 Expedition Camps 298
Ritter & Company New Berne Operating Contract 299
Michel's Six Colonies and Maryland Refuge 304
Sorting Out Michel/Michael Genealogy 305
Misconceptions Corrected 312

Bibliography 316

Index 325

Endnotes 343

Illustrations, Maps, Tables, and Slideshows

Illustrations   Page
Michel von Schwertschwendi coat of arms   139
Hand-drawn front page of Michel's 1702 journal   139
Ralligen Castle exterior   140
Ralligen Castle interior   140
Portrait of Michel's grandson, Andrew Michael II   141
Portrait of Johann Rudolph Ochs   142
Ancestral home of Johann Rudolph Ochs   143
Worb Castle, home of Christoph von Graffenried   143
Michel's 1702 drawing of Indians and waterspout   145
Michel's 1702 drawing of Williamsburg's Wren Hall   146
1725 Courthouse of King William County, Virginia   147
William Penn at 22   154
Implements *circa* 1768 from Michel Foundry   155

Maps
Competing Maryland and Pennsylvania land claims   127
Michel 1702 map of Tidewater Virginia   145
Placement of Michel's first Virginia colony   147
Michel's 1704 map of western Maryland   148
Michel's 1704 map of western Maryland, annotated   149
Placement of Frederick County in Maryland   149
First map of New Bern, North Carolina   151
Graffenried's map of Potomac River and environs   152
Migration routes of German-speaking refugees   153
Map of Michel's six colonies and Maryland refuge   154
Map of Michel's 1704 side trip   155
Areas in America settled by German-speaking refugees   225

Tables
German-to-English translation of Michel's 1704 map   87
Periods when Michel was known to be in America   195
The Lords of Ralligen by generation   278
Swiss social ranks in the 1600s and 1700s   279
Timeline of Michel/Michael's life   280
Michel's 1704 Maryland expedition camps   298
Michel's six colonies and Maryland refuge   304

Slideshows
Mac Users   tinyurl.com/FEKeynote
Non-Mac Users   tinyurl.com/FEPowerPoint
All   tinyurl.com/FEUnanimated

First Explorer

Foreword

Frantz Ludwig Michel's is the story of a rare daring vision and driven curiosity that gave birth in the early 1700s to the world's first large-scale intercontinental resettlement of refugees. His was a life as America's first explorer beyond colonial Atlantic coast settlements, and of how his adventurousness and particularly his humanitarianism gave new lives to thousands of European refugees as they reached colonies that he had established for them in the New World. As Michel explained, he explored unknown places "to satisfy my old curiosity, to seek out unknown things and to collect the wonders of nature." Explore, seek out, and collect he did, and much more.

When I conceived of this book, I had in mind privately producing a biography for the many descendants of its subject and for libraries, schools, and historians in western Maryland where Michel was the first European explorer in 1704. While *First Explorer* as published is particularly suited to these audiences, it became obvious as research kept revealing more about Michel that his was a story so extraordinary that it deserved a wider audience beyond one family and one region of a single state.

To an extent, biographies write themselves as their subjects' lives unfold, then their biographers do their best to portray. As Michel's life evolves in these pages, we see him making breakthrough history in five of Britain's North American colonies, his native Switzerland, Great Britain, and war-wracked German-speaking areas of Europe. As the veil of three centuries is drawn back, we see Michel as the scientist that he was, as one who respected the Native Americans who he met as his human equals, as that special spiritual breed, the long-distance trekker, and most revealingly as career-long humanitarian with an extraordinarily ambitious vision. Once in sharp focus, we see Michel as Michel the visionary that he was and as glowing material for the biographer and reader. My hope is that publishing *First Explorer* for the mass market will introduce this remarkable, history-bending change-maker to a broad audience bound to appreciate him.

The conclusion of *First Explorer* discusses Michel's sons who made their own marks in America in the 1750s, settling in Maryland at two locations precisely where their father had explored and noted on his landmark 1704 map. Because of conflicting material found in researching *First Explorer* as to whether the four settlers were actually Michel's sons, an appendix here analyzes the fatherhood in depth. While no conclusive proof is known after three centuries confirming one, perhaps two, of the father-son relationships, a provisional body of evidence points to the relationships as presented here.

If Michel did father the youngest son attributed to him, the author is a fifth-great-grandson of Frantz Ludwig and Anna von Lerber Michel. Particularly because I am a Michel/Michael family descendant of the subject of this biography, I have taken special pains to stay away from writing flavor which might appear hagiographic. I have asked reviewers of *First Explorer* to be especially watchful on this score and they report no transgressions into undue praise, avoidance of critical assessment, or familial favors. I have not been reluctant to take Frantz Ludwig Michel to task in instances in which he erred, which weren't many.

At the same time, I have found that it was not always easy to write with an objective hand given a subject who accomplished so much of importance and deserves far more recognition than he has received. In this circumstance, I have made special effort to give Frantz Ludwig Michel his complete biographical due while at the same time avoiding embellishment. This has not always been a simple balancing act. *First Explorer* would have been easier to write if I were not related to Frantz Ludwig Michel.

The reader will notice that the name of the capital of Switzerland is sometimes spelled as Berne and other times as Bern. At some time in the past, the accepted spelling changed from Berne to Bern, the form used today. References here to the city during the era when Frantz Ludwig

— First Explorer —

Michel lived in the late seventeenth and eighteenth centuries use the spelling of the time, Berne. When referring to the modern city, Bern is used.

Retaining focus in writing *First Explorer* required a measure of brevity. A more detailed biography of Frantz Ludwig Michel could have included additional material on his many diplomatic dealings with the British government in London and colonial governors in America. But the tedium and minutiae of lengthy official transactions would have bogged down the book unnecessarily and detracted from its intended focus to portray the lively person who Michel was and how he affected the destiny of thousands. Those wanting deeper detail into Michel's bureaucratic dealings are referred to the very professionally researched work of Andreas Mielke and Sandra Yelton listed in the bibliography.

Before moving on, it would pay to have a brief tutorial on the pronunciation of the Michel name and to point out incorrect assumptions about it in some of the sources cited here. To most English speakers, Michel would be assumed to be the French name pronounced mee-SHEL. However, the Michel family here is German-speaking Swiss, and the surname is pronounced in the German as **mee-KEL**. Switzerland then and now has had German, French, Italian and Romansh as its native languages, reflecting the country's ancient ethno-linguistic make-up. German is the most spoken language in Switzerland.

In his 1916 articles on Frantz Ludwig Michel in *The Virginia Magazine of History and Biography,* author William Hinke mistakenly referred to Michel in the French as Francis Louis Michel. In the United States, Hinke's seminal work became a go-to source for some scholars and others, and Hinke's error sometimes stuck in their later writings. Apparently, Hinke picked up the error from the Swiss petition to Britain to grant Michel permission to found colonies in America. The petition was written in French, the diplomatic language of the time, with Michel's name in French.

FIRST EXPLORER

English-speaking colonial officials with whom Michel dealt in South Carolina in 1712 referred in writing to Michel in the English as Louis Mitchell, and this name, too, has persisted occasionally to the present. However, sometime after Michel took British citizenship in 1709, he did Anglicize his name by 1718 to Francis Michael, which he went by for the rest of his life In *First Explorer*, our man is referred to by his birth name, Frantz Ludwig Michel, up until he is forty-three in 1718 by which time he goes by Francis Michael, his adopted American name.

Abundant evidence of the Michel name originating as German comes from the German given names in the family from the thirteenth century to the children and grandchildren of Frantz Ludwig Michel in America; from marriages only to German-surnamed women almost exclusively over the same span even into the family's third American generation; from still-spoken German by American descendants into the twentieth century; and from handed-down German recipes still in use today among Michel's American descendants. Recent DNA analysis of a Frantz Ludwig Michel direct descendant shows Celtic Swiss but no French ancestry.

In his American travels, Frantz Ludwig Michel interacted with at least eight Indian tribes ranging from Pennsylvania to the Carolinas. His journal entries during his first exploration in Virginia during 1702 make it clear that Michel approached Native Americans with an open-minded acceptance of them as his human equals. When he received his large Virginia land grant that year that included the traditional lands of the Mattaponi and Pamonkey nations, Michel did not chase them off as was the growing practice of European settlers but welcomed them to stay and included himself among them as their neighbor. The direct result of this peaceful inclusion was the two tribes being the only two existing in Virginia today recognized by the federal government.

Michel befriended the Canoy during his 1704 exploration of western Maryland and the Shenandoah Valley, respected a treaty with the Conestogas of Pennsylvania in 1708, prevented the slaughter of a Tuscarora village in South Carolina in 1712, and generally befriended America's original inhabitants in his characteristically humanitarian way. Michel's encounters with Native Americans were so regular that they ended up comprising such a significant current in *First Explorer* as to deserve commentary in the book's epilogue and timeline appendix where the fates of the eight tribes Michel dealt with are recorded.

Early in Michel's time in America, he co-founded the colony of New Bern, North Carolina with another Swiss figure, Christoph von Graffenried. Their strained relationship and Graffenried's sad downfall, being an important chapter in Michel's story, are presented factually here and could not be made complimentary to Graffenried. Having to dredge up Graffenried's tumultuous life cannot be pleasant reading for his living descendants who include accomplished and distinguished people, for example the mayor of Bern, Switzerland, as of this writing. I want to extend my respect to this long-illustrious Swiss family for what of historical necessity has been included here about one of their ancestors.

Peter H. Michael
Adamstown, Maryland

November, 2022

Suggestion to the Reader

Because *First Explorer* proceeds along the multiple lines of Frantz Ludwig Michel's life, his wife's, refugee resettlement, war, and other strands, the reader may find it advantageous to begin with the timeline provided as an appendix here.

First Explorer

First Explorer

First Explorer

A biography of the Swiss humanitarian Frantz Ludwig Michel, first to explore beyond the Atlantic coast, who in the 1700s resettled thousands of European refugees to America

FIRST EXPLORER

First Explorer

1. An Improbable Life

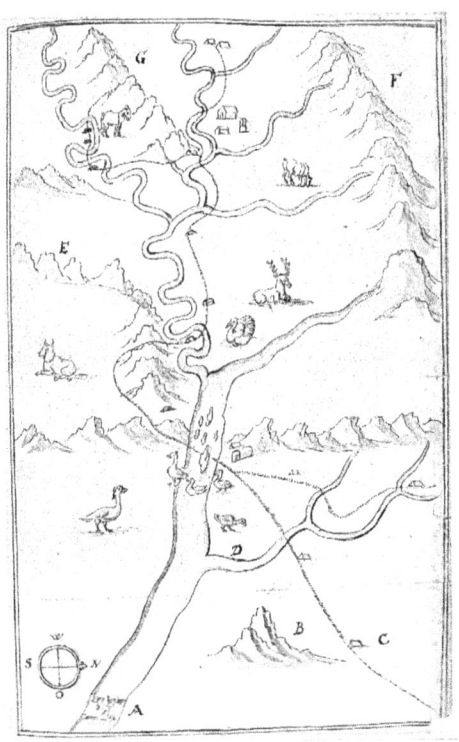

Frantz Ludwig Michel's map of his epic 1704 exploration of western Maryland and the Shenandoah Valley

The Visionary

Today it would seem unimportant to most as to when in life newborns would be formally received into their family religion, but for 300 years the timing of this was a life-or-death proposition in Europe.

Within two decades after the Protestant Reformation began in 1517, several Protestant denominations had adopted the belief that baptism should occur only after a person had become old enough to understand and consent to its meaning. This was at odds with the practice of Europe's major Protestant denominations and the Roman Catholic Church which all baptized infants shortly after birth.

The political implication of adult baptism was growth of a third-way movement that had the potential to drain off membership from the two dominant religions. As much of a threat were the new groups' spreading beliefs of pacifism and leave-taking from civic life, which in the minds of those holding power posed direct challenge to established order.

Opponents of these new sects began referring to them collectively as Anabaptists, from the Greek *ana-*, against. Included under the Anabaptist umbrella term were Mennonites, Hutterites, Amish and Quakers—the major sects practicing adult baptism—and offshoots of these.

By the 1600s persecution of Anabaptists by both church and state was in full swing with the most common method of suppression the execution of Anabaptist leaders. As others stepped up to lead, suppression was extended to ordinary parishioners with horrific results. In 1660, the Dutch writer Thieleman van Braght documented Anabaptist persecution of more than 4,000 executions by imprisonment, burning, stoning, drowning, and even live burials, numbers that only accelerated into the 1700s.

Religious persecution of Anabaptists became widespread in Europe with only a few places offering refuge and then only sparingly. German-speaking areas where Anabaptist doctrine seemed to have greatest appeal became prime hot spots for persecution, especially Switzerland, Alsace and along the Rhine River in the German-speaking area of the Federation of the Rhine.

By 1700 in Switzerland, persecution had long been official and ruthless, often involving draconian measures of imprisonment, involuntary expulsion from Switzerland, confiscation of property without compensation, extraction of an emigration tax upon eviction, and loss of citizenship. Those caught re-entering Switzerland after expulsion were subject to life in prison or execution.[1]

Bearing the brunt of this overt religious persecution was Switzerland's sizable Mennonite community concentrated around Berne, the political center of Switzerland's confederation of twenty-six jurisdictions called cantons. However, while the Great Council of Berne—the Berne canton's governing body—was enforcing its policy of expulsion against the canton's Mennonites, by 1700 significant opposition to the practice had arisen among many in the general populace including some of the influential.

In 1701, into the maelstrom strode three well-positioned Bernese Protestants having family relationships with Mennonites, determined to alleviate the suffering among their in-laws and friends. Within a decade, the three would create an organization of refugee rescue and relocation on a scale never before conceived, found friendly American colonies to receive refugees, and arrange refugee transport to the distant new continent by a public-private partnership far ahead of its time. What the trio would create would take on a permanent life of its own in the 1700s and eventually evolve to become the United States Federal Refugee Resettlement Program very active today. All three men would devote the rest of their lives as humanitarians bettering—or outright saving—the lives of thousands of European religious and war refugees.

The role of the youngest of the trio, barely in his mid-twenties at the turn of the eighteenth century, was to explore the New World for suitable refugee resettlement sites and establish friendly colonies there to receive refugees rescued by his two associates in Berne. Resulting in six such colonies, his American explorations were the first westward by a European into the American interior beyond the Atlantic seaboard and two generations before those by the next deep explorer, Daniel Boone. The young scientist-explorer would accomplish his six history-bending refugee colony foundings in a brief fourteen years as the resettlement experiment began playing out in full.

This is the story of Frantz Ludwig Michel, later in life to become Francis Michael, the all but forgotten humanitarian hero of earliest American exploration, who planted the first seed of transcontinental refugee resettlement.

Nobleman by Birth

Frantz Ludwig Michel descended from a long line of Swiss nobility dating at least as far back as the fourteenth century to one Itel Michel von Schwertschwendi, the Lord of Ralligen, of Berne Canton in the Swiss Confederation, the name of Switzerland at the time.[2] From the Confederation's coalescing in the thirteenth century until the establishment of the unified Swiss federal state in 1848, each canton of the confederation was a fully sovereign republic with its own nobility, customs, border controls, military and currency, an arrangement similar in some respects to the European Union today.

The hereditary Michel title of Lord dates back at least to the time of Itel Michel and the closer association of the Swiss fiefdoms after the year 1291 when the Swiss Federal Charter began allying Swiss cantons, and apparently before that when the fiefdoms were parts of the Holy Roman Empire. Beginning in 1291, the new Swiss federation titled certain local Lords as *Landvogt* and charged them with administering a canton or group of cantons on behalf of the new Swiss central authority in Berne and serving as judges for capital crimes. The closest English language equivalent to the landvogt title would be a state governor or mayor of a large city.

From 1415 on during the reign of Itel's son, Lord Berthold Michel von Schwertschwendi, the Lords of Ralligen held the title of landvogt and were responsible for governing cantons to which they were assigned. For example, Berthold was assigned as the Landvogt of Burgdorf, a district ten miles from Berne and twenty-five miles from Berthold's home at Ralligen. At the time, a landvogt need not permanently reside in the place of which he was landvogt.

From at least the time of Lord Berthold Michel von Schwertschwendi, the Michel family consorted in noble circles including European royalty. Aside from the author, among Berthold Michel's direct descendants today are King Charles of Great Britain and Juan Carlos, former King of Spain. Both are fifteenth-great-grandsons of Lord Berthold Michel von Schwertschwendi.[3]

The German Schwertschwendi means "wasting sword," wasting in the sense of dispatching, eliminating or fateful.

"Lord" is a title within the classes of European nobility ranking below royalty. Dating back to the Middle Ages, the title Lord is one of the most ancient and prevalent of noble titles. In the feudal system of the Middle Ages, a Lord was the ruler within a kingdom of a prescribed area or domain of serf fiefdoms, which he controlled and usually owned outright. There would be multiple Lords within a kingdom but only one king or queen, and only they and their prescribed blood relations would be classified as royalty. However, Switzerland, being a confederation of republics at the time and since, never had royalty and was therefore not a kingdom though it was governed largely by those with noble titles.

Seven generations after Itel Michel, we come to the father of our explorer, David Michel von Schwertschwendi (1634-1696), who served in a series of high capacities, first as the Lord of Ralligen after the death of David's father, also named David Michel. Ralligen is an estate twenty-five miles (forty kilometers) southeast of Bern, within the Bern Canton, along the north coast of the *Thunersee*, Lake Thun, a large lake at the foothills of the High Alps. Ralligen castle served as the estate's and the Michel family's manor house from at least the fourteenth century from which it dates and is where Frantz Ludwig Michel is believed to have been born and raised. Two views of the home are shown in the center pictorial pages here. Today Ralligen castle is a Swiss national historic landmark operated by monks of the Christustraegern Bruderschaft, the Christ-bearers Brotherhood, as a guest house and retreat.[4]

From 1673, Lord David Michel served as a member of the Great Council of Berne (as it was spelled then), the equivalent either of a national parliament if one takes Berne as a sovereign independent entity at the time, or of a state legislature if one regards the Swiss Confederation as having been more of a unifying entity then. In 1682, perhaps simultaneously with his Great Council tenure, David Michel was appointed as Landvogt of Gottstatt, a stewardship of Berne Canton. In Switzerland, a canton is the nation's top-level administrative unit, the equivalent a state in the United States or a province in other countries. A stewardship is the equivalent of a United States county or large municipality. Since 1848 Berne (now Bern) has been the Swiss national capital.

In 1667, David married Ursula Fels in Bremgarten, Switzerland. The couple had ten children, the fifth of whom was our explorer, Frantz Ludwig Michel, the apparent heir to the title of Lord of Ralligen. Another of David's sons, Johann Ludwig Michel, became Lord of Aarau and Revenue Commissioner in Yverdon, then and now a pleasant assignment because of its hot springs and baths dating to Roman times. David's daughter, Johanna Esther, married Abraham Wild, the Landvogt of Buchsee. In an era of extreme elite privilege, worse even than in the United States today, the Michel von Schwertschwendi clan was able for at least six centuries to use its own blood lines to preserve advantage.

FIRST EXPLORER

Dying in 1696 at sixty-two, Lord David Michel von Schwertschwendi did not live long enough to know of the unprecedented exploits to come for his son, Frantz Ludwig Michel, then twenty-one, who would cross an ocean to explore a far distant continent five years thence and go on to rescue or cause the rescue of thousands of persecuted Mennonite and European war refugees.[5]

Frantz Ludwig was born July 24, 1675, almost certainly at the family home at Ralligen, and was baptized five days later.[6] Most likely, the young Frantz was schooled by tutors as was the custom of aristocratic families at the time.

It is easy to imagine that the explorer in him was baked in at birth and that growing up the young Frantz hiked the nearby mountains at the foot of the Alps with local trailheads literally a short walk from Ralligen's back door. At Ralligen, Michel grew up at the foot of the Emmental Alps, a major sub-range of the Swiss Alps. Residents of Ralligen and nearby can walk from their homes and in minutes be on trails leading to the 6,729-foot Sigriswiler Rothorn and Mount Burgfeldstand, at 6,768 feet the highest point in the area.

Later in 1704 as he would hike along the base of Maryland's Catoctin Mountain and further on gaze up into Virginia's Massanutten Range, he must have fondly reminisced about his much higher mountains at home. On his returns to Ralligen, perhaps using the relic of his Maryland expedition knapsack, it is easy to imagine that Frantz took off again taking hikes up behind his castle and into the Alps. Why wouldn't he? There is, and likely was then, good skiing up there, too.

Once it sets in, one's love of long-distance hiking tends never to abate. For some, the lure of the trail sets in deep on that first multi-day hike, as the far wilderness horizon beckons, and embers of the night campfire summon reflections that can seldom surface in the usual day-to-day humdrum. Not all to be sure, but some who experience this utterly fresh take on life never want to go too long without it ever again. For the ultimately hooked, lives get rearranged to open the way for multi-day through-hiking. For them, backpacking in quiet beautiful realms becomes a spiritual undertaking and a must. For Swiss hikers, the Alps, their continent's highest range, lie at their doorstep. For Americans, there are the border-to-border Pacific Crest and Continental Divide Trails and the Georgia-to-Maine Appalachian Trail, which Michel would cross on his epic 1704 exploration of western Maryland and Virginia's Shenandoah Valley.

By his fondness in reporting his explorations, Frantz Ludwig Michel leaves little doubt that he was an enamored long-distance hiker. His 1702 journal, 1704 map,. and the inferences possible from them make plain that he liked, even reveled in, "being out there." When he reached as far as he wanted to go up the north branch of the Shenandoah River and turned around in 1704, he had seen enough to form conclusions about the territory and could have begun his trek back to Annapolis. Instead, he went overland to the south branch of the river, hiked upstream along it just to see what was there (more of the same), and then decided for the adventure of it to climb Massanutten Mountain, the most strenuous thing he would do on his exploration.

On a history-altering sidetrip during this exploration, he did not have to divert from his planned route to make the sidetrip up Maryland's Monocacy Plain, but his "old curiosity" called and off he went, finding beautiful places where his sons would choose to settle a generation later.

In the Shenandoah Valley and the sidetrip we see in full flower the curiosity of the long-distance hiker in Michel, who seemed glued to the horizon as avid hikers are. *What's over that next mountain there, and the one beyond that?*

Author William Hinke states that, "In his early life Michel had a military training. He probably served as an army officer, as his whole later conduct, as well as his interest in military affairs, point in that direction."[7] A later researcher expands on this, stating, "For a while Frantz Ludwig fought for the 'Sun King' Louis XIV most likely in the Regiment Erlach, a regiment raised in Bern in 1672. This was not an uncommon experience, as Swiss men had served under the *fleurs-de-lis* for more than two centuries and would continue to do so for another 120 years. Possibly at the end of the War of the League of Augsburg in October 1699, Michel returned to Berne."[8] However, Frantz Ludwig Michel's having seen combat is doubted by yet other scholars including Andreas Mielke, who had compiled the deepest work on Michel.

When and where Frantz acquired his scientific education are not clear from any sources examined here, but that he did is evident in his writing by his commentary and drawings, astute for their time, on botany, zoology, anthropology, geography, cartography, and geology, among other disciplines. Unless he had gone abroad, he would have studied at one of the three Swiss universities existing in the late seventeenth century, the universities of Basel founded in 1460, Lausanne (1537), or Geneva (1559). Given the emphases in his 1701-02 travel diary, Frantz appears to have concentrated his university studies in what at the time was called natural philosophy. References indicate him as being what in his era was termed a naturalist, today referred to as a scientist. That so much of what is known today in science was unknown then permitted naturalists of his time to explore interests in multiple scientific—"natural"—fields as Frantz Ludwig Michel seems to have done. The meaning of "natural" in this case is in the sense of nature.

Explorer by Nature

His most prolific researcher has described Michel as the "Extraordinary, ingenious, indefatigable America explorer" and "The most important American traveler of his time."[9] That he was.

While the Spanish had explored what would become the American Southwest as early as the 1500s, and the

French, Canada and along the Mississippi River by the 1600s, there was nothing at the dawn of the 1700s that could be considered Appalachian exploration of any of Britain's Atlantic seaboard colonies. As example, by 1700, nearly a century after the first English colony at Jamestown, all twelve of the Virginia colony's counties had an Atlantic shore, none was inland, and there is no record of exploration as far west as the Appalachian Range in Virginia until Michel's in 1704. Richard Thornton has catalogued eight explorations of the western reaches of the Virginia piedmont up to 1671, which resulted in exploration parties going as far west as the foot of the range's first mountain, the Blue Ridge, but then turning north or south exploring along the foothills but not up onto the mountain itself. It appears that that first range of the Appalachians was accepted as a limit not needing to be challenged.

The single possible exception among these early Virginia explorations was that of Johann Lederer in 1669. Thornton writes, "In 1669 Johann Lederer led a small party of explorers up the York River to its headwaters. They climbed to a high peak where the heart of the Shenandoah Valley could be seen. Apparently, his party did not enter the valley. He is generally described as 'the first white man to see the Shenandoah Valley.' This is probably not true. Nevertheless, there is no evidence that Lederer actually entered the valley."[10]

The same long diffidence about probing the Appalachians is true of the other English colonies along the Atlantic coast. While the Spanish and French had fanned out early wanting to know what lay beyond their original landings, the English had arrived in America and stayed put along the coast for nearly an entire century. In contrast to what was happening on the western side of the continent, when the Virginia colony needed a new capital, the new one was built only twelve miles from the old one and *closer* to the Atlantic coast. Except perhaps among a few in the halls of power in London, the English vision of its New World presence was coastal and fixed.

FIRST EXPLORER

The closest that might be claimed as inland exploration along the Atlantic seaboard was Henry Hudson's sailing up the Hudson River on September 11, 1609, but soon turning around and leaving. All of the North American explorations listed for the 1700s[11] are west of the Rocky Mountain Range until David Thompson's through Canada to the headwaters of the Mississippi River in 1798, but by then we are nearly into the nineteenth century.

Frantz Ludwig Michel's unprecedented 1704 exploration two ranges deep into the Appalachians in Maryland and Virginia would prove to be far ahead of its time. The next recorded explorer to probe the Appalachians, Daniel Boone, would not find his way through Virginia's Cumberland Gap into the wilds of Kentucky and Tennessee for another four decades. Heading west from the Atlantic, Michel was by far America's first explorer to proceed from the eastern seaboard.

However, in 1660 the Bohemian immigrant surveyor Augustine Herman was hired by Cecil Calvert, Proprietor of the Maryland colony, to survey his Maryland domain as far west as the foothills near the Appalachians. Herman spent ten years traveling extensively to produce his highly detailed 1670 map of coastal Maryland and nearby parts of Virginia, Pennsylvania, and New Jersey. One edge of his map extends as far west as the mouth of the Shenandoah River beyond which Michel would explore in 1704. Unlike the rest of his intricate map, Herman shows no detail for western Maryland, only the rivers' names. He identifies the Potomac River as such and the Shenandoah as the Acconachena, a possible corruption of "Shenandoah."

The configuration of the Shenandoah River on the Herman map is far from conforming to the river's actual geography of continuous pronounced loops that go on from its mouth 156 miles to the river's headwaters. All other places of the Herman map are dense with names of landforms, waterways including creeks, Indian communities, settler communities, counties, regions, and fine cartographic accuracy for the era, including river courses. While the map is precise in showing, for example, the location, names, and longhouse symbols of the Indian villages of coastal Maryland, none such appears for anywhere else farther west in the Maryland colony including Indian villages that Herman would have gone by on his way up the Potomac if he actually got that far. His map does show the Monocacy River which he identifies as the "Northeast Branch" of the Potomac, so he probably got at least that far but the Monocacy River is still in the Maryland piedmont well inland from where Michel would reach.

Herman may have relied on Indian reports of the large tributary of the Potomac River—the Shenandoah River—to fill out that edge of his map, as the rest of the Herman map's meticulous cartography is at odds with the bare sketchiness of how the Shenandoah River and the few western Maryland features are drawn. Further up the Potomac, Herman has it being fed by the Monongahela (his "Monanloch") River of Pennsylvania. The Monongahela River rises in far western Pennsylvania and drains westward to the Ohio River, the Mississippi River and the Gulf of Mexico. Its headwaters never join those of the Potomac. The Appalachian Range lying between the Potomac and Monongahela Rivers drains to both east and west on opposite sides of the range's crestline, the continent's eastern continental divide. In this error, Herman was doing his best to patch together the sketchy geographic knowledge of the time when Europeans had been in Maryland for only a generation.

Augustine Herman was surveying as he was appointed to do, not exploring which wasn't in his assignment. For him, it was quickly in and out of western Maryland to get the area approximated on his map if his surveying actually extended that far. It would be left to Michel thirty-four years later to produce his fully detailed map of western Maryland and Virginia's Shenandoah Valley as the result of well-documented, extended personal exploration. Michel's highly detailed 1704 map shows the twists and turns of the Shenandoah, territory well upstream from the fork of the great river, locations of Indian villages and his fifteen

FIRST EXPLORER

campsites, and three ranges deep into the Appalachians. Herman might have been the first European to set foot briefly as far west as the entry to the Appalachians, if he actually got that far, but not the first to explore there or beyond. That was left to Michel.

Augustine Herman's map, the first of Maryland, became justly acclaimed for its cartographic precision and beauty. The cartographic detail and superb draftsmanship of this map are considered among the best of American maps of the time.

From 1702 to 1716, Michel would cross the Atlantic Ocean to America multiple times. During his visits he would found six colonies for refugee resettlement, two each in Virginia and South Carolina, one in Pennsylvania and one in North Carolina. He would also extensively explore and publicize the upland piedmont of Maryland to which more refugees would find their way. The dates and locales of his explorations (E) and colony foundings (C) are these.

1702	Tidewater Virginia (55 days on site)	C E
1704-05	Maryland, the Shenandoah Valley of Virginia, and Pennsylvania	E
1707-08	Western Maryland and Pennsylvania	E
1710-11	Virginia, Pennsylvania, North Carolina	C C C
1712-13	South Carolina	C
1716	South Carolina (briefly)	C

Where Michel spent time during the intervals between his explorations and colony foundings is the enduring mystery of his life, along with when and where he died and who his children were. His own journal shows him at home in Switzerland between his first two explorations but then he becomes hard to track after his third exploration. He could have been in America, Switzerland, London where we know he was for a time, gathering refugees along the Rhine River, or all of these places. Deep research presented later here offers a few clues as to Frantz Ludwig Michel's whereabouts at certain times but not until late in life a clearcut life itinerary and conclusion as to where he and his wife called home.

The origins of the idea of North American exploration and the founding of colonies by Michel involve two Bernese friends with whom Michel would be closely involved for the rest of his life, not only in their mutual humanitarian work to resettle persecuted Swiss religious refugees but also through their wives' situations as the men married.

Georg Ritter (1667-1723)[12] "is said to have been twice in America"[13] prior to 1705 but this is disputed. One source shows Ritter as a "well-to-do grocer" but this is at odds with other references that describe him as, for example, a "druggist by profession."[14] Ritter, who was wealthy and influential, but not of the noble class that held political power, was more likely to have been what today would be called a botanicals importer and pharmaceuticals manufacturer and perhaps foodstuffs wholesaler or broker.

As was Ritter, Johann Rudolph Ochs (1673-1749) was Michel's trans-Atlantic correspondent to whom Michel floated his earliest ideas of founding North American colonies as sanctuaries for Swiss and other European religious refugees. Professionally, Ochs was a dealer and artist in precious stones and master engraver who would be called Europe's best of the era. It would be Ochs (pronounced "Ox" rather than "Oaks") as apparently the last man standing who, after Michel and Ritter had died, would continue into mid-century the intercontinental refugee resettlement program that the three men would organize.

From the dawn of the eighteenth century, Michel, Ritter and Ochs, working in close concert, would devote themselves to aiding religious refugees, the entire time in contravention to official Swiss positions. Resented by officialdom and continually skirting established authority, the three were able to be stunningly effective in their venture in large part because of Michel's high noble status and Ritter's and Ochs's as prominent merchants. Status alone though would have gotten them no more than jail time had they not held the high card in dealing with the Great

Council of Berne: as this government went about ridding Berne Canton of its unwanted religions, it could do so with much less upheaval and bad notice by endorsing the Michel-Ritter-Ochs humanitarian relocation venture and putting the trio in charge of humane resettlement rather than the government continuing coldly to running people out.

By 1705, Ritter and Company, with the endorsement of the Great Council of Berne, would submit a petition to the British Crown for permission to establish a colony of Swiss settlers in Virginia's piedmont or Pennsylvania's hinterland. Frantz Ludwig Michel had given Ritter and Ochs a full report of his tidewater Virginia exploration of 1702, in which Michel did not get far from the Atlantic coast, until his trailblazing deep exploration of western Maryland in 1704.

Michel and Ritter and possibly Ochs had been collaborating at least since Michel's 1704 Maryland exploration on a venture to establish Swiss colonies in England's Atlantic coast provinces. Michel and Ritter may have begun their discussions before Michel's first visit to the New World with the 1701-02 Virginia exploration by planning that trip as a reconnaissance of opportunities. It might have been that the two had together struck up the notion of a North American venture or, more likely, that Ritter had done so alone and then recruited Michel probably in 1700 or 1701.

At the turn of the century, Ritter was thirty-three, married, and busy with an enterprise large enough for him to bankroll foreign expeditions. Michel was single, noble, fit from his recent military service, well educated, and, among the idle rich, available. But would Michel be interested in leaving his privileged comforts and hauling off to a wild continent afar to explore? In Michel, Ritter had found one of that special breed possessed of a never satisfied curiosity about what lies down that long path, beyond that next mountain, across the ocean. By all appearances, Ritter had found himself a born explorer. What Ritter had also recruited was a member of Berne Canton's social elite who had ready access to the small oligarchy of Bernese nobility who ran the canton and its government, the Great Council of Berne.

The match was made but the two had a stronger motivation than just exploration in getting to know the New World.

Humanitarian by Choice

Michel, Ritter and Ochs were men of conscience who had developed strong reservations about the increasingly harsh official persecution of Swiss religious minorities, particularly Switzerland's Mennonites, Amish, Quakers and Hutterites. Nowhere in the Swiss Federation did the persecution exceed that practiced against Mennonites in Berne Canton, the richest and most powerful of the Swiss states then and now. While persecution sprang from reaction to the Mennonite doctrine of pacifism which forbade the bearing of arms or swearing of allegiance to civil authorities, other than these refusals members of the persecuted sects were generally model citizens who caused little trouble.

At the time, Prussia and the States General of the Netherlands were alone in willing to accept Switzerland's refugees and then only in limited numbers. The only other practical escape route was through England all the way to her Atlantic coast provinces which were beginning to try to attract European settlers and would tolerate religious differences to do so. England herself did not want refugees but would permit transit through her ports. For the refugees and those aiding them, the most attractive destination at first was William Penn's colony of Pennsylvania founded in 1681 on Quaker Penn's principle of complete religious tolerance. Equally attractive was the English colony of Maryland which in 1649 under colonial governor William Stone[15] had passed its Toleration Act granting freedom of conscience to all Christians. Since even before the founding of the colony that Michel would create in Virginia in 1702, Virginia had been open to immigration of all faiths, and had already begun accepting religious refugees.

The exception to Switzerland's intolerance toward its Mennonite minority was in the case of marriages between Mennonites and Protestants or Catholics, though the exception may have been only for Mennonite wives. Because of the official ostracism of the Swiss toward their Mennonite countrymen, friendships between the two groups were less frequent and inter-marriages fewer. In this context, it is starkly conspicuous that Michel and his two close Bernese associates, all of the Swiss Reformed faith, became intimately involved with the Mennonite community including by marriage.

Because of his good rapport with Bernese Mennonites, Georg Ritter, at his suggestion, was appointed by the Great Council of Berne as overseer of the canton's resettlement of them. Until his death in 1723, Ritter would personally deliver hundreds if not thousands of Bernese and other Swiss Mennonite refugees to safe haven in The Netherlands and to England and then Great Britain[16] for passage to America. For example, in 1711 when Swiss Mennonites fled the country to settle in The Netherlands, Ritter led five boatloads of them from Basel to Amsterdam from July 16 to August 3. Until 1709 when Michel was delegated the role, Ritter would also administer negotiations with the British crown to successfully propose American settlements of refugees and others.

At this point, let us keep in mind that by 1702, as the trio discussed the prospect of Mennonite resettlement, Ochs had taken a bride with Mennonite family relations and that Michel in 1705 would marry a Bernese Mennonite refugee. Part of Michel's motivation might have been to provide legal cover for his bride, but there is no escaping that he, Ochs and Ritter were primarily acting on their genuine humanitarian impulses as matters of conscience in their resettlement work.

Ritter would spend two decades, Michel and Ochs four, devoted to redeeming the futures of thousands of gravely threatened European religious and war refugees, and arranging for new lives for them in America. While Ritter and Ochs devoted considerable time, energy, and personal resources to the trio's humanitarian project, of necessity they continued their professional work in Berne. Michel pursued the humanitarian project as his full-time occupation for the rest of his life including the brief interlude in 1710-11 when he simultaneously held the job of William Penn's Pennsylvania's Commissioner of Mines.

The three spawned what appears to have ranked as the largest American humanitarian refugee rescue project until the United States Food Administration was created after World War I and the Marshall Plan after World Ward II.

Theirs is one of the most under-told of American heroic stories.

II. Virginia Expedition: Testing a Vision

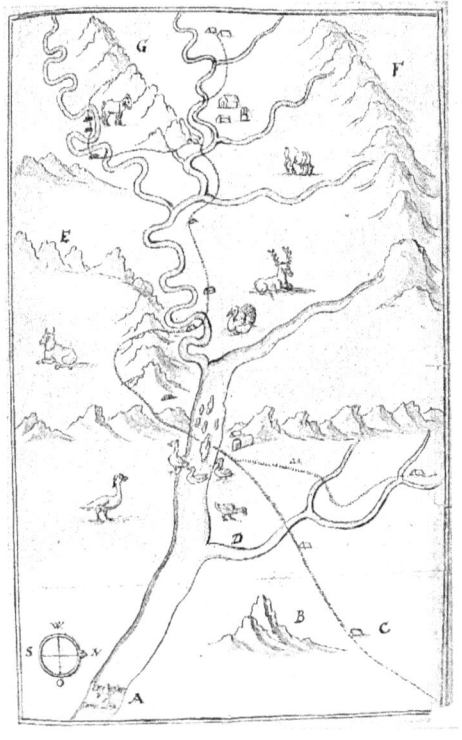

Under Way

On October 8, 1701, Frantz Ludwig Michel boarded a ship at Basel, Switzerland, and sailed down the Rhine River to Rotterdam, The Netherlands, arriving twenty-two days later. There the following day he essentially hitched a ride aboard the yacht of the English Lord Galway to London via Brielle, arriving at the River "Tems" as in his journal (the Thames) the night of November 4. Writes Frantz, "As it was already dark and as I was unacquainted with English customs and the English language, I had great difficulty in finding a lodging place for the night. But in the morning a Frenchman showed me a room, in the so-called Quarter Gracq [Greek], which was rented by the week, where I stayed till my embarkation."[17]

Here we first encounter Michel in his own voice as he records his impressions in the journal that he assiduously kept during his expedition to and from Virginia and on his next New World visit to Maryland in 1704 up until the time that he began his epic exploration into the Appalachians. Through this journal that was preserved by Michel's brother Hans, we are able to directly experience Frantz Ludwig Michel the person in his own voice for two and a half years in his mid-twenties until afterward when we must rely on a hard-to-research patchwork of other sources that tell his story mainly through extant references, such as they are, and inference. To capture the spirit of the man, his journal is quoted liberally here until we reach its end.

For want of a ship sailing to Virginia, his planned destination, Frantz spent the next three months in London as a tourist seeing the sights including the nearly completed St. Paul's Cathedral and outlying castles and familiarizing himself with the city's charms.

He may also have been in discussions with Lord Galway and others about relocating religious refugees to England's North American colonies. Galway was a French Huguenot, who himself may have been a religious refugee, had become an English Earl, and before that had spent time in Berne raising military recruits. This plus Michel's so readily embarking on Galway's yacht make it appear that the two did know each other, or that their rendezvous had been arranged by others, perhaps Ritter, and that plans or at least the concept of refugee resettlement may have already been in the works.

To outfit himself as a traveler of his station in life, Michel went shopping, purchasing "a mattress, linen, whiskey, ready-made clothes, hats, stockings, shoes, rifles, all kinds of household goods and implements, knives, scissors, shoe buckles, hair powder, especially amber, all kinds of perfumes and laces; in short everything that a man needs, except food."[18] As we will see, many of the provisions that he bought were for trade in Virginia to help pay for his expedition.

By mid-December, the travel broker Frantz had hired, a retired ship's captain, arranged Frantz's passage on His Majesty's Ship *Nassau* set to sail the following month. On December 15, Frantz moved his provisions and himself aboard, securing "a well-located cabin" and "with some effort" made himself comfortable, now fully prepared for departure. Between this time and when the *Nassau* set sail, she had a change of captains as Captain Thomas Fowlis was transferred and Captain George Byng, the future First Viscount Torrington of Devon, was given command. In protocol, but not in naval command, the captain was outranked by his noble Swiss traveler-scientist, the young Lord of Ralligen. This also explains why Michel often dined at the captain's table. In 1727, John Byng would be named Admiral of the Fleet and First Lord of the Admiralty, the top positions in the Royal Navy.

No sooner had Frantz become ensconced than a month of windless doldrums set in, which left him spending Christmas and the New Year waiting. After weighing anchor in vain for the fifth time, finally enough breeze came up on January 14, now 1702, and *HMS Nassau*, its passengers and crew were underway. Making it down the Thames and into the English Channel, the doldrums set in again leaving the *Nassau* and a great many other ships to tack back and forth unproductively trying to get to open sea on fits and starts of contrary winds. At one point the *Nassau*'s captain sent for his wife who shared his cabin until the *Nassau* was finally able to fill her sails on February 18 and be off into the Atlantic.

The first of at least three trips that Frantz Ludwig Michel would make to America had begun. Especially in those first few days on the great Atlantic Ocean, the young adventurer, now twenty-six, must have assessed the risky life path that he had chosen. What explains why a person born into all of the comforts of the upper aristocracy with privilege, title, and security would choose to venture off to a wild distant continent entirely lacking in the comforts he knew, with no guarantee that he would come back alive or even make it across the Atlantic?

Frantz Ludwig Michel was probably just born that way, as science has now shown that wanderlust appears to go beyond personal inclination all the way into one's genes and heredity. Scientific researchers make a good case that adventurousness is a genetically inherited biological trait, and that hauling off to explore a mystery continent is an especially good example of it. They point out that, "Dopamine, a pleasure-inducing brain chemical, is linked with curiosity, adventure and entrepreneurship, and helps drive results in uncertain environments." They have found that, given that only about two percent of people have high enough dopamine levels to fuel their curiosity to the extent of going off on risky explorations, high-dopamine individuals and the nations they have populated end up having wanderlust actually hard-wired into their DNA.[19] In fact, following the indigenous populating of America, itself a high-dopamine undertaking, it had to have been people adventurous enough to uproot themselves, vault an ocean, learn a new language in many cases, and confident enough to carve out a living for themselves in a land they had never seen—dopamine two-percenters from across the globe—who came. Once on the shores of their new continent, their inborn wanderlust didn't abate as they flowed across a broad continent east to west. Frantz Ludwig Michel appears to have been no different and it would be he who in two years would be the first to explore North America's east coast beyond its Atlantic fringe.[20]

Though on his trans-Atlantic voyage Michel would witness a would-be mutiny, burials at sea, a waterspout tornado, deprivation below decks, and other distresses unthinkable on a large passenger ship today, he nevertheless was being transported in the grandest style known at the time. With railroads more than a century away and ornate carriages used by the very few the epitome of land travel, people traveled almost exclusively on foot or, if they could afford it, by horseback, wagon or small watercraft. Surpassing any of the latter by orders of magnitude in size, convenience, capability, technology and sheer splendor in the early eighteenth century were the mighty ocean-going ships of Europe.

English Lord Anson in 1756 first devised the system by which warships were rated when he sorted ships of the Royal Navy by size into six categories according to the number of cannon or guns that they carried. The largest of the war ships, labeled as "first rate," carried a hundred or more guns on three decks.

Here we encounter a discrepancy between Michel's description and British naval records as to the size of the *Nassau*. Michel's subtitle of the journal of his first trip to North America is "On the Ship *Nassau*, built for 700 tons and forty pieces." Pieces means cannon or other large guns.

The Royal Navy's historical inventory of its ships shows a series of war ships named *Nassau* in service before, during and after 1702 with no two existing at the same time. From 1672 through 1880, six ships of the Royal Navy bore the name *HMS Nassau*. The *Nassau* in service in 1702, the second of these, is listed as a "third rate ship of the line" with seventy guns. Given the official nature of this listing and that only one ship at a time could hold a name, this record is taken to be correct.

Since the use of the *Nassau* on Michel's voyage was to transport passengers and cargo, it could be that she had been repurposed, at least for this particular journey. She had had nearly half of her guns removed to allow for more cargo. In fact, Michel notes that when the captain's wife went back ashore so did two guns, reducing the number still aboard to thirty-eight.

With this number of guns, the *Nassau* fell into the fifth of the six rates of war ships, those with at least thirty-two guns. Though Anson's classification system did not come into being until fifty-four years after Michel's first ocean voyage, it suffices to get an idea of the *Nassau*'s size. Despite her size, the *Nassau*, minus half of her guns, was therefore classified as a frigate, a smaller, nimbler warship that could outmaneuver an enemy of greater force, run down one of lesser force, or patrol to disrupt enemy shipping lanes.

The naval inventory description shows the *Nassau* with 150-foot length, forty-foot beam, and seventeen-foot depth in her hold. Her displacement was 1,097 tons but this was counting seventy guns aboard. While first- and second-rate ships were larger and more powerful, mid-size ships like the *Nassau* struck an optimum considering speed, handling, firepower, and cost. Such ships of the line typically had six decks and a crew of about 650 when staffed for battle.

In 1695, the Navy had contracted with Elias Waffe of the Portsmouth Dockyard to build the *Nassau*, which was commissioned in 1700 when it began its first service as the Royal Navy's flagship in the Baltic Sea. After the *Nassau*'s return from America, she would be assigned to the Mediterranean where she participated in the capture of Gibraltar in 1703. The *Nassau* served only seven years until being wrecked on October 30, 1706, on Bembridge Ledge off Spithead, England where she ran aground.

As she set sail for Virginia in 1702, the *Nassau* had 218

people aboard. Of these, Michel notes, there were 130 "that had been sold." As the ship was being readied for its voyage, Michel witnessed that, "During this time merchandise and provisions were daily taken on board, and also some poor English people, or persons who had been guilty of some crime, young and old, sold into servitude for four years. Those who are not of age must serve, according to law, till they have reached the 21st year, for food and clothes. When they are sold in Virginia the ordinary price is from 10 to 18 pounds. It should be known that there are people in England and especially in London, who sell foreigners and simple-minded people to go on West India ships."[21] West India referred to the Caribbean.

The other eighty-eight aboard consisted of the captain, officers, sailors, merchants, and other passengers. The indentured and kidnapped passengers were kept confined in close quarters on the *Nassau*'s lower decks while other passengers enjoyed far roomier quarters on upper decks or in top-deck private cabins such as Michel had if they could afford it.

Shortly after passengers had been lodged and the ship was still idling at its London wharf waiting for winds, a group of the indentured attempted a mutiny. As Michel described the incident, "I cannot omit to relate briefly what happened on the 22nd at night, at ten o'clock, through those sold into servitude. About fifty of these deceived and liberty-loving people plotted together, supplied themselves secretly with sticks, to be used in case they would meet opposition in their effort to seize the sloop by force and to return to the land. But they had to come up the stairway, close to which I and four French families had settled. We looked in upon the commotion for a while, not knowing of their intention, until they all made a furious rush to seize the stairway. We thought their object was to attack us, hence four of us seized swords and held the passageway, until the ship's owner, together with twelve sailors, who had heard the uproar in their beds, came down in their shirts with their guns and anchor bars, saw the tumult and knocked down everybody who resisted and did not escape. Many were gravely wounded and beaten. They took twenty of the leaders, whom they laid, during the whole cold night, backwards across the cable and the anchor-ropes. The noise was heard on shore and became known in London. The captain came to hear what was the nature of the tumult. After he had heard of their plan, he ordered twelve of the chief ringleaders and also two women, who had incited the revolt, to be locked up in irons. They had to suffer for it during the whole journey. The owner of the ship and also the captain were very grateful, that so few of us had held up the mob, and had taken the part of the ship's owner, in return for which we were well treated."

And so, the adventure of the questing young naturalist had begun.

Life and Death Aboard *HMS Nassau*

Frantz's seventy-nine days on the high seas were probably no more of a trial than the typical trans-Atlantic crossing at the time, but what he witnessed, were it to happen today, would surely result in inquiries, arrests, quarantines, and vessel impoundment.

At about the time of his first meal aboard, Frantz described in his journal the daily routine of what came from the galley. "We were also sufficiently supplied with all kinds of provisions. Food was henceforth distributed in the following manner: Five passengers had to club together. They received daily four pounds of biscuit, one quart of beer, two quarts of water, two pieces of beaf [beef] and pork, weighing six pounds, in addition every noon, which was mealtime and announced by the ringing of bells, a dish full of large peas. On Sundays and Wednesdays, we received in place of the meat two pounds of flour and half a pound of pork lard, out of which a thick paste is made, which is put into a linen sack. It is cooked with the meat, but not as long as the latter. Grape juice is often put into it, which is a good dish, called *boudin* [pudding]. It happens often that instead of meat fresh and large beans with butter are given out. The food is often, on account of the heat and because it is not salted sufficiently, like the water, of such bad taste that we suffered considerably, especially because the large number of mice spoiled our bread altogether. The captain and those that eat at his table are always supplied with fresh meat, nor do they use wine and strong beer sparingly. It costs ten pounds for the journey outwards and six pounds for the return trip to eat at his table, besides the transportation fare."

With the *beaf* and *boudin* and more spellings to come, keep in mind that this is a German speaker doing his best to put to parchment what he hears in English.

As the *Nassau*'s galley used older and older food during the crossing, some of it inevitably began to spoil with predictable results of sick passengers. There were also days of rough weather when many would suffer seasickness and either be unable to eat or otherwise couldn't keep down what they did. More serious maladies arose from passengers who had boarded with a contagious disease, knowing it or not, and lain ill in cramped quarters, especially among the 130 unwilling people jammed into the lower decks.

In mid-March Michel records that, "The acute fever prevailed among us very much, so that about forty men and women were sick, and every week one or two were taken off. They were all thrown into the ocean. Hitherto I have kept well, except getting sea-sick, but on the 11th I fell asleep on the stern of the ship, lying in the sun. The climate of this region is said to be warm throughout the whole year. During this time there died among others an English lady, of high family and great wealth. As she had been guilty of some indiscretion, her family was sending her to Virginia. The captain had a coffin made for her, in which were placed stones and through which holes were bored, so that it might sink more readily."

For each distressed journal entry he makes, Michel has optimistic observations dealing with "beautiful sailing weather," depth soundings, and daily calculations of latitude and longitude telling the ship's position.

On April 1, Michel notes the sighting three miles distant of a "waterspout"—a tornado—and drew a sketch of it in his journal. His sketch is shown in the center pictorial pages here. The ship's officers enlightened the scientist on the nautical phenomenon, eliciting the following journal entry.

"We saw, upon our left, about an hour's distance from us a waterspout which are usually seen at certain places, when good sailing weather is coming, but they are terrible and dangerous to the ships, if one cannot escape from them, or break them up through cannon balls, which are shot off at them. They appear like a cloud on the water and in the air. From the lower cloud rises a stream of water like a serpent into the upper cloud. Experience shows that when a ship comes near and breaks up the waterspout, a mass of water falls down, which, if it does not sink the ship, damages it seriously."

Alongside the travails of mutinies, enslavement, burials at sea, rotted rations, diseases, and tornados were pirates, an ever-present threat on the high seas at the time. More than once during the *Nassau*'s crossing, ships not flying the colors of any nation would appear on the horizon and tail the *Nassau* menacingly. It was probably the presence of the *Nassau*'s guns, showing her as a war ship rather than a freighter, which kept the mystery ships at bay.

But not always. Wrote Michel, "At daybreak, we discovered a ship on our right, about twelve miles from us. As the wind carried us toward it, it made every effort to approach. In this latitude pirates are commonly found. We saw that it approached us and was sailing better than we, hence we prepared our defence. The masts were fastened with chains, the cannons and firearms were loaded, the broad swords and short pikes were laid out. All the men were assembled, the women were locked in the hold. The sailors had to fix their beds and hammocks on the quarterdeck as a breastwork, so that we might be safe against the small arms. Forty bottles of whiskey were ready to fill the people with courage. Meanwhile we approached closer. We saw through the field glasses that it was not as large as ours, but we could not discover the nationality or whether it was a pirate. Finally evening came and, because of the darkness, we saw it no more. But we kept a good lookout and changed our course, so that in the morning we had lost sight of each other."

However, not all encounters with other ships were unwanted. "On the 2nd [of April] we had beautiful warm weather. We saw a ship in the morning behind us, well provided with sails. It was approaching us. We made ready for a fight if it had to be. Toward evening we were still close together. We thought it was surely a pirate. Finally the captain hoisted the English flag. It was answered by the same, which pleased us very much. We did not feel much desire to fight. Finally we came together so closely that the captains could talk to each other through the speaking trumpet and could drink to each other's health. The ship was from Bristol and like ourselves on the journey to Virginia. As this was the first company we had, the captains would have liked to come together to celebrate, but the high sea did not permit it."

On another occasion it did. On May 4, two ships flying the British flag approached the *Nassau*. "As it was good sailing weather, the captains came to our ship, where they were hospitably entertained. The large ship, which we had taken for a warship, was one of the most beautiful merchantmen, named "Indian King" or "Wild King," because it had been built in Virginia. Three years ago it fell into the hands of the pirates not far from land, but was rescued after a hard battle by the governor. Sixty pirates were taken prisoners, of all kinds of nations, nearly all of whom were later hung in England."

Not long after the waterspout, Michel begins writing of shallower soundings, the ocean turning from blue to green, shore bird sightings, and the ship's navigator's reports of being ever farther west. By the time of the two visiting captains, they confirmed that the *Nassau* was then not more than fifty miles from land. That day, the young naturalist also saw his first whale.

Then on May 6, 1702, "At break of day we heard from the mast the pleasant call, Land, land!" On the evening of May 8, the *Nassau* sailed up Virginia's York River and eased into her berth at Yorktown amidst six other ships lying at anchor. The first of Frantz Ludwig Michel's American explorations was about to begin.

Colony Founded

After all of the travails of his nearly three-month voyage, Frantz Ludwig Michel would spend only fifty-five days in Virginia before returning to Europe, but made the most of his time during his brief stay, not only as the naturalist recording what he saw but as prospective colonizer seeking favorable locations. As to his frame of mind in reaching Virginia, Michel expresses it plainly later when he writes to his Bernese friend Johann Rudolf Ochs as "to satisfy my old curiosity, to seek out unknown things and to collect the wonders of nature."

At first it might not seem clear from his journal or other sources whether Michel went to Virginia planning to look for colonizing opportunities or was so taken with what he saw after he got there that he then began considering the possibility. It is known that during his Atlantic crossing he conferred with Pierre Sabattie, a French clergyman among the four French Huguenot refugee families aboard who had crossed the Atlantic to found a colony in Virginia. Rev. Sabattie and his charges were fleeing religious persecution in France. British government permission had already been granted and Sabattie had with him a letter of introduction to Virginia Governor Francis Nicholson. Michel had his own letter of introduction requesting that courtesies customarily accorded to travelers of his noble rank be extended to him.

In 1700, several hundred French Huguenots had migrated from England to Virginia, where King William had promised them land grants. When they arrived, colonial author-

FIRST EXPLORER

ities offered them land twenty miles above the falls of the James River at the abandoned Monacan village of Manakin Town. On May 12, 1705, the Virginia General Assembly would pass an act naturalizing the 148 Huguenots still resident at Manakintown. Of the original 390 settlers in the isolated settlement, many had died, others then lived outside town on farms in the English style, and others moved to different areas. Gradually they intermarried with their English neighbors. In the Manakintown area, the Huguenot Memorial Bridge across the James River and Huguenot Road were named in their honor, as were many other modern local features including Huguenot High School.[22]

Sabattie was scheduled to meet with Governor Nicholson soon after arrival, which happened with Michel present at Sabattie's invitation. Was Michel on the same kind of colony-founding mission as Sabattie to begin with? Had the two known each other before travelling to Virginia together? Or was Michel invited to Sabattie's audience with the governor on the spur of the moment based on sudden interest? Based on two relationships that Michel had in Berne, it appears likely that Michel's going to Virginia was for the planned purpose of investigating the feasibility of founding a settlement there or actually going ahead and doing so.

Letters to and from Michel, Georg Ritter and Johann Rudolph Ochs in 1703 when Michel was in Maryland indicate that the three had known each other for some time. Their letters explicitly discuss establishing settlements for immigrants in England's North American colonies and the tone of the letters isn't toward commercial gain. Ritter and Ochs are wealthy, established Bernese merchants who will soon become, with Michel, the Swiss and then the continental leaders in resettling religious refugees. All three would become intimately involved with Berne's persecuted Mennonites and soon be arranging resettlement of them to refugee colonies that the trio would create along the American east coast. The best explanation for Michel's 1702 presence in Virginia, if not a sure thing, is that he was on a scouting mission planned by the three. Michel's rendezvous with Lord Galway in Holland and then with Pierre Sabattie aboard ship fit the same conclusion that Michel had set out from Berne on a mission.

Governor Nicholson and Colonial Secretary Edmund Jenings received Michel and Sabattie enthusiastically at Williamsburg, Virginia's new capital then under construction. Jenings, a royal appointee and member of the Governor's Council, issued all of the colony's land grants and naturalization papers, and had taken the lead in implementing the 1701 Act for the Better Strengthening of the Frontier, which promoted immigration of Europeans to Virginia. This was just what Sabattie and his Huguenot religious refugees had emigrated to Virginia for, and what now, if not before, Michel had his attention fixed on. During the meeting, Michel expressed willingness to organize a Swiss colony in Virginia, to which Nicholson gave immediate consent and directed the two to the newly formed King William County founded only the month before. This was the Virginia colony's first inland county.

As the location of the new Huguenot colony was yet to be chosen, Michel and Sabattie set out on May 23 to visit the existing French colony of Manakinton or Manakin Town, and a nearby Swiss immigrant family both fifty miles up the York River. This location is where today's county seat, the village of King William, is located. The two men liked what they saw. Despite their having been offered part of his 10,000 acres by James Blair, Episcopal bishop of the colony and president of its parliament—"a learned, sensible and well-to-do man" wrote Michel—he and Sabattie preferred areas not far from Manakinton for their colonies-to-be.

Michel wasted no time in securing his land grant. With a letter in hand from Manakinton colony minister Benjamin De Joux addressed to the governor, Michel went back to Williamsburg and filed his grant application, requesting the same terms that the Manakinton settlers had been granted two years prior. Sabattie made essentially the same request for his proposed grant and the two requests were granted immediately. Michel then returned to King William, as the governor had named Michel's grant, and left it in the care of a hired overseer, Monsieur Dutoit of the French Huguenot colony. Michel stored some of his belongings at his new property. After returning to Williamsburg in early May, Michel wrote in his journal, "Truthfully that there is no other country where it is possible with so few means and so easily to make an honest living and be in easy circumstances." Less than three weeks after his arrival, Frantz Ludwig Michel had become a major landowner and social figure in Virginia.

The governor had named the new Swiss colony after King William, the British monarch who, still unbeknownst to Virginia, had died on March 8. Also yet to be heard in Virginia was that William had immediately been succeeded on the throne by his sister-in-law, Anne, now Queen Anne. Anne would reign until 1714 when she died at forty-nine and would be a pivotal figure in creation of the public-private venture that would see Britain bear the expense of transporting Frantz Ludwig Michel's refugees to North America. We will encounter Anne at several important junctures further along here.

Michel's large land grant comprised either all or a good portion—it isn't clear which—of the new County of King William. Today's village of King William, the county seat, has a population of only about 250. Today's population of this still very rural county is about 16,000. Built in 1725, the county courthouse is the oldest in continuous use in the United States. The courthouse, King William Training School, Sharon Indian School, and Sweet Hall are listed on the National Register of Historic Places.

Manakinton, whose name devolved to Manquin, is today a small community along US Route 360 nine miles northwest of King William.

Michel's establishing his King William colony soon led to its settling of new Swiss religious refugees joining a small group already there. Over the next fourteen years as

Michel would found five more refugee colonies in America, the flow of refugees to his colonies would mount into the thousands, and would never stop even up to the present.

His were not the first religious or other refugees to reach America. The Massachusetts pilgrims of 1620 had fled religious persecution in England for the tolerance of seventeenth century Holland. In the 1650s, Catholic refugees found refuge in Maryland, the first of the thirteen colonies to establish freedom of worship. A few years before Michel founded King William, the Lerber sisters and their mother had fled Berne finding refuge nearby along the Mattaponi River at the edge of Michel's new colony. But each of these relocations was accomplished without much assistance to those who relocated. With King William, what Michel and his two humanitarian partners had created was a program of America's first, organized, aided, end-to-end means of refugee relocation and resettlement. In doing so, they had also launched a permanent American tradition of generous refugee resettlement that has been in place ever since. The 1702 trickle would by mid-century become a torrent. The three organized it with their own money and sweat.

Colony Vanished

During these early days when he almost certainly thought that Jamestown was England's first North American colony, Michel learned that it was the second and that the first had mysteriously vanished more than a century earlier. In what is the longest entry in his journal, Michel elaborates on what he had heard since he landed about the enigmatic disappearance in 1585 of Britain's Roanoke colony in what later became North Carolina. His entry contains several historical inconsistencies indicating that the handed-down accounts he was told had partly morphed into local tale, but what Michel heard was mostly correct.

After 400 settlers had been left to found a colony near present-day Manteo, North Carolina, the following year a two-ship resupply expedition with another 800 settlers arrived to find the site deserted with no sign of what had become of the earlier group except for "CROATOAN" carved into the trunk of a tree at the site. Croatoan or Croatan was the central community of the Croatan Indians at nearby Cape Hatteras.

Wrote Michel, "They had a long and troublesome journey. But finally they landed, expecting to encamp with the above-mentioned settlers, in order to learn from them how they had fared thus far. To their great consternation they found no one, not even a trace of their labors. They were much surprised and fearful that there might be Indians nearby. They concluded to supply themselves with provisions for several days and, following the river, to march into the country, in the hope of finding a trace of their people. But they were unable to find anything except an immense quantity of game of all kinds. . . . In time they learned that they had been killed by the Indians, for, when they fought with them later, they found many things among the Indians which had been taken from the four hundred."

"Learned that they had been killed by the Indians" was what Michel had heard but this is at odds with the later shown fate of the Lost Colony.

What happened to the disappeared colonists has never waned in the collective imagination since, with various theories abounding for more than 400 years without hard proof surfacing for any of them. What appears to be convincingly leading among clues are reports in generations immediately following the disappearance that Native Americans with European features and bits of English vocabulary were present in the area, and that European objects existed among natives at the time. There is also the intact oral tradition of North Carolina's Lumbee Tribe that they partially descend from assimilated Europeans.[23] Then the question becomes, were the Roanoke settlers captured or did they in desperation assimilate by choice. Frantz Ludwig Michel, as all then and since, was left to wonder.

A convincing explanation has been put forth by North

Carolina writer Joel Stegall who is mixed Lumbee and White. In early 2022, Stegall wrote, "Some of the English appeared to have married with the Native Americans in the area and gave up all remnants of the English language and customs. On the other hand, it also seems clear that at least one mixed-race group emerged that was not absorbed into an existing tribe. Members of this new community not only looked different, but they held on to remnants of English language, culture, and religion. It is not a great leap to imagine that if they were not accepted by existing tribes, they would have sought a place where they could live in peace.

"[R]ecords indicate that two centuries later Scottish explorers moving through the wetlands of the Lumber River, 250 miles south[west] of Roanoke Island, came across people who identified themselves as Indian but had lighter-colored skin and spoke English. With names such Goins, Oxendine, Dial and Lowry, they lived in two-story houses, farmed in an English style, and practiced a form of Christianity. Their ancestors, they said, were 'white people' who could 'talk in a book' and 'make paper speak'."[24]

Stegall's account is but one over the years to the same effect, that the 400 colonists of 1585 became native and were assimilated by choice or otherwise.

Building Boom

What Michel encountered in Virginia was not a vanishing colony but a rising one now spread out along Virginia's Atlantic shore fifty-five-miles northward from Jamestown to the Potomac River and the colony of Maryland. In 1702 nowhere in Virginia was as busy as the new provincial capital being built at the Middle Plantation, a pleasant place about to be renamed Williamsburg.

Michel's arrival in Virginia coincided with the transfer of the colonial capital beginning in 1699 from Jamestown to a safer and less mosquito-ridden location. The change was driven by the wooden colonial statehouse at Jamestown having burned down for the second time and the government, needing a place to meet, choosing the newly constructed College of William and Mary at the Middle Plantation, a fortified settlement twelve miles away. Originally, the move was to be short-term but, finding the "temporary" location safer and more pleasant than Jamestown, members of the House of Burgesses voted to keep the capital at the Middle Plantation, renaming the place Williamsburg in honor of King William III of England.

After Williamsburg's designation as the colony's capital, an immediate local building boom ensued with construction of the colony's new masonry capitol building, platting of the town-to-be around the college's sites and the new Bruton Parish Church, and the sprouting of a proliferation of ordinaries, inns, tradesmen's shops, and homes. By 1710, Williamsburg had had ravines filled, streets leveled, and more college buildings, another church, and a magazine for the storage of arms built. It was this new budding boom-town capital in which Frantz Ludwig Michel found himself conducting his business and taking in his new continent. He devotes quite a bit of ink in describing Williamsburg.

The College of William and Mary, the continent's second oldest institution of higher learning, was the center of the town's social life. Its first graduating class was in 1700. Michel recorded his impressions of the new college as, "The youth is instructed in the higher branches in the College there. But, because most of the people live far away, only the more well-to-do parents, who have the means, can secure boarding for their sons there, which costs yearly twenty guineas. There are about 40 students there now. Before this it was customary for wealthy parents, because of the lack of preceptors or teachers, to send their sons to England to study there. But experience showed that not many of them came back. Most of them died of small-pox, to which sickness the children in the West are subject."

Michel got to know the college perhaps better than he had

imagined he would. After attending a fireworks display at the college one evening, he confesses that, "I had taken my place in the highest part of the tower on the building, whence the best outlook was to be had by day and night. As it was eleven o'clock at night and my lodging place was two miles away, being also compelled to pass over a miserable, misleading road, I stayed up there over night, although I was afraid that, if somebody should find me there, it might be misinterpreted of me, being a stranger, but no one came. When day dawned, I left the building, without anybody noticing me." So, the intrepid young nobleman was not above a streak of mischief.

On his rounds in Williamsburg, Michel meets with the governor, the colony Secretary who was second in command, the colony's head cleric, the college president, and other officials high and low, all in short order. It seems that there was nothing like showing up with a noble title to open doors and facilitate introductions. Michel notes that the colony's military is almost entirely composed of uncompensated militia volunteers, and has one general and twelve colonels, one for each of Virginia's counties at the time. (Virginia has ninety-five counties today.)

Michel, who was raised in the Swiss Reformed faith, remarks on the official lack of religious toleration in Virginia which practices the British state religion of the Church of England. But he records that the colony's French Huguenots are permitted to practice their Calvinism and the Swiss colony, its Mennonite beliefs. He notes the absence of Catholics in Virginia but that, "There are also some Catholics, who can hold their religious services in Maryland. But there are only a few of them."

During his time in Williamsburg, Michel entered his drawings of four of the capital's new civic buildings into his journal[25]. These, the oldest existing images of the architecture of colonial Williamsburg, have been a boon to historians and preservationists ever since.

The Naturalist Explores

Michel spent his remaining five weeks in Virginia exploring and adding heavily to his journal in which he wrote in his native German. As there were few written place names or road signs, if any, in use in 1702, Michel learned place names by hearing them spoken rather than seeing them spelled. In his journal, he thus spelled what he heard as if the words were German. Some amusing results are *Willemsburg* for Williamsburg, *Falensgrig* (Falling Creek), *Jemston* (Jamestown), *Jorgtown* (Yorktown), *Jorgk Rivier* (York River), *racon* (raccoon), *mocketbort* (mockingbird) and *pons* (punch refreshment).

His observations on nature and rural customs were made for the most part along an exploration of several weeks from Williamsburg to the Virginia side of the Potomac River and back, about 180 miles round trip, all on foot. For part of the way, Michel's journal has him on the Great High Road, an ancient Indian trail running from the Carolinas up the Virginia coastal plain to Maryland. In Virginia, parts of this trail had been widened to handle settlers' wagons. Michel notes wayfinding as, "For the guidance of those not knowing the way it is only necessary to watch the signs that are found on trees along the great high road. Every year white places are cut into the trees with hatchets, by the removal of the bark. There are so many ways that otherwise one could easily go astray." The Great High Road in the area where Michel went is more or less today's US Route 17.

It is not clear why Michel walked instead of rode, as he had written that horses were so cheap that "it must be a poor man who can not afford one." Hiker Michel observed plenty but did not plan adequately, leading to a roadside collapse in exhaustion one day and heat prostration on another. What aided him was the local standard of hospitality providing the shelter and feeding of total strangers who happened by or were in distress. Michel had to suspend his old-world courtesy of offering to pay for the meals and bunks he was provided, as he found such offers insulted his hosts. "At first we were too modest to go into the houses to ask for food and lodging, which the people often recognized, and they admonished us not to be bashful, as this was the custom of rich and poor. We soon became accustomed to it." Michel's "we" here is poetic license in the translation as there is no indication that he did not hike alone.

One of Michel's goals on this exploration was "to travel to *Mattabany* [Mattaponi], where Swiss people were living, especially a man named Willion, known to me from military service, another of the Pays de Vaux de Bex, back of the bailiwick of Aehlen, who was lieutenant captain under Sacconay." Pays de Vaux de Bex and Aehlen are places in Switzerland. A passer-by "told us that not far from that place Swiss people were living. I was anxious to see them. We reached the house in a short time. I expected to find Swiss but met there the four sisters Lerber from Berne. I do not want to stop to describe their condition. It would be very desirable if they had someone, who could manage their place and secure servants for them. Their mother died shortly after their arrival."[26]

The four were the Mennonite daughters of Frantz Ludwig von Lerber, Secretary to the city treasurer of Berne. The sisters and their mother had left Switzerland because of persecution of Mennonites, which they were. Frantz would encounter the eldest of the sisters, Anna Barbara, again before leaving Virginia for home.

The small Swiss settlement of Mattaponi (Algonquian: MAT-tah-po-nye) that Michel visited was named for the local Indian tribe that still resides in the area. The settlement was along the Mattaponi River upstream from the present-day Mattaponi Indian Reservation about five miles from the center of Michel's King William land grant colony. The Mattaponi place name where the sisters lived has since disappeared along with their Swiss hamlet. This place is not to be confused with two other places not far distant in Virginia with the name today.

Another of Michel's goals on this exploration was to cross into Maryland to inquire about its disposition toward receiving organized groups of new settlers but he was advised when he reached the Virginia side of the Potomac River, the boundary between the two colonies, that without a high-level official letter of introduction he would be arrested upon entering Maryland. Thus began an arduous walk back to Yorktown where he would seek return passage to Europe, but Maryland would come on his next trip to America.

In his travels in Virginia in 1702, it is doubtful that Michel ever got more than fifty miles from the Atlantic coast, as few if any European settlers had yet ventured that far inland. Indeed, all twelve of the colony's counties at that time had Atlantic shorelines. Perhaps a handful of adventurers had pushed farther west, though no record showing that was found in researching *First Explorer*. Michel's new King William colony forty miles from the ocean was considered to be far into the hinterlands at the time. In 1702, little was yet known of what lay beyond the allure of the Blue Ridge Mountains, Virginia's first fold of the Appalachians within far distant sight of the coastal piedmont on a clear day. In fact, up to that time nearly the entire British experiment in colonizing North America was coastal, extending westward usually only as far as sea-going ships could go before reaching the fall line of rivers draining the Appalachians. There were as yet few if any explorations beyond this coastal fringe, but Frantz Ludwig Michel would famously conduct his own two years in the future.

Describing the boundaries of Virginia, Michel notes, "The length [read width] extends into the wilderness, which is not known to any one and the end is impossible to find." Michel likely did not realize how true that was: Virginia's founding grant set her western boundary at 200 miles beyond the "Western Sea," the Pacific Ocean. This and similar "western land grants" to five other of Britain's North American colonies would delay the formation of the United States eighty years hence until John Hanson would resolve the western lands impasse in March of 1781, opening the way for the thirteen rebellious colonies finally to legally unite as a nation on November 5 of that year. For his breakthrough, Hanson was elected as the first President of United States under the new nation's original government chartered by the Articles of Confederation. Hanson was from the future Frederick County, Maryland, which in 1704 Michel would explore a quarter century before other Europeans began to discover the area. More coincidental is that the author descends directly from Michel and collaterally from Hanson. The two families became joined when the author's parents married in 1940.

The Naturalist Records

As scientists, or naturalists in their day, are inclined to do, Michel's journal gives the appearance of his much enjoying the recording of his observations on man and nature as he wandered one corner of the New World. Some of what he saw was identical to what he knew from his European Old World, some familiar but different, some altogether new.

His observations on nature show wonderment as when for the first time he sees porpoises, catfish, oysters so large that they cannot be eaten whole, groundhogs, raccoons, squirrels four times larger than what he is used to, flying squirrels, hummingbirds, fireflies ("glow-worms" in his journal), and the general "abundance of game, a real 'zoological garden'" as Michel puts it. He reserves special affection for the "nicest apples" and for turkeys, which he has by then enjoyed at one table or another.

Michel exclaims at the ease of growing crops, herds, and gardens in Virginia's temperate climate and rich lowland soil, and notes, "But fresh seeds must be imported every year from Europe, for, if the seed of this country is planted, it turns into the wild kind again." He marvels at the proliferation of fish, shellfish, and oysters, and how easy it is to find and harvest them. He finds turtles and tortoises everywhere and is fairly ecstatic over the enormous oyster beds he takes from. A harvest festival that he observes reminds him fondly of those at home in Switzerland.

What Michel doesn't comment on, which as a naturalist he could have, is Virginia's man-nature balance that, at the time, still permitted nature to flourish. In 1702, Virginia's European population was approaching 60,000 but growing slowly and then almost entirely due to immigration, hence the colony's easily had land grants. Nevertheless, Virginia was by far the most populous of Britain's thirteen American colonies, having nearly twice as many people as second-place Maryland. In mid-century, Virginia's population took off as its immigration did, and by the Revolutionary War had passed a half million.[27]

By the twenty-first century in Virginia and adjoining Maryland, the American eagle was almost wiped out, the crab catch in the Chesapeake Bay, which the two states share, had dropped ninety-eight percent, and spotting a turtle became something to talk about. What Michel observed in 1702 was a natural abundance that had probably already begun to slip. As today, many didn't make themselves aware of human impact on nature as when Michel wrote, "Partridges are numerous and tame. I was surprised to see them sitting on trees and hear them sing. I have shot many of them for their good meat and because they are found everywhere, *but never only one of them.*" (Emphasis added) But now, the partridge, too, is harder to find. Over the last half century, the United States has lost nearly a third of its bird populations, close to three billion birds, due to the mounting human-caused world ecological debacle.[28]

One of the sharpest natural declines already happening by the time Michel arrived was the wrecking of Virginia's soil by tobacco cultivation. Introduced to the plant by their native neighbors, it hadn't taken long after the first successful English settlement at Jamestown in 1607 for Europe to become wildly fond of smoking the American plant *nicotiana tobacum*. The novel recreational pastime swept Europe, immediately creating export-dependent economies in Virginia and Maryland, themselves dependent on their soil.

As Michel explains, "It grows best in new soil, but the land must be very good if it is to bear tobacco for twenty years. However, it is not done. Hence the inhabitants do not live close together and the country is not settled in villages, because every twenty or thirty years new ground must be broken. When the tobacco field does not want to bear any more, he sows corn in its place. A workman must plant yearly from 1500 to 2000 pounds of tobacco."

Tobacco quickly came to play such a central role in Virginia that it became the medium of exchange and primary asset of taxation. Michel explains that "Tobacco is the principal article there, with which trade is carried on. It passes for money, because gold and silver are seldom seen there, especially among the common people. All purchases or payments are made in tobacco. It is planted in such quantities that this year 150 ships, large and small, but not more than twenty small ones among them, left the country laden with tobacco. When the inhabitants need something, they go to the nearest merchant, who gives them what they want. It is recorded according to agreement. When the tobacco is ripe, the merchant arrives to take what is coming to him."

The tobacco economy didn't stop with the common man. Rather than from the collection plate, clerics were paid in tobacco at 16,000 to 20,000 pounds yearly. Members of the colony's Court of Assembly, the lower chamber of the legislature, each received one hundred pounds of tobacco daily for the two-week session, with a member's county paying the cost.

The market only grew as more Europeans discovered tobacco and most who did became habituated to the most addictive substance known, nicotine. Unwittingly, Virginia, Maryland and then other colonies had found a sure-fire export strategy as the sole source for an addictive drug. But their price to pay as fertile lands were taken up with new tobacco-growing settlers was soil exhaustion, leaving entire areas of early settlement in economic depression.

The author's mother's Hanson ancestors faced exactly this in 1769 when they sold their played-out tidewater Maryland tobacco lands and moved west to the then frontier of Frederick County, Maryland, where they then raised mostly political office holders.

Native Survival Against All Odds

The pressures on fauna and soil that Frantz Ludwig Michel witnessed in Virginia, as severe as they would become, were not nearly as devastating or as sad as the toll that the continent's new inhabitants were already exacting on its original ones. Before looking at the fates of the tribes that Michel met, it is instructive to recall the continent-wide saga of the American Indian from Michel's time onward. The story of the Plains Indians is as instructive as any.

Estimates vary widely but one gauges that Europe's diseases, then gunpowder, then dishonored treaties, then officially sanctioned genocide reduced the North American indigenous population by an estimated ninety-seven percent, from eight million in 1491 to a census-measured 248,000 in 1890. Another estimate has a drop from seventeen million in 1491 to one million by 1650. Another shows the virtual annihilation of New England's Indians by 1720, only a century after the Pilgrims' arrival.[29]

Native American historian and Fulbright Scholar Al Carroll has reported that the estimated population of Native Americans in the future United States before the arrival of Columbus was reduced ninety to ninety-eight percent by the beginning of the twentieth century, the worst of it coming *after* the Civil War when the Great Plains and west were settled. As illustration Carroll cites, "In California for example, a typical tribe might have been 15,000 people. A century and half after genocide ended, most California tribes today are under 200, some only a few dozen."

Whatever the estimate, the historical picture comes out the same: North America's White newcomers nearly exterminated those whose continent they seized and did so not mostly incidentally as from the diseases they brought but deliberately by force. The hard fact is that this was a methodical four-hundred-year genocide, in percentage terms the most nearly complete in known history.

The nadir for the American Indian came in the census of 1890, the same year that the United States government declared that the nation's frontier was then "closed," code for the First Peoples finally having been completely subdued with the assassination of Sitting Bull that year.

Then the American Indian, now with an accurate identity of Native American, began a slow comeback. As demographer Jeffrey Passel describes it, "For decades through 1960, the American Indian population, as enumerated in U.S. censuses, grew little if at all. From a population of 248,000 in 1890, American Indians increased to 524,000 in 1960. While this does represent a doubling of the population, the average annual population growth rate over the entire 70-year period was only 1.1 percent—an exceptionally low figure resulting from high fertility and very high mortality."[30]

Nearly exterminated by the white man's diseases, guns, forced marches, massacres, child snatching and official genocides, Native Americans today are largely shunted off into inhospitable places where the buffalo no longer roam, commerce chooses not to settle, and despair hovers as the constant death angel. Fergus Bordewich's *Killing the White Man's Indian*, one of the best tellings of the story of the contemporary Native American, opens with the massacre of every man, woman and child who had been pushed off to live on Indian Island in northern California's Arcata Bay. Drunken whites with no apparent motive other than sheer wonton slaughter rowed out to the island before dawn on February 25, 1860, and in a froth-mouthed few minutes depopulated the entire band of several hundred peaceful Wiyots.

Five of the seven poorest counties in the United States are in South Dakota, all five are within Indian reservations, and Oglala Lakota County where the author once visited while researching a book[31] is the second poorest of the nation's 3,144 counties. Oglala Lakota County's 2012 per capita income of $5,213 was less than a twelfth that of the nation, and less than one-twenty-fifth of that of the nation's highest per capita income county, Teton County, Wyoming, where the second (or third) homes of billionaires abound. Nineteen of every twenty county residents are Indian. In 2012, Oglala Lakota County had the highest proportion of its residents receiving food stamps of any county in the nation, with nearly three-quarters of the reservation's food stamp recipients children, elderly or the disabled. The "assistance" at the time amounted to $1.50 per meal.

The nation's poorest county, Buffalo County, South Dakota, is home of the Crow Creek Indian Nation. Five of every six Buffalo County residents are Native American. In 2012, the county unemployment rate was fifty-seven percent and two-thirds of children lived below the poverty line. Median home value was less than $38,000 with many of the county's barely 500 households lacking kitchens, running water or both. The county had no businesses larger than its single country store. Gann Valley, the nation's smallest county seat, had a population of fourteen.

But since 1960, the nation's Native American population has nearly quadrupled, growing from 552,000 to nearly two million. Part of the growth has come from better public health on reservations resulting in lower mortality, but a larger cause has been people with partial American Indian ancestry now identifying as Indian when they hadn't before.

Amidst the contrast of deepest poverty and exaggerated wealth, but not because of either, an unexpected beneficial trend is underway for Indians, though it is confined mainly to the Great Plains. As the Plains states, the Dakotas in particular, have been depopulating for several decades (Kansas has more ghost towns than any state), the Indian population has been rising, more so from Indians moving back to the Plains than from natural increase. Perhaps their swelling population in the Dakotas will eventually give them political power that might improve their situation.

More than sixty percent of Great Plains counties have lost population. A broad vertical stripe of nearly 900,000 square miles, more than a quarter of the area of the forty-eight contiguous states, now has so few people that it once again meets the population density definition of frontier—six or fewer people per square mile—and a good part of that swath has regained the official classification of vacant. In North Dakota, all but six counties have lost population and the few that have gained are populated mainly by Indians. Half of South Dakota counties have lost population, but the state's second-fastest-growing county is majority Indian. All but four of the Great Plains counties of Montana have lost population, but three of the four gainers have reservations where tribal diasporas are reassembling.

As many parts of the Great Plains were losing up to a quarter of their population since the 1980s, Indian populations have grown by similar rates in the Dakotas, Montana and Nebraska through steady net in-migration. As a typical example, Donald Lake, a Santee Sioux who is director of the Inter-Tribal Bison Cooperative in Rapid City, South Dakota, and came home after a long spell living in Los Angeles, says he doesn't miss LA's hectic pace, high prices or near absence of Indian life. Lake says that he "feels alive again" as he gets involved at the top in Indian, bison and Great Plains causes. The wellspring of this Plains Indian counter-diaspora is a deep longing to reconnect with a native identity of spirit, heritage, place, and people.

It is virtually exclusively the White counties of the Great Plains that are depopulating while significant numbers of Indians, having given a try to life elsewhere, usually urban, are heading back to their ancestral homes and increasing the Great Plains Indian population. The abandoned farms of Whites are giving way to resurgent prairie grassland and to buffalo now numbering 300,000 just on the northern Great Plains alone, up from 300 animals—yes, 300—nationwide at the turn of the twentieth century. Across the Great Plains their decimated flora and fauna are also making hearty comebacks.

White settlement of the northern and central Plains has always been driven by government incentives, first the 1862 Homestead Act, then the 1904 Kincaid Act, and now very generous pork-barrel agricultural subsidies mainly benefitting large corporate agribusinesses with absentee owners. With homesteading incentives discontinued (the last homesteader was an Alaskan in 1976), non-Indians still finding the Plains attractive are mainly the large food companies but their owners don't live in the Plains. Today, annual government subsidies of $20 billion are the main incentive keeping non-Indian farming and ranching communities from depopulating the Great Plains faster than they already are.

Economists now argue convincingly that White settlement of the northern Plains was all along a government-induced mistake through handouts to railroads, homesteaders and now corporate interests, and that European agricultural settlement of the prairie was thus an accident of history.

What we see now is what happens to Plains life when economic distortions begin to be cured even as a more modern one—the pork barrel—is introduced. It is instructive to contemplate what the future of the Plains would be if Congress finally did away with the corporate welfare doled out to large agribusinesses: would it be Plains depression or healthy re-establishment of Indian vitality, power and political influence?

So the Plains miraculously are coming full circle from their primeval state of a short 200 years ago, through a century and a half of near annihilation of indigenous peoples, the buffalo, grasslands and native fauna and flora, to today's restoration of what was before. There are now more Indians and bison on the Plains than at any time since the era of Sitting Bull and the last Indian wars. Nearly three dozen northern Plains tribes now manage their own large bison herds, and a third of all Indian colleges offer bison management.

This re-emergence of a Great Plains of Indians and bison is recreating a historic Buffalo Commons of the ancient Plains animal now again beginning to thunder over the land. One is called on to believe that this coming back will lead to a restoration of the clear-eyed Native American spirit of old that will open the way to eventual recovery from poverty, despair, and decimation of culture. All should note that this transformation is occurring not through any sudden government or dominant-culture largess to Indians, but on their own initiative, by their own ways, a coming home of their diaspora, and the passing away of many of their occupiers' ravages that Indians have long prayed would go.

May the dark American chapter of mistreatment of First Nations peoples finally be succeeded by light, which might now be happening. In 2021, Deb Haaland, a Native American of the Navajo Nation, became Secretary of the United States Department of the Interior, which oversees the heretofore notoriously poorly run Bureau of Indian Affairs. Expect reform.

While the pendulum swings back toward recovery for Native Americans of the Plains and Southwest, progress lags or was long ago obliterated for Indians in most of the rest of the Americas. What of the eight eastern tribes that Frantz Ludwig Michel met with?

While the Indians of the Great Plains forge an inspiring comeback, the populations of most tribes elsewhere remain so severely depleted that they either have no critical mass to build on or are too small or too scattered to qualify for the White man's official federal recognition as a tribe eligible for Bureau of Indian Affairs assistance. Some small federally recognized tribes get by operating tribal casinos but others, including those Frantz Ludwig Michel met, either barely exist, were long ago annihilated, or were "removed" for the convenience of White settlers as with the French settlement that Michel visited.

In his journal, Michel pays special interest to the new race of people he encounters as he visits Virginia. In multiple entries, he makes note of their agricultural replenishment practice of field burning, "secret" antivenin for snakebites, finely worked silkgrass basketry, trading and commercial practices, superior archery skill, use of allspice as medicine, and Indian spiritual beliefs, among many of their ways of life that he records.

Michel also mentions battles between settlers and the tribes of the Powhatan Confederacy occurring as far back as the Battle of Jamestown a century before in the year that the colony was founded. He pays particular attention to the two tribes living within his newfound colony, the Mattaponi and the Pamunkey. His lengthy descriptions on the culture, social life, behavior, values, and languages of the Indians he meets are an early, sympathetic and astute anthropological treatise on them, this long before the field of anthropology was born. A good bit of what he learns of Indians is firsthand as when he goes on a hunt with them, is fed as their guest, is impressed by partaking of their village life, and trades British goods for pelts with them.

Michel describes at length Indian participation in a multi-day memorial service in Williamsburg in May after the death King William[32] and the following celebration of the ascent of Queen Anne to the throne. "The representatives and principal men of four different tribes, about forty in number, appeared on the appointed day. . . . Those who were present at the proclamation brought with them as much as they could carry of all kinds of wild animal skins, prepared or fresh. They also brought a large number of baskets, carried on the arms, of different colors, made very artistically. They weave into them all kinds of animals, flowers and other strange things, very beautifully. Everything that they bring is brought to send it as a present to England. They also make tobacco pipes, very beautifully cut out and formed. When they are summoned, their king or queen, as also their princes and nobles wear crowns of bark, a little more than a buckle wide, round and open above, with white and brown stripes, half an inch long, set in beautifully in spiral form, so that no bark is visible. The women, especially the queen and her three servants, were overhung with such things, on big and small threads or something similar, in place of chains. I wondered what kind of material it was. I examined, therefore, the finery of one of the maids of the queen. I cannot compare it to anything better than to strips of leather, hung over the harness of horses in Switzerland. They are not unfriendly and ugly people, but their language is very wonderful, so that I cannot describe how it sounds and how they change their voice. Regarding their religion, I have heard from reliable people, who have had much intercourse with them that they fear Satan, who torments them frequently. They also say that water is stronger than fire, because fire can be extinguished by water, hence water was to be feared and honored more. They further believe that if they are disobedient to one of their superiors or kill one of their people or live badly otherwise, after their death they will come into a land in the north, cold and evil, but those who live honorably, according to their opinion, will come into a land in the east, good and warm."

Here we hear the voice of the humanitarian Michel who would not drive off or seize the lands of the two tribes residing within his King William domain but establish a neighborly respect that shielded the two tribes and had much to do with their intactness in their ancient homelands down to the present.

As of this writing, there are 574 federally recognized American Indian and Alaska Native tribes and villages, each with its own set of beliefs and cultural truths. Perhaps it was Michel's scientific bent and openness to native peoples that had to do with the two tribes living on his new land grant being the only two officially recognized by the federal government in Virginia today. Eleven are recognized by the State of Virginia. With nearly all of the rest of the state's Indians slaughtered, long ago expelled, scattered to the winds, or diluted into other races, it was much against the odds that the Mattaponi and Pamunkey tribes could survive but they have. Their reservations are a few miles from the village of King William, the center of Frantz Ludwig Michel's land grant.

The Mattaponi were one of the original core tribes of the Powhatan chiefdom. The Mattaponi Indian Reservation was created from land long held by the Mattaponi by an act of the Virginia General Assembly in 1658, making it one of the oldest Indian reservations in the United States. Through the years, both the reservation's land area and its population have dropped. The reservation today covers 150 acres housing seventy-five residents, with another 375 members of the tribe living elsewhere. The reservation borders the Mattaponi River six miles from King William. Facilities include living quarters, Baptist church, museum, trading post, fish hatchery, marine science center, and community tribal building that was formerly the reservation school.

From the tribal website, the Mattaponi Tribe stresses that it has maintained its heritage and customs despite strong pressures to assimilate completely into "mainstream culture." The Mattaponi River has kept the Mattaponi alive for centuries with its shad, striped bass, catfish, herring, and perch, staples of the Mattaponi diet. Although some Mattaponi maintain jobs in nearby cities, tribal members still farm the reservation land. The Mattaponi people also fish, hunt, trap, and turtle. Efforts are underway to revitalize the Mattaponi language.[33]

The Pamunkey [pah-MUNG-kee] Indian Reservation, established in 1646, is thought to be the oldest inhabited Indian reservation in North America. The reservation's 1,600 acres are located along the Pamunkey River nine miles from King William. The tribe numbers 415 persons who reside on the reservation and elsewhere. The tribe has operated a fish hatchery on the reservation since 1918, the Pamunkey Museum and Cultural Center, school, pottery school, pottery guild, and program to assist its low-income citizens with home heating and utilities.

A burial mound containing the remains of Chief Powhatan, father of Matoaka (Pocahontas), is located on the Pamunkey Reservation. Also buried there is Powhatan's brother Opechancanough.[34]

Both reservations are governed by tribal councils. The two reservations are nine miles apart by road. Several miles downstream the Pamunkey River and the Mattaponi River join at West Point, Virginia, to form the York River, one of Virginia's major rivers, which empties into the Chesapeake Bay near its mouth at the Atlantic Ocean.

This long chapter on Indian life is not an unintended straying from this book's story line but the taking of American writers' underused opportunity to shine light on First Americans and their own holocaust at the hands of Whites. It is worth re-emphasizing that Virginia's only two federally recognized tribes happen to be the ones living within Frantz Ludwig Michel's land grant and that his humane inclusiveness to their ancestors may have set the tone that had much to do with the two tribes' survival.

FIRST EXPLORER

III. Twice Perilous Journey Home

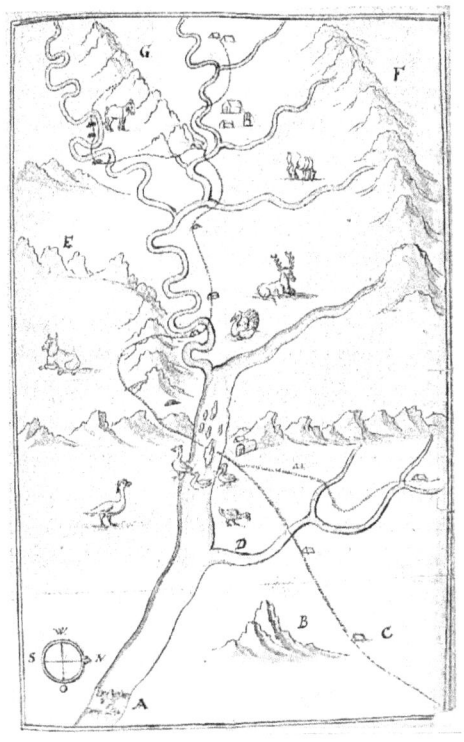

Chance Encounter?

After the disappointment of not being able to cross from Virginia into Maryland, Frantz Ludwig Michel had little choice but to turn around and head back. Having successfully secured a generous land grant, made the acquaintance of the colony's highest officials, gotten to know Indians and their ways, explored extensively, and recorded his impressions of New World fauna and flora, Michel had little more on his check list and headed for the port at Yorktown to seek passage back to Europe. He had accomplished all of this in five weeks.

His trudge back proved to be more difficult than the one out had been as in Michel's following journal entry. "To travel alone is not good and I do not want to undertake it again, because one is subjected thereby to many dangers. I was often made to sleep in outhouses,[35] and when tired and sleepy had to be apprehensive of some accident that might happen to me, because I was often compelled to take lodging in remote places where there was but a single house. If they had committed an overt act against my life or property, who could have made a complaint? Otherwise I lived better while traveling than when not. I made good use of their hospitality. One must, however, be surprised when lodging with poor people, for better food is frequently met with there than among the rich. At other places where I stayed I exchanged merchandise for food, and thus supplied myself with provisions. There is little opportunity to sell eatables, except in harbors and at inns. At these places it is expensive, for a meal usually costs a shilling."

Along the way when Michel came down with a fever, he was taken and in and cared for by two men who kept house together until he felt well enough to go on. He was weak for the rest of his trek back and had recurrences of the fever afterward including aboard ship when returning to England. Common causes of such relapsing fevers are ticks, lice, viruses, tonsillitis, and untreated infections, any of which the long-distance hiker could easily have picked up.

After making it back to Yorktown, Michel rested before finding a ship making ready to sail. As the ship still had a cabin available, Michel gathered his belongings and moved them and himself aboard to await departure, but this proved temporary.

While biding his time in Yorktown harbor, Michel encountered Anna Barbara von Lerber, one of the Lerber sisters he had met at Mattaponi, as she prepared to board another ship to return to England to buy clothes and other things for her sisters. She chose a particular ship because she had sailed to Virginia on it with its captain who had shown her and her family much kindness. Frantz Ludwig Michel would come to know the Lerber family well.

After eight days, Michel had an offer to transfer to "Captain Schmid's ship," which he doesn't name, when Schmid offered to take him to England free of charge if Michel would agree to do guard duty in rotation with others every four hours during the voyage. Owing to his continued weakness and recurrences of fever, Michel did not accept. Schmid then offered passage at forty shillings and would not compel Michel to work, but this, too, Michel declined "because it was a little ship, having every place filled with tobacco to such an extent, that there was no place of shelter in case of rain."

Then down the York River from Point West came the *Nassau* and Captain Byng, and Michel's decision as to how to get back to Europe was easily made. As he explained, "I rather preferred to go to my old captain, who showed me much kindness at all times and all of whose sailors I knew. Besides, the doctor, a Saxon, was my friend and the ship was better supplied with provisions than any other ship in the fleet. Experience confirmed this, because the other ships frequently sent for provisions from ours. Hence I thought, if sickness should overtake me, I would be among people who would render me assistance."

Fraught Voyage

As when trying to leave London, Virginia's July winds blew in fits and starts, halting much progress until July 2 when sails billowed at last and got the fleet of 154 ships including the *Nassau* underway, sailing as a convoy for protection against pirates and unfriendly warships of other nations. During the voyage, Michel's fever came and went and twice hit him hard but usually he was able to carry on through it.

Not far into the voyage, death, as it had on the westerly voyage, made its appearance when "Captain West, who commanded the ship *Bristol*, died. He had been on our ship four days before, because he was a good friend of our captain. The carpenter came to fetch a box from our ship in order to make a coffin. On the following day he was lowered into the ocean. All the captains who knew him gave each a salute of four shots, every minute a shot. After a large number of shots had thus been fired, the pilot, who took over the command in the captain's absence, expressed his thanks by firing all his cannons slowly in succession."

Michel again records at length on what goes into and comes out of the galley. As to meats, what went into the *Nassau*'s galley came aboard live but was only good for a day after being cooked. Part of the pantry was a virtual zoo with its "45 pigs, small and large, on board of ship, 1 calf, 3 sheep, more than 20 turkeys and turkey hens, 14 geese and more than 100 roosters and chickens," plus "what Mr. Foes, the preacher, brought with him, who had taken along many fowls and much strong drink, of which many of us had a share." And once again, as on the way out, "Our biscuit was full of worms, so that the smallest particle could not be broken off without finding them in it. This caused a general and great longing for the land."

A fleet of 154 ships sailing closely together faces special challenges of coordination. To begin with, to remain together the entire fleet can't move much faster than the slowest ship, requiring extra provisions and expense on what would otherwise be the fastest ships. Communication is limited by relying on cannon shots signifying one meaning or another based on the number and timing of the shots. Ships near one another may communicate by what Michel calls a speaking trumpet, a megaphone.

As Michel explains the coordination challenge, "Whatever wind may prevail (unless a storm is raging) the ships are turned against the wind, catching the wind with one sail and holding up the ship with another. As a result, the ship hardly leaves its place. The ship often yields to such an extent that it rolls to and fro on its sides, as we did almost daily towards evening, when we waited for those in the rear. This is the most disagreeable thing about a fleet, because some of the ships are not well provided with sails, or otherwise sail poorly, hence there is constant waiting for them, and often the best time is lost. The fleet commander has a war ship of 70 pieces of cannon and wonderful sails, for he often sailed faster with half a sail than we with eight."

Most important in a large fleet, real damage or even sinking results if ships collide. A large fleet of 154 ships must strike a balance between staying far enough apart to be safe from each other versus getting so spread out as to lose sight of one another. Even with a prudent balance, carelessness will cause problems as one night when a loud commotion arose. "There was no ship which did not fire off several shots to signal to others. This continued throughout the night. They thought pirates had fallen upon the fleet. The war ships sailed back at once to the place of the fire signals, but they found that two ships had merely stuck to each other, being entangled in their ropes. The bowsprit, which extends forward, had become entangled, and through the action of the waves, the ships bumped together, so that they would have done great damage to each other, if others had not come to their rescue. Especially when a strong wind blows and when it is dark and stormy, there is great danger in a fleet, because the ships often come so close to each other that they frequently pass less than four feet from each other and thus cause great anxiety."

The naturalist in Michel again hits its stride in his descriptions of flying fish, "their enemy, named dolphin by the English," giant sea turtles, seaweed blooms, kelp, and stray pigeons that, being too far from land, always return to the ships. On July 24, somewhere in the mid-Atlantic, the young naturalist turned twenty-seven.

Entangled ships, spoiled food, and a dying captain were not, by a long shot, the worst to come to the fleet and the *Nassau* as in early September what was possibly a hurricane barreled down on them and nearly sank the *Nassau* with all aboard. Michel's lengthy journal entry tells of the saga.

"On the 2nd of September we saw a dull sky and the wind began to blow from the south with such force that only the foresails could be used. But all this was nothing compared with what happened on the 3rd of September, old style.[36] I cannot possibly describe our condition and the terror of death at that time. When day was breaking, the wind increased to such an extent that we all feared a disaster. The fleet at once scattered, that we might not be hurled against each other to our destruction. The weather was dreary and black. The wind took the water and drove it along like clouds and fog. The waves rose to such a height and broke down upon us with such a roar that it was terrifying to behold. The wind also howled awfully through the masts and sails. That, however, was like nothing. But when the storm tore the sail away and the helm or rudder refused to work, so that the ship was laid over on one side, and was thrown about from one side to the other, then such a quantity of water dashed over and into the ship that, when they tried to pump it out and wanted to work, it was impossible to stand upright, and they had to hold fast to the ropes, that the water and wind might not sweep them out.

"The greatest terror was caused by the fact that, when

they measured how much water was in the ship, they found that there were already five feet in the tobacco room, as the color of the water soon showed, for when it was pumped out it was all yellow from the tobacco. In addition, the coner [the helmsman's mate] announced the bad news that there was a hole in the ship. Truly, hope for our rescue was small at that time, even among the most experienced. Death was depicted upon the faces. Everyone moaned so that it was pityful to hear. Whatever was not well tied or nailed down, was partly thrown into the ocean, partly broken to pieces, for nothing of such things was safe. The greatest damage was done when one of the highest waves broke down upon the ship from behind, injured the stern and knocked out the windows above and below. It dashed over the upper part of the ship, knocked down the captain and the physician, who were on the quarter deck, then it covered us on the main deck to such an extent that we could hardly bear the weight of the water and thought nothing else but that we were all drowned.

"At the same time the cry was raised that we should run to the cannons, fire off two shots, hoist our flag at half mast and thus signal our distress. But we saw none to help us, nor would it have been possible at such a time. When the storm had raged for four hours, it began to clear a little. The sun came out and the merciless wind subsided slightly. But then the waves began to rise still higher, that one's hair stood on end, so to speak. However, we succeeded so far that we were able to hoist half of another sail, in order to let the ship run before the wind. We also made every effort to pump out the water as best we could. We succeeded so far that it did not increase, and then we began to have some hope. The captain and Mr. Foes distributed brandy and strong ale to encourage the people. It helped not a little. We all worked till evening to hoist up the tobacco and to let down pumps with chains, which was our salvation. Afterwards four pumps could be used. Before night a ship came near to offer assistance, which we needed much. On account of the high seas we could not approach each other.

"But they promised through the speaking trumpet to keep us company during the night, which made us happy. During the night we had a fairly good rest, except the work of pumping out the water, as the ship was leaking very much. In the morning of the 4th we saw no fleet. Soon there was a call from the mast that about 90 ships were in sight."

Frantz and the *Nassau* had most likely experienced a hurricane. Of the fleet's 154 ships, twenty were missing, another four were sinking, and the sea was full of the flotsam and jetsam of destruction. Hundreds of lives were lost. At the *Nassau* captain's urgent request, the fleet commander sent his carpenter to the *Nassau* who nailed a patch of lead sheet over the hole in the *Nassau*'s hull, which slowed but couldn't stop the leak. The patch and round-the-clock pumping of all four of the ship's bilge pumps barely saved the ship.

"We had to work day and night to pump out the water. Double rations were distributed from now on till we reached England, because we had to pump so hard and incessantly day and night. This fear did us more harm than death itself, for it was a slow death and we felt it for some time afterwards. At that time, every one would have given all he had if he could have been on land, and I thought I would never venture into such danger again, but I soon forgot it."

Such a rebound is the spirit of the adventurer.

The *Nassau* was still 900 miles and about two weeks from land. It sailed on in good weather until September 18 when again it had to contend with "very boisterous, stormy weather" though nothing like what been endured before. "We were not a little afraid at that time, because we were not far from land and the condition of our ship was very poor. We could not leave the pumps nor dry ourselves. We met also another ship, and passed each other so closely that we threw up our hands in fear, but we did not touch. Whoever has not experienced the terror of the water, can hardly believe what the feelings are. But finally we saw land, which was the Isle of Wight."

Days later toward the end of September, the gravely injured *Nassau* limped into port at Gravesend on the Thames twenty miles downstream from London. Here it would be repaired and put back into service in the Mediterranean. Fevered, exhausted, emaciated, wet and forlorn, Frantz Ludwig Michel repaired to London, on the way delivering a letter for the *Nassau*'s captain to his wife.

During Michel's London stay, Captain Byng offered him a position to "keep book for him" compensated at half an English crown daily. After initially accepting, Michel reconsidered that constant traveling on the ocean did not suit him. When he thanked and paid Byng for the return voyage, the captain refunded him two crowns because Michel had labored alongside his sailors during the storm. Captain Byng then took his intrepid passenger to dinner and wished him well in completing his journey home to Berne. This is the same man who a quarter century later would command the Royal Navy.

Frantz Ludwig Michel's travel difficulties would take a different turn between London and Berne. As soon as he had reached Britain, he learned that mainland Europe was aflame with the War of the Spanish Succession, which had burst across the continent in July.

War, Sentries, Detours and Nerve

The global Spanish Empire at the time included the Spanish Netherlands, large parts of Italy, The Philippines, and extensive swathes of the Americas from Chile to California plus Florida and Texas, all taken together a tempting plum for dismemberment by Spain's foes.

The embers of the War of the Spanish Succession erupted in November 1700 when the childless King Charles II of Spain died and Britain and France attempted to use the unresolved question of who should succeed Charles as wedges to parcel out pieces of the Spanish empire to themselves. Charles's closest blood heirs were Austrian Habsburgs and French Bourbons. What led directly to war was the custom of European royals marrying other European royals, creating complex webs of cousins and distant cousins who often had conflicting political aims. Politics being thicker than blood in this case, the war was on.

The conflict would drag on until 1714 when three separate treaties would finally put the war but not the animosities to rest. The Spanish Empire remained largely intact, France was left financially exhausted, and Britain came away with Gibraltar and Menorca, which it captured during the war, significant trade concessions in the Spanish Americas, and Britain's displacement of the Dutch as the leading maritime and commercial power. Regarding Gibraltar, the *Nassau* had a hand in its capture after undergoing repairs and being reassigned to the Mediterranean. Under long dispute over more than three centuries, Gibraltar to this day remains a British outpost.

By the fall of 1702 when Frantz Ludwig Michel needed to make his way up the Rhine River back home to Ralligen, the war was raging full tilt in Europe. On October 8, 1702, a year to the day after he had set out from Berne for Virginia, he left Britain to go home. It appears that Michel already had another trip to London planned as before departing London he left some of his belongings with a Swiss resident of London named Bornas "to keep them for me till my return."

Since the dawn of human wandering in Europe, the most direct route between the northern Atlantic Ocean and landlocked Switzerland has been along the Rhine River, which falls more than 700 miles from its rising point in the Swiss Alps to the river's delta in The Netherlands and into the Atlantic. By the 1700s, sailing ships such as Michel had taken beginning his journey had begun plying the Rhine upstream and down as far inland as Basel, Switzerland, below the river's alpine fall line. Taking the river is how Michel almost certainly would have elected to get home had the war not eliminated most river traffic and made the remainder too risky to use. Instead, Michel was left with the well-travelled land route connecting cities and towns running along the eastern side of the river. On the river's western bank was France, which at the time was more heavily involved in the war, and on the eastern side, German-speaking peoples severely affected by the war's spillover onto their lands.

For much of its length, the Rhine today is the border between France and Germany. In 1702, the border was between France and what was then the Federation of the Rhine, a collection of German-speaking duchies, baronies, provinces, principalities and other small independent entities that were essentially the last of Europe's feudal fiefdoms before their consolidation into modern European nation-states. But it would be another 169 years before these German lands would coalesce into the nation of Germany. This multiplicity of jurisdictions meant many borders for Michel to cross, all of them now with wartime travel restrictions. The route taken by Michel and the travelers he met and helped guide began at Amsterdam in the Kingdom of The Netherlands and took a southerly course zigzagging back and forth across the Rhine through the Grand Duchy of Luxembourg, the Province of the Saar and Lorraine, the Province of Alsace, the Duchy of Wurttemberg, and finally to Switzerland's northernmost canton, Schaffhausen on the banks of the upper Rhine.

Ordinarily, going 400 miles (560 kilometers) from Amsterdam to Switzerland on foot would take three to four weeks, less if by boat. It would take a hazardous seven weeks for Frantz to be reunited with his family. Straight away upon sailing down the Thames, an incoming boat warned of hostile actions at sea along the sailing route to The Netherlands, causing Michel's voyage to be postponed until night for a safer crossing. Michel arrived at Briel at the mouth of the Rhine delta on October 10 where his latest adventure would begin. From the outset of this trip, Michel writes in the first-person plural but does not make clear who the "we" are if not poetic license by his 1916 translator meaning just Michel himself. A guess would be others headed to Switzerland from his ship or picked up along the way.

Day one of the overland trek brought sentries, being stopped for interrogation, and having to apply for a certificate of passage to be able to proceed. Michel reports that, "A few days before, Rheinberg, which can be seen from here, had been bombarded by the Brandenburgers, but, according to their own statement, they had lost about a hundred men."

When being blocked from proceeding for lack of high-level clearance papers at Duysberg, Frantz Ludwig Michel, the Lord of Ralligen, pulls rank on the local commandant to bluff his way through for himself and what by now is an entourage of other travelers headed for Switzerland. Along the way, he meets more travelers hoping to get to Switzerland including at one point a group of twenty "Switzers" (Swiss), two from the Canton of Berne, who join his growing group. A sizable neutral noncombatant group led by a nobleman stood better chances.

Further on, Michel meets two travelers who had been headed for Switzerland until they were stopped and robbed of their rifles by locals. At Muelheim, a guard warns Michel and his party of "the double and even threefold danger of traveling, as daily unfortunate accidents were reported on the one hand from the French, who make strong raids from Bonn, on the other hand, the farmers in Bavaria and in the Spessart Forest who are said to be very dangerous. Whenever they met a person, they would take his clothes and often his life."

During a long detour for safety through a forest, Michel talks down twenty riflemen who demand money for passage. Later, he learns that, to avoid four hostile companies of the French army farther along on the Great High Road that they were on, his group would have to detour three days "through wild regions, already covered with snow, to Hagen, Siegen, Dillenburg, Wetzlar, where the imperial chamber meets. Thence to Freyburg, in the Breissgau, finally to Frankfort, where we were strictly examined."

FIRST EXPLORER

As the group moved haltingly closer to Switzerland, lodging did not seem to be a problem since in towns they were able to find room in hotels and inns that had a surplus of space because the war was keeping travelers away. Nearing Switzerland as members of his party begin peeling off to get to their destinations, Michel numbers his remaining party at twelve. "The rest of us traveled safely to Tubingen, in Wurttemberg, where we had to pass through between the French and the Bavarians. In the center were the dragoons. Everybody told us how unsafe it was to travel and that some people had lost everything. We told them that wolves do not bite each other. We were soldiers too, who had swords and pistols."

With this bravado, pass through the twelve did, crossing the border between the Duchy of Wurttemberg, and the Swiss canton of Schaffhausen on December 1 after their fifty-three-day odyssey. The troubled return from the first of Frantz Ludwig Michel's expeditions to the New World had delivered him safely home. There would be more expeditions and more returns to come, but we know of nothing as fraught as Michel's first return through hurricane and war. Of his 422 days from Switzerland and back on this first New World visit, only fifty-five days had he spent in Virginia taking in what he had set out hoping to learn but that was long enough to determine the rest of his life's course.

Setting foot on Swiss ground again, the greatly relieved Frantz Ludwig Michel closes the record of his first expedition to the New World in gratitude for still being alive with "God be praised for ever! Amen."

The 1701-02 journal of his expedition to Virginia and back became supplemented in 1704 with Frantz's account of part of his time in Maryland. This single volume is nearly all that is known today in the hand of Frantz Ludwig Michel himself. From this single volume, we gain more insight into Michel the person than is available from any other source. The journal resides in Bern's central library, the Burgerbibliothek Bern.

With the exception of a few pages in that same diary at the start of his second American sojourn in Maryland in 1704, this marks the end of knowing Michel up close from his own journal, and the beginning of observing him from a step back through a few surviving letters and the vivid historical marks left in his wake. Nevertheless, his American expeditions to come go far in revealing him more deeply as explorer, scientist, colony founder again, humanitarian, and progenitor of a large American family.

FIRST EXPLORER

IV. The Dawn of Refugee Rescue

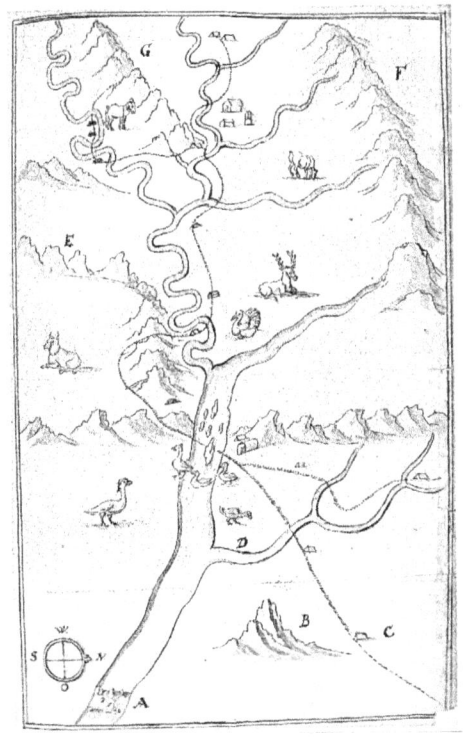

Three Humanitarian Families

Two letters from Frantz Ludwig Michel to Johann Rudolph Ochs survived when Michel's brother Hans donated them along with Frantz's journal from his 1702 Virginia exploration to the Bern Public Library. The first of the letters was written from May 6 to 16, 1703, when Frantz was in London, and the second a year later from May 20 to 30, 1704, from Annapolis. Other than his Virginia journal and a brief continuation of it in Maryland in 1704, these two letters and Michel's 1704 map are all that are known to remain from Frantz Ludwig Michel in his own hand until 1728. The letters give us one more firsthand look at the man, what is on his mind, and his inclinations. The two letters to Ochs illuminate the friendships among Michel, Ochs and Georg Ritter, the intimate connections among their three families, and the moral origin of their career-long refugee rescue venture.

Michel, Ritter and Ochs were born within twenty-one months of each other between 1673 and 1675. During the same brief period, Anna Barbara von Lerber, Michel's future wife, was born. Two others who would play vital roles in giving life to the grand plan that Michel, Ritter and Ochs would conceive were born on either side of the three men, Queen Anne in 1665 and Virginia Governor Alexander Spotswood in 1676. The five, working in concert, would alter history.

In 1702, Ritter's wife, Elisabetha, sponsored the marriage of Ochs and Anna Katherina von Lerber, daughter of the Governor of Landshut, a district fifteen miles (twenty-three kilometers) north of Bern.[37, 38] From 1702 to 1715, Johann and Anna Katherina Ochs would have eight children. Elisabetha Ritter served as godmother at the baptism of the last Ochs child named Elizabetha in her honor.[39] No record found shows Elizabetha and Georg Ritter ever having children.

Johann Rudolph Ochs's grandmother, Eva Ochs, was a

Lerber who may have been Mennonite. Her husband, Hans Ochs, was a prominent mill owner and mayor of a town in Berne Canton. In 1652 he became a member of the Grand Council of Berne. An image of the Ochs home and mill is shown in the center pictorial pages here.

Official Swiss persecution of Mennonites was already running strong in the early 1600s when the elder Ochs couple lived but to some extent Eva, if she was Mennonite, would have been shielded from expulsion and official sanction because she was married to a Protestant, a member of the canton's governing body no less. The young Johann Rudolph Ochs, born in 1673, would have been familiar with the stories of Mennonite religious discrimination, perhaps also experienced by his grandmother, that he heard growing up, and this was likely the root of his empathy toward the plight of Switzerland's Mennonites.

In 1705 Frantz Ludwig Michel would marry Anna Barbara von Lerber, the Mennonite refugee he had met twice in Virginia, and spend the rest of his life on his single-minded humanitarian quest of resettling refugees, especially Mennonites.

Here we encounter the question of how closely the Lerber families that Michel and Ochs had married into might have been related. The answer isn't revealed by the available record, but we do know that the two Lerber families resided only fifteen miles apart in the same canton, that both had high Swiss social status, and that the men they married would devote the rest of their lives to the rescue of Mennonites. These associations suggest that the two wives were likely related which made Michel and Ochs, if not brothers-in-law, then related by marriage.

We see that the Michel, Ritter and Ochs couples were a tight-knit group in marriage, outlook and purpose, with all six of them having special interests in protecting Swiss Mennonites.

Michel, Ritter and Ochs were themselves not Mennonite but of the Swiss Reformed faith, otherwise they, too, would be refugees or under the threat of becoming so.

Their status as nobility in Michel's case, and high figures in Berne's commercial community for the other two, gave them the social heft that they were able to exercise in their close relations with the Mennonite community. The three also had the clinching advantage of having something that the Bernese government badly wanted: a humane solution to ridding the canton of its Mennonites.

Though the three men appear to have discussed the concept of refugee resettlement before Michel's visiting Virginia, the earliest known record of any of the three proposing a project to find safe haven for Berne's unwanted Mennonites is Michel's letter[40] of 1703 to Ochs, written while he was biding his time in London, in which Michel, in the words of historian Andreas Mielke, ". . . evaluates the possibility of forming a colony with a purpose that is not primarily economic. The idea as expressed is that of a humanitarian: the purpose is the establishment of a refuge for Swiss people in times of need. Michel, who is usually referred to as a military veteran, speaks here as if he were a pacifist, a Quaker or a Mennonite. His is an uncommon idea, not only for his times."[41] Here Mielke accurately characterizes Michel as the humanitarian that by this time Michel has chosen to be. Michel is twenty-eight and has heard the call.

Ochs took Michel's letter to Ritter who liked the proposal.

The Trio's Grand Vision

In his letter, Michel tells of his purpose of being in London, which is to be granted an audience with William Penn, proprietor of the English colony of Pennsylvania. As Michel reports to Ochs, "Thus far I have been unable to have an audience with him, but I have been requested to appear in the mornings. I have handed in a memorial, in which the matter is presented in the best possible form. I am now waiting with eagerness for the outcome. Otherwise, I enquired to my satisfaction about the land and am decided to sail with a Pennsylvania ship that will leave within two months. I found it annoying that twelve days ago I had to see the fleet leave for America and could not go along."

The "memorial" of which Michel writes is a proposal to Penn from the Michel-Ritter-Ochs partners to permit their group to resettle Swiss Mennonite religious refugees to the German settlements of Pennsylvania. Quaker Penn will enthusiastically agree. Over the next several years, Pennsylvania's refugee intake would grow substantially to include not just Mennonites but refugees of other persecuted sects from German-speaking areas within and outside of Switzerland, and refugees fleeing the raging War of the Spanish Succession in their lands. Michel's and Penn's meeting may be regarded as the beginning of what would become the permanent American practice of organized humanitarian refugee relief.

Michel also relates the misfortunes of his voyage to reach England from The Netherlands, which sound as harrowing as his near fatal passage from Virginia to England in 1702. His letter relates bad weather that beached ships in The Netherlands, then doldrums that delayed sailing, pirates seizing a mail boat, and his ship colliding with another, all of this just in crossing the English Channel.

Finally, Michel mentions the "stones" belonging to Ochs that Ochs had entrusted Michel to take to Penn for Penn's inspection for a possible purchase. These are gemstones which Ochs the lapidarist artisan has cut.

A year later in May of 1704 finds Michel in Annapolis, Maryland, writing letters to Ochs and Georg Ritter. His letter to Ritter would lead in 1705 to Ritter's request to the Great Council of Berne for the Council to make a formal proposal to English Queen Anne's Council of Trade and Plantations to allow the trio to found refugee colonies in America.

In this second Michel letter to Ochs[42] what he mentions first, referring to Ochs, is, "I hope that I shall in due time be able to receive such a worthy friend in my soon finished cabin, not one built according to new fashion, to be sure, but according to the old simplicity." Where Michel is building he refers to as *Arundel Conti*, which is Anne Arundel County, Maryland, where the colony's capital, Annapolis, is located. This cabin will serve as Michel's base as he confers with Maryland Governor John Seymour and others and plans his epic exploration of the far interior of Maryland months hence. The cabin would also become one of the suspected places where Michel may have stayed during gaps when the record runs dry on him.

Mainly this 1704 letter serves as a report and updating for Ochs's benefit on Michel's activities since he left Berne and headed for America. In the letter, Michel reveals that, "My daily journal with all details will follow with the next opportunity." This is the only known indication that Michel kept any journal beyond his 1702 Virginia log. This journal was written in the same volume as was his first, filling it. As Michel's brother Hans ended up with the journal, we are to assume that Michel mailed the journal as promised and that Ochs, after reading it, gave it to Hans Michel for safekeeping within the Michel family. This is the journal that eventually Hans Michel donated to the Bibliotheque Berne, the public library of Bern.

While passing through Rotterdam and London, Michel gathered a collection of materials including his own report on Philadelphia with a city map, and others' reports on Pennsylvania, "in short, a complete guide for those who want to travel there."

His letter describes his second trans-Atlantic voyage: "This distressing weather scattered our fleet to such a degree that even now ships are still arriving, which because of lack of water, loss of masts, diseases and other such events were forced to seek land at Bermudos, Barbados, Carolina, and other places. The loss of the ships has already been reported and there are too many accounts to repeat here. The governor here [Seymour] was on board of the commander's ship that arrived here only four weeks ago. We were about one hundred sails strong, among which were four warships, but some left us and sailed to

Guinea. As to our ship, it was one of the best; it was the second to reach land, that is on January 16th. Such a long and dangerous passage is unusual."

We see that Michel waited four months to compose his letter, but he had reasons for the delay: "We found such an unusual cold here, but only for five days, as I have never seen. Most of the waters were frozen and hence I was forced to postpone my journey to Pennsylvania until spring and get a house here."

Eventually it warms enough that Michel can visit Philadelphia for the first time. He is impressed: "Philadelphia is a city of twenty-two years, whose growth and fame to be preferred to most English-American cities. I was amazed to see the difference with other cities in this country, in view of its size, huge buildings, daily construction of new houses and ships, the regularity of the streets, the abundance of food at a much lower price than in the neighboring towns."

Michel also pays close attention to the personal rights that William Penn told him to expect in Pennsylvania when he writes, "Most important, there is such an influx of people from other provinces which is mostly due to the liberty which all foreigners have to trade, to believe, and to live as each understands it."

He visits the nearest of the colony's German settlements: "Six miles from here lies a large village, a mile long, named Germantown where almost all inhabitants are Germans. A Frankfurt company bought 30,000 acres land with this objective, that, when they and their people should be compelled through war, religion, or other events to leave their home and fatherland, they there find a certain and safe residence. I found the place very convenient . . . because it is just like living in Germany. Three large tracts of land of equal size adjoining each other were also for sale at a small price. I found the place convenient and intended until a better opportunity to live in the neighborhood."

Concluding his letter to Ochs, Michel tells of his plans for his coming exploration with which he would become most identified, his epic deep probe beyond the English colonies' Atlantic coast into western Maryland, Virginia's Shenandoah Valley, and the Appalachian Range. Here he articulates his audacious vision of melding exploration, colonization, and public-private partnership to pull off what up to that time would appear to be the world's first large-scale refugee rescue enterprise. As to scale, Michel's grand vision would join Old World and New World across an ocean for thousands who would be able to lead newly peaceful lives.

In his words, "The reason why I returned to Maryland the beginning journey to the still rather unknown western regions, of which the Indians here know to tell wonders, on account of high mountains, where warm waters, rich minerals, fertile land, large rivers and an abundance of game are found. To that end I associated myself with eight well-experienced Englishmen and four Savages, together with eight horses, two of which are to carry furs at my expense.

"Although we are taking provisions for not even six days, we do not expect to return before four weeks. Game, however, is so common that daily one faces more than one can use. Some have the intention to take up land, as do I, if it is feasible. Others go to hunt, some to discover mines. I for my part go to satisfy my old curiosity, to seek out unknown things and to collect the wonders of nature, as I have already not a small number of specimens that cannot be seen without amazement. Last evening I shot two *racon* [raccoons] in a tree. I have also a live *poson* [opossum]. It carries its young in an open belly and lets them out and in again at will."

Michel then explicitly explores the proposition of using the thinly populated New World for the resettlement of European refugees: "I am quite of the opinion that the government or mostly private persons will in time get a better knowledge of this country. How praiseworthy and easy would it be to establish a colony similar to that of other nations, which would bring more glory and praise than to send a large number to the butcher block just for money.[43] We think it may be an honor; other nations, however, speak of it differently. What was the intent of Hollanders, Swedes, Finns, Germans etc. and other nations, which send people to this country, other than to be able to use such places in case of need?

"I have already noticed sufficiently how willingly the English government would consent to that. Who has more reason to look for expansion and places of retreat than just our country? I cannot but conclude than the authorities become guilty in that they do not assist in this matter with word and deed the many empty hands and hungry bellies. How easy it would be to present a proposal to the English Crown, the answer would soon show whether it is feasible or not."

It was this suggestion that led to Ritter drafting the trio's first proposal that would be submitted to the English government. Here in Michel's 1704 letter to Ochs we see revealed the first appearance of the grand vision that would have Michel, Ochs and Ritter relocate thousands of refugees from one continent to another and become a permanent humanitarian fixture in governments around the world. Grand indeed.

Let us be clear though that theirs was not quite the first such undertaking. That distinction belongs to William Penn who between 1671 and 1677 made three trips to German areas of Europe where he gathered Quaker, Mennonite and other persecuted religious refugees and got them to Pennsylvania and freedom. It was Penn's prototype which the trio expanded upon into a permanent, large-scale international phenomenon.

In closing his letter, Frantz Ludwig Michel tells Ochs that, "Writing this is accomplished with difficulty." No ink was available in *Arundel Conti* so Michel had made his own from gunpowder, which is one part charcoal. His letter with its gunpowder ink survives today.

Michel's Choice

We now come to the remarkable impetus of the young Swiss scientist, not yet near his thirties, who became the first in any of the English colonies of North America to explore inland much beyond the Atlantic coast. With his second exploration in 1704, Frantz Ludwig Michel virtually single-handedly was able to get England's Atlantic coast colonies to pivot their eastward gaze away from their mother country across the ocean toward their own promising land to the west and on into the Appalachians. In doing so, Michel opened to English, German, and his own Swiss settlers, and to thousands of European refugees, a welcoming home that would transform the newcomers who, in their newfound freedoms and comforts, would before long begin to think of themselves as that new breed calling itself American.

But before venturing off to America for the second time, Frantz Ludwig Michel had to have had a reckoning with himself as to risk. On his outward Virginia trip in 1702 he had experienced a mutiny, a tornado, food poisoning, the threat of pirates, and witnessing burials at sea all before ever setting foot in Virginia. There he suffered heat prostration, fever and exhaustion. On his return home, he barely survived a hurricane, near sinking of his ship, exhaustion again, and having to dodge warring armies to get home. Only a combination of luck and fortitude had kept Frantz alive as he negotiated this fourteen-month gauntlet.

Just seventy-five days after making it safely back to the comforts of home, what could make Michel willing to gamble against high inestimable risk a second time? At this point, no one would have blamed Michel if he had said "never again" to the perils through which he had just come. Why not settle in comfortably at Ralligen and pursue his humanitarianism there by relocating Swiss and other European refugees from the front of the pipeline as Ritter and Ochs were planning to do rather than at the far

American end?

The answer to his choice seems to lie only in the character of Michel the man. In fact, despite Michel's travails in Virginia he had also had his successes there and they were major: making the acquaintance of virtually all of the colony's top officialdom, securing a large land grant and establishing it as a refugee destination, exploring colonial Virginia south to north and back again, and taking his wide-ranging naturalist's observations back to Europe and making them available. This tide of smash successes in Virginia—all in fifty-five days—would have been forefront in Michel's calculus as he pondered his next move. It must have been that, in his mind, the good that he was able to accomplish in Virginia outweighed the difficulties that he had endured getting there and back, as bad as they were. The adventurer and risk-taker now evident in Michel won out over conventional assessment.

At this point we also recall Michel's frame of mind as he was closest to perishing in the barely afloat *HMS Nassau*. After weeks of pumping bilge to save his life, he had this to say in his journal. "At that time, every one would have given all he had if he could have been on land, and I thought I would never venture into such danger again, but I soon forgot it."

"Soon forgot it" is the kind of sentiment that issues from a born adventurer.

But behind all of this, we see that what also had to have propelled Michel were inborn determination, courage, an extremely far vision, and the deep fulfillment that comes from having chosen a humanitarian life. These traits are what propelled him.

Frantz Ludwig Michel was rare and just getting started.

V. Maryland Expedition: Bending History

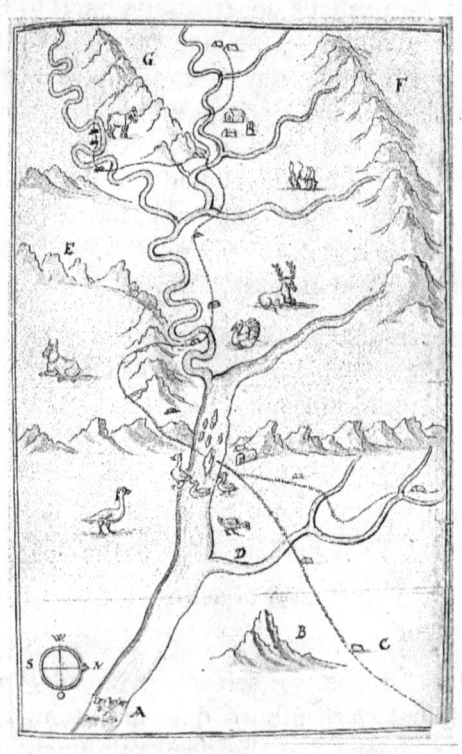

First Beyond Atlantic Shores

The remarkably busy Frantz Ludwig Michel once again left Berne on February 14, 1703 for London and America. It had been only eleven weeks before when he had reached home from his first trip. As on his initial New World trip to Virginia, Michel continued his journal on this second trip but this addition only goes up through the time that Michel spent in Annapolis preparing for his exploration of western Maryland and the Appalachians. We know from his famous map that he drew during his Maryland exploration that he recorded that much of his exploration and that the map ended up in the British archives as part of the Bernese trio's application to found other colonies in British America. Does that mean that he kept another journal on this second expedition? We don't know. If so, it has been lost to time but the map survives.

Nor is Michel known to have kept a journal on his other explorations yet to come, or, if he did, their whereabouts have also been lost to time. We are also limited by the relative paucity of the archival record of a subject who died more than three centuries ago, including for what little remains of what Michel accomplished on this, his second trip to America. What we do have is the important and, for its time, highly detailed map of Michel's exploration far deeper into the North American continent's eastern rim than any European had dared go before. In addition to everything else that this broadly erudite man was, he was a commendable cartographer for his era.

Michel's 1704 exploration of western Maryland was the first in any of England's thirteen Atlantic seaboard colonies—what would evolve into the United States seven decades later.

It took a century after the Maryland colony's first European settlers arrived aboard the *Ark* and the *Dove* in 1634 and began settling along the Chesapeake Bay's shores until their great-grandchildren would begin to filter as far west as what today is known as Western Maryland, less than seventy miles away. It would take until 1649 until Governor William Stone would found the colony's capital at Annapolis, 1729 before Baltimore budded into being, and 1748 before the colony had its first noncoastal county, Frederick County, which when chartered covered the entire colony west of its string of bayside counties. In 1704, exploration as far inland as the Appalachian Range was no more than a concept if even that. "Western Maryland" was a hazy abstraction.

Western Maryland as it is thought of today begins a few miles east of the Monocacy River Valley, a rich alluvial north-south plain draining the Potomac River's largest tributary forty miles west of Baltimore and Washington, DC. Beginning a few miles farther west, Western Maryland extends 150 miles across most of the Appalachian Range to Maryland's western tip where the range then drops down and fades into its western foothills at the Ohio River.

Western Maryland's earliest known settlement, Monocacy, with its Moravian log church, was founded sometime between 1725 and 1730 at a now forgotten site near the present-day hamlet of Creagerstown in Frederick County. By 1730 small numbers European settlers began trickling into Western Maryland from the bayside and from pioneer German settlements in Pennsylvania around Pequea where Michel would found a refugee colony in 1710. In the 1730s and 1740s the trickle became a regular flow of settlers moving the eighty miles from Pequea down the ancient Susquehanna Path, today's Maryland Route 194, to the area that in 1745 would become Fredericktowne, Maryland. This influx of newcomers from Pennsylvania was almost entirely German speaking.

By 1736, the Evangelical Lutheran Church, the region's oldest still in operation, was founded and by 1741 Thomas Cresap began operating his remote trading post at a site deep into the Appalachians at present-day Oldtown. When Fredericktowne was platted by Irish immigrant Daniel Dulany the Elder in 1745, Dulany began recruiting settlers from the Pequea area to settle his new town. The County of Frederick was chartered three years later with Fredericktowne as its seat.

But a quarter-century before any of this early settlement began, when there had never been any Europeans of record in western Maryland, came Michel in 1704. It was during Michel's second sojourn to America in that year that he would map and record his impressions of Western Maryland and Virginia's Shenandoah Valley as he extensively explored scouting for sites for more colonies. This utterly novel, continent-opening undertaking would soon unlock the territory he explored to settlement that, for better or worse, would forever change North America.

But before Michel, indigenous explorers, of course, had roamed the Americas as far back as 18,500 years ago and perhaps earlier. And explorers they were, traversing the entire 11,000-mile length of the American continents from Alaska, where they arrived from Siberia, to Tierra del Fuego at the southern tip of South America, apparently over only about a thousand years.

Better Prepared

On Frantz Ludwig Michel's first expedition in Virginia in 1702, he explored from Williamsburg up to the border of Maryland and back to Yorktown, never leaving areas of European settlement, barely populated as some of them were. It is doubtful that he ever got farther inland than seagoing ships reached going up Virginia's wide rivers or that he went as far as halfway into the Virginia piedmont from the sea. He mentions mountains that he saw in the distance, Virginia's first line of the Appalachian Range visible on a clear day from where he was but he never ventured close to them during his 1702 exploration. Neither had any other European or at least any who left a record.

Michel's 1710 expedition when he would venture to the Carolinas and try to stabilize a Swiss colony there, was much the same as he had experienced in Virginia. Like

Virginia, the Carolinas were a proposition of where and how much to explore, or should be explored, being unable to assess the risks of venturing deeper inland.

For both Virginia and the Carolinas, Michel earned full credit as an explorer for the adventure and risk that he faced to probe as far inland as he did. But nothing he undertook in any of those colonies would come close to matching the extent or daring of the exploration that in 1704 he would make into western Maryland and beyond two mountain ranges deep into North America.

On this second of his expeditions Michel would venture far beyond any place of European settlement or where Europeans had ever explored, use personal skills to relate well to and avoid confrontation with the Indian villages that he passed through, and produce the world's first map of the broad area that he covered. His 1704 expedition would introduce the European world to distant valleys, rivers and mountains that, because of this exploration, would begin to attract settlers within thirty years. This second expedition more than 300 years ago, opened up the very area of western Maryland where the author lives today.

Like the detailed journal that Michel kept on his first expedition that has long been so useful to writers and historians, Michel's 1704 letter to Ochs mentions that he was continuing his journal on this second expedition. On his Maryland trek, he did produce his famous annotated map and mention his discoveries in a very few letters. Perhaps the most telling description was written by Frantz's brother Hans Ludwig Michel whom we would assume listened intently to his brother by the hour describing his New World exploits. Frantz's Virginia journal quoted herein is actually Hans's transcription of it into his own finer hand.

As seen from his map, Michel landed at Annapolis when arriving in America on his second visit. At this point, the reader is referred to the map in the pictorial pages here as we make our way along Michel's expedition path, which leads out in a mid-coastal direction from Annapolis. The map is presented twice: as Michel drew it and as annotated by the author. In both versions, sites A through H are as in Michel's original map; in the annotated version's sites H through Q have been added by the author. Note that north faces right the way that Michel drew his map. The original map is in the possession of the Public Record Office of Great Britain's National Archives in London.

As it was translated into English when it was filed as part of the Michel-Ritter-Ochs colonization application in 1707, the legend of Michel's original map appears as follows along with modern place names. A list of Michel's fifteen campsite locations is provided as an appendix here.

German-to-English Translation	*Modern Place Names*
A. Rocks in the River called Potomack, as far as one can ascend in barques and beyond in small boats	Great Falls, Maryland, 20 miles upstream from the Potomac River fall line
B. A spring which flows 60 miles from Annapolis	At foot of Sugarloaf Mountain, possibly the rising point of either branch of Bennett Creek or of the Little Monocacy River
C. First hut which was made to sleep in on the trail on the route	The pup tent symbol denotes Michel's campsites. He probably didn't construct huts.
D. A river called Quattaro	The Monocacy River
E. Mountains of Virginia	The northern Virginia reaches of the Blue Ridge Mountains
F. Region of the Mesesipi	All westward from Virginia's Massanutten Range to the Mississippi River
G. Mountains of Cenentua	The Massanutten Range (Cenentua is Michel's hearing of Shenandoah)

The route that Michel took works out to be 230 walking miles or a little more from Annapolis to the point in the Virginia mountains where he turned around to retrace the route back, so a total of about 500 miles when Michel's sidetrip from Conoy is counted. Without multi-day layovers along the way, this would have entailed a minimum of four weeks of hiking at nearly twenty miles a day, an ambitious pace, which assumes no delays and trails mostly in existence. But, as on his map, there were at least two sidetrips, one up the Monocacy Plain, the other up Massanutten Mountain. Michel's route, in territory generally familiar to the author, was along rivers and so was mostly flat, however often brushy along riverbanks. Thus, he could have made good time and four weeks may have been possible but longer would have been required if Michel wanted to make the most of his exploration. Four weeks is a baseline.

Michel would have encountered pleasant spots such as Great Falls, Canoy, and the extremities of his trek where it would have been tempting to linger, and Indian communities where to rest, mix and learn. Then there were true obstacles of terrain where the going was slow, and possibly illnesses or injuries needing to be mended. Also taking time were Michel's campsites in close proximity to one another at the end of his route up the north branch of the Shenandoah River and then again on the south branch. According to his map, these stays took five nights minimum and more if Michael was using them to explore.

Six weeks at least is a more realistic estimate of how long Michel's second expedition lasted, with seven weeks or more well possible. One source has Michel setting out in late February of 1704[44] but, aside from the seasonal impracticality of this, it is at odds with Michel's May letter to Ochs telling of the trip forthcoming. We are to assume then that this was a summer or fall trip for the man in a hurry to "satisfy my old curiosity."

After learning from his bad experiences on his Virginia exploration, Michel would certainly have prepared better this time. In Virginia, Michel had the benefit of nightly hospitality not available in the unexplored territory where he was headed in Maryland. He thus had to plan for shelter and food. In Virginia, he had traveled lands earlier largely purged of Indians but now was venturing deep into the home of uncontacted tribes, so he had to plan for personal protection. Considering all of these needs and more is the challenge of the long-distance hiker.

On his Virginia expedition, Michel wrote of his "sack," probably the kind of basic leather or canvas rucksack or haversack that hikers and climbers used in eighteenth century Switzerland. Being from a mountainous country, Michel might well have gained useful hiking and camping experience. Given the season, Michel likely wore a light longcoat or perhaps leather clothing to protect against rain and took along a broad-brimmed hat. Heavy boots would have been in order.

In his sack, Michel had to provide for shelter, warmth, food, safety and comfort, all in under twenty percent of his body weight, the rule of thumb for backpackers. He would have had to forage and hunt to feed himself and plan for berries and other fruits being in season when he set out. He probably took along lightweight dried foods such as fruits, pemmican, jerky, and hardtack but the amount of these would have been limited by weight and volume. He may or may not have carried a rifle which is a nuisance on a hike and little help if attacked in numbers but useful in getting fed. He may have carried a pistol which would have given a measure of security against animals. His calculus for security would seem to have been betting on his practicing friendly behavior rather than relying on gunpowder. He probably carried with him a store of light-weight goods that he could have traded for food or given as gifts with Indians.

Michel would have taken fishing gear, canteen, eating utensils, steel-and-flint fire starter, rope, towel, a sleeping roll, a good knife or two, and perhaps an oil cloth, tent, compass, salt, and medicines. He would have bathed and washed underclothes and socks in the rivers and streams he found. He likely preferred to camp at Indian settlements rather than in the wilderness where he and his party could become prey to large carnivores. He probably did build a campfire in the evening and tend it once or twice during the night. He would have begun walking at dawn to warm up.

Frantz Ludwig Michel either took along writing materials to record the invaluable map of his second expedition or produced it from memory later. If he was keeping a new journal on this second trip to the New World, he most likely used it on his hike. If only had it survived.

Lone long-distance hiking is a bad idea for obvious reasons but some long-distance hikers, the ones who long to restore through far-off solitude, wouldn't have it any other way. Think Cheryl Strayed and her 2012 book *Wild*. Based on his choices during his Virginia exploration, our man here would appear to be of that breed but on his Maryland exploration he did elect to take along the group of twelve hired hands who he gathered in Annapolis and mentioned in his May letter to Ochs. One source mentions one of the twelve as a Mr. Clark. Was Clark hired for his backwoods acumen? As a porter? Just for company? Safety in numbers? We don't know but his and the others' presence obeys a cardinal rule of wilderness hiking which is, for safety's sake, avoid going solo.

Where His Sons Would Go

As Michel sets out on this second expedition, we come to the end of his surviving journals. For the remainder of *First Explorer*, we no longer have the benefit of Frantz Ludwig Michel's own voice and the further authenticity that it would provide. However, from his highly detailed map of this 1704 expedition, we are able to make a number of reliable inferences that do help to round out Michel the person.

His route first took him from Annapolis along the few

trails of the day to Great Falls on the Potomac River. His map does not show this sidetrip but Michel refers to the falls. A beautiful spot much visited today, Great Falls is twenty miles upstream from the limit of navigability of the Potomac River, along the fall line of the eastern seaboard. From there his map shows that Michel went to Point of Rocks, Maryland, from there across the Potomac upstream along its Virginia banks to the Shenandoah River, then crisscrossing the Shenandoah's northern fork several times until reaching Virginia's Massanutten Range. From there he went overland to the river's southern fork, explored it upstream to the other side of the Massanutten Range, then turned around and retraced his route back to Annapolis.

Proceeding from Great Falls (A on either map), Michel would have made his way through heavy virgin forest and occasional prairie until crossing the Linganore Hills within sight of Sugarloaf Mountain (B), a monadnock landmark since earliest aboriginal times. Here Michel, Clark and the rest of the party camp (C) near a spring (B). The spring could be the rising point of any of three creeks originating on the slopes or at the base of Sugarloaf. These are either branch of Bennett Creek or the Little Monocacy River.

Their path then dropped down into the Monocacy Valley, the rich alluvial plain that drains the Potomac's largest tributary, the Monocacy River (D). Here Michel begins to find what he had especially hoped to, rich prime soil with good water. A generation later, Michel's sons would emigrate to this valley.

Looking up from the Monocacy Valley, Michel at last saw close up that mysterious range he had seen in the distance in Virginia, the Appalachians (F), now right in front of him within an easy half day's walk. He was looking at Catoctin Mountain (N), the first mountain of the Appalachians heading west in Maryland. Catoctin Mountain is a lean north-south ridge running fifty miles from Pennsylvania through Maryland, finally tapering off in Virginia where it is called Furnace Mountain. Catoctin Mountain is no more than four or five miles wide and only 1,300 feet high, but in the worn-down Appalachians, the world's second oldest range,[45] this counts as a mountain. Since the 1920s, Catoctin Mountain has been home to the Camp David presidential retreat.

Vanishing Home of the Canoy

Tramping across the Monocacy (Algonquian: "river of many bends") Plain to the foot of Catoctin Mountain where the mountain is cleaved by the Potomac River, Michel came upon the Indian community of Conoy, the major native settlement of the area. The place name Canoy, coined perhaps by Michel himself, was named after the Conoy people who lived there. "Potomac" is an English corruption of the Algonquian *Patawomeck* meaning "great trading place." The location of the great trading place was at a prominent point of rocks jutting out from Catoctin Mountain overlooking the river at Canoy. At this easily recognizable landmark, the northern and southern tribes would meet to trade goods and news with one another.

As it winds its way through this part of Maryland, the Potomac River broadens to the extent that it becomes shallow enough in places to walk across without becoming more than chest deep most of the year. This affords convenient crossings dating from aboriginal times up and down the river from Canoy. Using these crossings, entire armies with their horses, wagons and cannon went back and forth across the Potomac here during the Civil War. Before that, the physical safety of the crossings funneled Underground Railroad freedom seekers through the area.

The combination of the easily identifiable promontory located directly at a shallow crossing made the location especially convenient for the northern and southern Indian nations to meet at the point of rocks for trade. Today, where Conoy used to be is the old railroad and canal town of Point of Rocks, Maryland. The promontory itself was blasted off in the 1830s to make room for the Chesapeake and Ohio Canal and the Baltimore and Ohio Railroad to both pass around the point as their routes were being laid out.

As the Maryland colony first began to be settled along the Chesapeake Bay in the mid-1600s, the Piscataway Indians were the largest and most powerful tribal nation between the Chesapeake Bay and Potomac River and up into the first foothills of the Maryland Appalachians. Piscataway means "people who live where the waters meet" in the Algonquian, the mother language of the Piscataway. "Where the waters meet" is the peninsula between southern Maryland's Wicomico River and Saint Clement's Bay.

As Europeans arrived, the Piscataway lost control of their ancestral lands as the tribe's bands splintered and fled westward seeking new territory unthreatened by European incursion. Some of the largest band of the Piscataway, the Conoy, migrated from their ancestral riverside home in Charles County, Maryland, to the county's Zekiah Swamp a few miles away where they were mostly left alone and able to survive into the present.

In 1699, seeking to escape proximity of the southern Maryland settlers, many of the Conoy fled across the Potomac going ninety miles northwest to safety on an island in the Potomac River at the point of rocks. It wasn't far enough as that same year Virginians first began scouting farther upland along the river. On April 21, 1699, Giles Vandercastle and Burr Harrison, the first known European explorers of the upland Virginia foothills, came up the Carolina Trail, an ancient aboriginal route, to its well-travelled offshoot leading to the Great Trading Place where they found the Conoy. Vandercastle reported on the Conoys' fort on the upstream end of the island being "50 to 60 yards square, 18 cabins inside the fort, 9 outside, enough corn on hand to spare." The two saw what they estimated as seventy people but housing for eighty to ninety with the rest assumed to be out hunting.

One would assume that the Conoy were not pleased by being discovered and were just as glad when Vandercastle and Harrison rode off. But seven months later on November 3, 1699, Virginians David Straughan and Giles Tillett rode into camp where they were told by the Conoy that their fort had been built in fear of "strange Indians" and, candidly, that they were wary of the English.

Three years after Michel's 1704 visit, Colonel James Smallwood reported in December of 1707 that "few were at home" after "a great mortality" had struck felling fifty-seven men, women, and children dead from smallpox, that the Conoy had "temporarily abandoned the fort," and that "much corn was still in the cabins and last season's crop was still standing in the field." As it would be everywhere else in the Americas, European diseases, against which New World people had little immunity, had killed off most of the Conoy.

After the first European visits, the Conoy in 1701 requested and received permission of the hospitable colony of Pennsylvania to move there and in 1705 some of the Great Trading Place Conoy did, settling at Conejoholo near present-day Bainbridge, Pennsylvania. Remnants of the Conoy remained on Conoy Island until 1712 when the rest of the band moved north to Pennsylvania's Susquehanna River where they sought the protection of the German refugee colony at Pequea that Frantz Ludwig Michel would found in 1710.

The American Revolution took a toll on many eastern tribes whose villages were devastated including the Conoy who became scattered as far away as the Carolinas, upstate New York and Detroit. Their island in the Potomac retained the Conoy name until it was settled by the Heater family in the 1800s and became known as Heater's Island, the name found on maps today. However, one still hears a very few old-timers in the vicinity call it Conoy Island or just Conoy.

It isn't likely that Frantz Ludwig Michel's wandering into the Canoy village was enthusiastically received. *Here they are again.* One wonders how the meeting went. In his Virginia diary, Michel's tone toward Indians is at once sympathetic and wide-eyed anthropological. The character of Michel that reveals itself from what we are able to know about him directly does seem to lean toward his appreciative acceptance of those unlike him. In this light, it isn't difficult to imagine that Michel's time among the Conoy was cordial and that he may have received good advice from them on the deeper territory that he was about to explore. He may even have had the benefit of a Conoy guide on his sidetrip from Conoy but we don't know. His map shows that he camped at Conoy.

Sidetrip Previews the Future

While at Conoy, Michel explored eighteen miles up a local Indian path that was an offshoot of the aboriginal Carolina Trail. The name Carolina Trail was devised by the English after they had widened parts of what was an ancient footpath into a wagon road in the eighteenth century. In Michel's day, the old trail led northward from the Carolinas, through Virginia, across the Potomac River at several shallow crossings and joined the Susquehanna Path through Maryland into Pennsylvania. When Michel trod the offshoot path in his 1704 visit, it was just that, a path. Not long after European settlement of the area began in the 1730s, the old path was widened into a wagon road and named Point of Rocks Road. In the late twentieth century, the name was changed to Ballenger Creek Pike, a pretty, lightly travelled country road running from the Potomac to Frederick, the county seat.

Michel's map shows that he took a sidetrip in a northerly direction (note the orientation of the compass points on his map), crossing a large tributary of the Monocacy, then diverting from the main northerly trail to explore alongside the Monocacy River, and ending at the confluence of the river with its next large tributary. All of the tributaries of the Monocacy in this area are designated as creeks today. If the map is depicting the two largest creeks both flowing in from the west as shown, those would be, going upstream on the Monocacy, Ballenger Creek and then Carroll

Creek. This being the case, Michel went as far as the precise location of present day Frederick where these two creeks flow into the Monocacy. What he found were abundant fresh water, soils of rich bottom land, and beautiful views, all of it running alongside the eastern slope of the long ridge of the mountain called Catoctin.

The map also shows two "pup tent" symbols representing where Michel camped along this sidetrip route, which tells us that he devoted time to investigating the area. A round-trip walk between the Potomac River and Frederick can be done in a long dawn-to-dusk day but Michel allotted at least four days and three nights to this sidetrip. The attraction would have been obvious: with their soils, water and views, Michel's scouting found ideal places for future settlement. In the 1760s, all four of Frantz Ludwig Michel's sons would emigrate to the area that their father explored on this sidetrip. Three would settle in the newly founded village of Fredericktowne, today's Frederick, and one of the three would in a few years purchase a large tract in the exact vicinity of their father's first sidetrip camping spot and settle there. That same tract remains in Frantz Ludwig Michel's family seven generations and more than 300 years after him.

But what led to the sidetrip in the first place? What could have convinced Michel to draw out his schedule and deviate from his plan to keep going up alongside the Potomac River?

He could have used the convenience of the Conoy village as opportunity to re-gather his efforts, mend any injuries to his men, or restock provisions, and, as long as he was there, explore locally. Perhaps thinking of favorable places for future European settlements, Michel had his men fan out looking for likely places and then visited the one that got the best report. Or the explorer in him could have simply been curious about where the major north-south trail through Conoy led as it went north. Or, perhaps less likely, the Conoy could have recommended to Michel that he have a look at where the Monocacy River gains its first large tributaries.

While these are all speculative motives, the result of the sidetrip would go far in setting the future of Frantz Ludwig Michel's descendants and of the very area that Michel took the opportunity to explore on his western Maryland sidetrip.

What Michel also encountered about halfway from Conoy to where he turned around was the junction of the trail he took with the Susquehanna Path, a major north-south route passing from Pennsylvania's Susquehanna River through Maryland to Virginia's Shenandoah River. The route exists today as highways running from Lancaster, Pennsylvania, to Harper's Ferry, West Virginia.

Where German Pioneers Would Settle

With his scouting from Conoy, Michel would have spent several days in the area before moving on, crossing the Potomac at the Great Trading Place into Virginia and heading upriver. Examining Michel's map, it shows the path he took to cover the twenty miles to where he came to the Shenandoah River just upstream from where it flows into the Potomac. The route was straight through the area in the northernmost tip of Virginia that in 1730 would see its first European settlers, who were German-speaking refugees, arrive.

That year a group of seventy-one families from the vicinity of Michel's Pequea refugee colony and the Tulpohocken Valley of Pennsylvania trekked down the Susquehanna Path and the Monocacy Valley and crossed the Potomac at one of its shallows, quite possibly at the Great Trading Place given where they ended up. Moving west five miles along the Virginia side of the river on narrow river plains at the foot of Furnace Mountain, these pioneer families came to the place of beauty rich with bottomland soil and pleasant views that the community they had left had heard about after Frantz Ludwig Michel's report on the area following his 1704 exploration through the spot.

Here the industrious seekers of opportunity stopped, built their homes, churches, schools, and well-tended farms, and founded what they had hoped for, a contented prosperous community in their new land. Perhaps the historian who has studied the history of this group of settlers most deeply is Eugene Scheel, a retired *National Geographic* cartographer who is the epitome of the dedicated local historian in whom much of the nation's rural history reposes.

In his characteristically clear style, Scheel, a modern-day resident of the area, portrays these hardy German settlers thusly.

"What the founders called their new settlement is also not known. However, very shortly 'outsiders' began calling it 'The German Settlement,' and the name stuck for about 100 years. From the very beginning, these people were prosperous, but their prosperity was no accident. They were sturdy by nature; and strengthened by past hardships, they did not shrink from hardships of life on this untamed frontier. With rare foresight and self-reliance, they planned their community. They saw to it that within their own ranks there were artisans who could work metal, make clocks, weave cloth, cobble shoes, make furniture and tools, and distill liquor. With them they brought horses, cattle, poultry, swine, sheep, and probably dogs and cats.

"They had chosen to become Virginians, but they continued to live as they had in the old country. They spoke only the German language and followed their 'Old World' customs, refusing steadfastly to be dependent upon others. They were geographically and socially removed from the English settlements to the south and east and continued in fact as well as in name to be Germans. In contrast to the colonial costumes of the English settlements of Virginia, the people of The German Settlement dressed in the simplest kind of homemade clothing. Thus, it is quite clear that these people followed a way of life peculiar to them alone."[46]

These settlers' independence also defied, but not confrontationally, Virginia's official position of urging worship according to the Church of England. As Scheel notes, "In Virginia, church and state were not separated. In fact, they functioned reciprocally as the parish rolls were used to collect taxes. Nevertheless, it appears that The German Settlement ignored the dictates of both church and state, for they established their own Reformed Church, which played a prominent role in shaping the early life of The Settlement. Their early church leaders performed the functions of both preacher and teacher. Although public education did not become common until many years later, the church leaders saw to it that all of the children were taught to read, write, and cipher."

The industrious settlers also built their German- and Swiss-style log homes and bank barns. As local historian Edward Spannaus tells it, "Log construction of houses was brought to the North American colonies in the 17th and 18th centuries by Scandinavians and Germans, including Swiss-Germans. (The English did not build log cabins and houses when they first came here.) Much of our early architecture in the Lovettsville area came from the Germans and Swiss who originally settled in Pennsylvania and then migrated south through Maryland into the Valley of Virginia. . . . The Pennsylvania bank barn [was] also brought to America from German and Swiss parts of Europe."[47] (Lovettsville is the modern name for the German Settlement.)

Before moving on with our explorer, it is worth mentioning that shortly before the German Settlement began in 1730, settlers from the same German-speaking communities in Pennsylvania had begun to arrive in western Maryland to the very areas a few miles north of the German Settlement that Michel had scouted on his sidetrip from Conoy. Enough settled near Ballenger and Carroll Creeks, mentioned earlier, so that the county seat of Fredericktowne would be platted there in 1745. As had the migrants to the German Settlement, so had those to western Maryland heard the reports on Michel's 1704 exploration of the area where they chose to settle. Fredericktowne and the German Settlement are twenty-three miles apart.

Michel wasn't the only influence that led to the two nearly simultaneous migrations of Germans from Pennsylvania, but both migrations did begin not long after reports on his exploration got back to the Pennsylvania refugee communities settled by Swiss and Germans beginning in 1710 when Michel and William Penn founded the Pequea colony. To these immigrants, it must have been all the more alluring that the reports were in German by a German-speaking explorer.

Terra Incognita

Up to the point on his expedition as far as Conoy, Michel was not the first European to explore that far, as the two pairs of Virginians mentioned above had gotten there five years before and someone else not long after that had come through with the smallpox that had ravaged the Conoy. But where Michel explored on his route west from Conoy, now one range deep into the Appalachians, there is no record of any European ever having explored there until a generation later in 1730 when the Shenandoah Valley first began to be settled. In 1670, John Lederer, looking for an Appalachian passage to the "Indian Sea" (the Pacific Ocean), had explored as far west as the summit of the Blue Ridge Mountains where he may have been the first European to look down on the Shenandoah Valley. Seeing range after range of the Appalachians off into the western distance, Lederer went no farther. Batts and Fallam the same year and Cadwallader Jones in 1682 had gotten no farther.

The Blue Ridge is the first ridge of the Appalachian Range heading west from the Virginia lowlands. When Lederer descended from the east side of the Blue Ridge heights, the Appalachian Range remained unexplored by any European. Sometime before 1670, the cartographer Augustine Herman may have briefly surveyed up to the entrance

First Explorer

of the valley to be able to approximate the Shenandoah River on his map of Maryland but he did not explore.

In what was summer of 1704 by this time, off west went Michel from Conoy into uncharted unexplored territory, pure *terra incognita*. Two or three days after departing Conoy, Michel came to the confluence of the Potomac and Shenandoah Rivers where the town of Harper's Ferry, West Virginia, is today. One must think that Michel was as awed by this supremely picturesque sight as are people today. Michel's map does not have him crossing the Shenandoah at its mouth where there are class-two rapids, but upstream at the river's second bend where the river is wide and shallow and the West Virginia Route 115 bridge crosses the river today. The author has inspected this crossing, which is broad, shallow, and placid except in times of high water. Michel's map indicates two nights of camping on this twenty-five-mile leg of his exploration up to the crossing.

In his map and writings, Michel refers to the Shenandoah as the "Cententua," what he had heard from the tribes that he encountered. This was the name of the principal Indian tribe that occupied the large lowland valley near present-day Bedford, Virginia. Early explorers wrote the name variously as Senantoa, Cenuntua, Shanantoa, or Senentoa.

The name comes from the Algonquian *shin-hahn-DOH-wee* meaning stream of the spruces. Shenandoah was also the name of two Oneida chiefs who lived after Michel's exploration of the Shenandoah region. There are inconclusive theories as to how the river and its region took the name but most likely it was from the tribe of the phonetically similar name in the Virginia lowlands. The earliest likely opportunity that Michel would have had to hear the name was probably at Canoy or possibly later from other natives as he reached the Shenandoah Valley.

After fording the Shenandoah, Michel hikes upstream forty miles on the north side of the river camping twice until coming to where the north and south branches of the

Shenandoah meet where, according to his map, the cartographer Augustine Herman had not gotten near. At the fork, Michel hews north, unknowingly taking the river's longer branch leading to the headwaters of the Shenandoah. On his map he draws in the buck deer, wild sheep, geese, and turkeys he sees along that stretch.

Upstream he crosses the north fork of the big river and records a camping location near a Shawnee community denoted by his symbol for a longhouse. Further along it is the crossing of a creek, probably Mill Creek, and to two more close-together campsites where he stops and goes no farther. He has reached the Shenandoah's rising point.

An unproven theory later abounded that Michel lingered in this area to prospect for minerals and that he found silver ore, the location of which he then always kept secret. This theory would be expounded repeatedly by Christoph von Graffenried, a troubled Swiss adventurer who would become a lifelong nemesis of Michel. We shall encounter Graffenried further along here. No one ever found any Michel "mines" that Graffenried conjured, and no silver was mined anywhere in Virginia until the nineteenth century and then not at this location. A more logical explanation for Michel's spending time at this point was that he wanted to rest and enjoy his surroundings before tackling the long hike back to Annapolis. Also, if Michel had prospected here there would have been no keeping it secret because he was not hiking alone as at least his hired hand, Mr. Clark, was accompanying him. As the Michel researcher Andreas Mielke has noted, Frantz Ludwig Michel " . . . is no expert in mines and is still not primarily interested in or 'clowdy' about them. His main interest remains what it always has been, a colony in America for the benefit of the Swiss in times of need."[48]

Over a week or more, Frantz Ludwig Michel has hiked about ninety miles from Canoy and is now at the source of northern branch of the Shenandoah River behind the Massanutten Range, three ranges deep into the Appalachians. He is near the location of the future village of

Mount Jackson, Virginia, which would be founded in 1746. He has now become the first European to explore as far west as the Appalachian Range and probe it three folds deep.

The intrepid explorer has completed the first leg of his exploration. After perhaps a few days of local exploring, Michel retraces his steps back nearly to the main fork of the river, where he swerves south, hiking overland from the northern tip of the Massanutten Range near today's Strasburg and Front Royal, Virginia, until he comes to the south branch of the Shenandoah River where he makes camp. From there he sets out along the riverside directly up the Shenandoah Valley, "up" meaning upstream. Twice he fords the river to shortcut through its seemingly endless loops as the river winds its way upstream from the Potomac. On this stretch of his exploration, Michel has the Massanutten Range to his right and the Blue Ridge to his left, west and east respectively. As he progresses, he denotes on his map wild horses, three of his campsites in quick succession to one another, and the terminus of his exploration at the foot of Massanutten Mountain, the highest point locally.

His spending at least three days here at three different campsites within five to ten miles of each other makes it appear that he had found a place of particular interest. Speculation and intrigue would ensue over whether this longer tightly local exploration was the result of prospecting for minerals or, as Michel would be accused of, discovering them and forever concealing the fact. However, as this would be the location for which he would successfully petition the British government for permission to settle a colony, his lingering here would appear to have been much more likely spent prospecting for a good colony site, not silver. In 1731, this very spot would receive the Shenandoah Valley's first European settlers, a group of Mennonite refugees sent from London by Johann Ochs.

Another entirely plausible explanation for Michel's changing campsites so close to one another is one that any long-distance hiker is familiar with: coming across a better campsite.

As on his map, Michel, born wanderer that he is, climbed Massanutten Mountain, which is just under 3,000 feet in elevation. The dead-end path shown at that location on his map indicates a day hike, what one would do to avoid climbing with the weight of a pack. The 360-degree view from atop the mountain would have exhilarated Michel. To the east he would have seen beyond Massanutten Mountain, the Shenandoah Valley and the Blue Ridge down onto the Virginia piedmont and perhaps on a clear day to the Chesapeake Bay 110 miles distant. To the west he would have seen ridge after long parallel ridge of the Appalachians off into the distance, each ridge paler than the one before it, the signature view of the Appalachians. Michel was the first European to take in this scene or to see the next ridge to the west, the first mountains of the Appalachian sub-range, the Alleghenies.

Then he descended Massanutten Mountain, completing his outward exploration. In long-distance hiking, upslope rewards with accomplishment and a view, then downslope begins to restore. As he hiked back down to his camp, it is easy to believe that Michel felt deep satisfaction with all that he had done and seen on this exploration, and with having found not just ideal but beautiful sites for colonies to which to relocate his refugees. He had no way of knowing that the Great Valley of Virginia that he had just looked down upon would long be reckoned as one of North America's most attractive places, a beauty spot. It is still thought of that way.

But he had more joy to contemplate. As he would marry Anna Barbara von Lerber within months after returning from his exploration, Frantz surely had her on his mind. As his hope of identifying suitable destinations for refugees like her was now proven feasible by his exploration, the supremely ambitious young man could see his humanitarian dream taking shape, that there were soon to be welcoming places such as he was seeing that would

FIRST EXPLORER

make ideal refuges for people like Anna. That night as he lay under Shenandoah stars, Frantz Ludwig Michel had the world by the tail.

From his last camp at the foot of Massanutten Mountain, one morning Michel turned around and began the last leg of his epic exploration, the long walk back to Annapolis 230 miles distant. His map does not show a return route other than the way he went out, so we are to assume that he simply retraces his steps. By now, Michel may be into the glorious fall of the eastern Appalachians with its dogwoods, fruit trees, maples and meadows turning their way spectacularly through the color spectrum. Few places on the continent put on a fall color show as vivid as in the uplands above the Shenandoah Valley.

Knowing the route, he probably spends two to three weeks returning, perhaps taking a break at Conoy to tell his Indian friends there what he had experienced. There he would have looked up along the long ridge that is Catoctin Mountain aflame with its annual show of fall color. As hiking is perfect for pondering, his trek back would have been good opportunity for Michel to contemplate his exploration. He now knows that the territory he has explored is inhabited with Indian communities small and smaller, and that they are about a day's walk apart from one another, most likely spaced such to demarcate hunting territories. He has witnessed a land chock full of game and fish where no one is going hungry. He has come across innumerable places offering good water, soil, and weather with abundant game and excellent views perfectly suited for settlement. He understands that his deep first-of-its kind exploration is historic and an unequaled success.

As he hikes back, he might not have been thinking in terms of having witnessed a healthy man-nature balance around him, but he was in the midst of it. He does understand that the beauty of the Virginia mountains and valleys would be a powerful attraction for European settlement. He now also knows that the going is not so difficult when sticking to river valleys. Michel is a scientist and born explorer who revels in nature and reporting on it, but he has now also ventured twice to the New World looking for opportunity. In the backcountry that he has just explored and along the coastal plain that he walks back to the Chesapeake, he sees ripe settlement potential as he had two years before in Virginia.

Sometime in late summer or fall assuming a six- to eight-week exploration, Frantz Ludwig Michel made his way back to Annapolis and the home that he had had built. He has just completed an eastern American exploration on a scale like none before it and opened the Appalachian interior to future settlement. His vision is one of transcontinental refugee resettlement on a scale not ever contemplated by others to colonies that he will establish himself. One day on his ambitious exploration, the young super-achiever had turned twenty-nine.

Back at his Annapolis home, Frantz bathed at one of the area's many springs, got back into his regular clothes, ate at the town's ordinaries, and made his accustomed rounds of the well-placed, learning their positions on prospective immigrant-established colonies in Maryland. He was pleased with the encouraging responses and recalls that Maryland had been the first colony to institute freedom of religion when colonial Governor William Stone, the founder of Annapolis, had declared it in 1649. As he had already met the governors of Virginia and Pennsylvania, most likely Frantz also calls on Thomas Tench, the governor of Maryland, or his successor, Colonel John Seymour who he had met aboard ship on the voyage to Annapolis.

Seven decades after Michel's Maryland expedition, as the United States was coming into being, there were still only the original thirteen colonies, by then states, along the Atlantic. There would not be a fourteenth or a non-Atlantic state until 1791 when Vermont joined, ninety years after Frantz Ludwig Michel first set out for the New World. With the nineteenth century approaching, explorers and settlers were just beginning to filter in earnest through the Appalachians to places with interesting-sounding Indian names like Ohio, Kentucky and Tennessee. Back in 1704, Frantz Ludwig Michel had been a man far ahead of his time.

Before he packed his bags and sailed for Europe, Michel says in a letter to Johann Ochs that he has been able to sell goods that he had brought with him from Europe at good margins in Annapolis, in some cases doubling his money. These must have been expensive goods and a significant amount of them as Michel had been able to afford to have had a residence of unknown size built for himself with the proceeds. In his 1702 Virginia journal, he had mentioned the same kind of trading except now he tells Ochs that his margins in Maryland are twice what they had been in Virginia.

This investing in high-margin goods begins to tell us how Michel financed his time in the colonies, at least in part. He would also later report the same means of generating income in Pennsylvania. When he began serving as Pennsylvania's Commissioner of Mines in 1710, presumably he was compensated for it and likewise when he later served in South Carolina as a senior military officer. It may also be that he drew pay for his service from Georg Ritter's Society for the Swiss Colony of Virginia as Christoph von Graffenried did when he would sign on as the group's representative in London in 1707. Finally, Michel came from one of Switzerland's wealthiest families and may have simply relied on its treasury to support his explorations. Michel comes across as thrifty and careful with money, and his years on and off in America give no sign of financial strain. Michel's frugality seems to be a good fit with his humanitarian instincts.

We know nothing of Michel's next voyage back to Europe or what travails he likely faced on his overland journey back to Berne while the War of the Spanish Succession was still disrupting travel. But by late 1704, we are to presume that Michel was back home at Ralligen. In Berne he would confer with Georg Ritter and Johann Ochs, and the three would begin putting together an unprecedented, far-reaching proposal for a three-cornered public-private partnership among themselves, the English government, and the Berne Canton government to resettle Swiss and other European religious refugees to England's North American colonies that England was trying to populate.

They would succeed on a scale never before seen. Michel, youngest of the trio, would eventually found six refugee resettlement colonies in America, all of them successful.

VI. Three Proposals

Before moving on to Michel's second Maryland expedition, we cover three developments that took root between the expeditions. These are Frantz's courtship of Anna von Lerber, the beginning of his professional association with William Penn, and the genesis of the public-private partnership between the trio and the British government. Of necessity, these accounts sometimes cover times before and after the two Maryland expeditions.

Anna Barbara von Lerber

In 1704, Frantz Ludwig Michel was conferring more widely than just with his two humanitarian partners, Ritter and Ochs. It would have been during this time when Frantz seriously courted Anna Barbara von Lerber if the two had not been engaged already.

We recall that during his 1702 exploration in Virginia Michel had made it a point to visit the small Swiss settlement on the Mattaponi River where four of the six Lerber sisters and their mother had settled after fleeing religious persecution in Berne. The eldest of the six sisters was Anna Barbara. The two other sisters had apparently remained in Berne with their father, Frantz Ludwig von Lerber, Secretary to the Treasurer of Berne Canton.

As earlier mentioned, a few weeks after his visit to Mattaponi Frantz Ludwig Michel and Anna Barbara von Lerber crossed paths again at Yorktown as they awaited their ships to travel back to London. They sailed in the same convoy aboard vessels that both survived a hurricane. Thus, Frantz and Anna landed in London at the same time. In the journal of his 1702 trip, Michel makes no mention of whether he and Anna had gotten to know each other better in London or whether Anna was in the group that he escorted overland from Holland to Berne. If romance was already afoot, he may have felt that his journal was not the place to mention it. At any rate, we see by what was to come that Frantz had been smitten.

From the available record, it isn't clear when Frantz began

taking an interest in Anna or began courting her. It is not improbable that the two families, his of well-known nobility, hers of near-senior officialdom, had known each other in Berne, perhaps even since the couple's childhoods as Frantz and Anna were born within two months of each other. (She was older.) Anna was born in the Bernese hamlet of Bumbach eleven miles through the Alps from Ralligen. Did the two already know each other when Frantz visited the Lerber home at Mattaponi? Was his purpose of that visit to see Anna? To propose? Were they engaged when they set sail back to England? By the end of the voyage? Not until later? She had gone to London to shop for goods for her sisters at Mattaponi. Did she then visit her home in Berne, stay for a while in London, or return to Virginia? When she completed her shopping, did she ship the goods to her sisters or return to Virginia with them?

A plausible theory is that, following the custom of the era, both went back to Berne so that Frantz could ask Anna's father for her hand in marriage. It is also possible that the two had first met at Mattaponi, become friends after disembarking in London, and gotten in touch again after reaching Berne with a bond by then having been forged by each having the same fantastic tales to tell of close calls at sea and on the walk home. Aside from speculation, what we do know is that over the three months from late June of 1702 until September 28, 1702, from Mattaponi to London, the couple was in close proximity to one another and may also have been together on the way to Berne in October and November of that year if that is where Anna went. Thrown together like this, a bond between Frantz and Anna certainly had been forged by shared adventure, perilous risk twice, and perhaps mutual reliance. What they also had in common, of course, was that they were both from the same hometown and could share all of the memories that that entails.

Whether or not the purpose of their long arduous trips was her father's consent, it was in any case expected by custom. If it was sought, the dad apparently said yes. After all, his eldest daughter was marrying up into nobility. The groom was transcending institutionalized Swiss religious prejudice to marry the woman of his choice, a religious refugee adventurous in her own right, which says much about the character of both of them. It helped the couple that his nobility conferred privilege enjoyed by only the few in Switzerland, that Mennonite wives of Protestant husbands were exempt from expulsion.

It may be that the lives of the roving adventurer and the on-the-move refugee may have offered little chance for romance until they crossed paths at Mattaponi in 1702. Genealogical information on both Frantz and Anna showing the couple marrying in 1705 does not include a marriage date, place or record. This leads to the question of in which church did they marry, the bride's Mennonite faith or her father's and husband's Swiss Reformed faith. A 2022 search of Swiss church and civil records by a skilled Swiss genealogist did not turn up a marriage record for the couple in Switzerland but there may have been none if the marriage had been performed in the Mennonite faith, as Mennonites were opposed to civil participation outside of their faith and may have shunned civil registration.

What can be deduced from known dates is that from Frantz's visit to Switzerland in late 1704 his courtship of Anna concluded with the couple's marriage sometime in 1705 but apparently not in Switzerland.

A very thorough records search in London by a skilled Cambridge genealogist in 2022 turned up no trace of Anna in Britain. The search included Mennonite and other marriage records. Known are Frantz's official dealings in London and his sailings from 1702 through 1710 but little on his personal life during this period. It is known that off and on from 1703 through at least 1710, Frantz spent significant periods in London and that he took British citizenship in 1709. He had to have lived somewhere but it could have been places where records of his presence may never have survived such as inns, rented quarters or friends' homes. As frequently as he moved around among

London, Switzerland, refugee areas along the Rhine, and six British provinces in America, as often we *aren't certain of* where he was than we are certain, at least until 1716.

If the marriage did take place in 1705 as genealogy websites consistently report, and with no marriage or habitation record turning up in either Switzerland or London for Anna, suspicion shifts to America as to where Frantz and Anna were married. A plausible scenario is that when the two arrived in London, they spent time together and made plans before Frantz walked home to Switzerland. Anna may have gone with him or may have remained in London and shopped for her family as planned. Whether she went on to Switzerland or not, Frantz could have asked her father for Anna's hand in marriage once he was there.

It is conspicuous that Frantz spent only seventy-five days at home before going back to London where he stayed for seven months working with William Penn and planning his return to America, this time to Maryland which he had not been able to visit before. More conspicuous is that as soon as Michel reached Annapolis, Maryland, where he landed in early 1704, he had a home built there. If he and Anna were now married or were about to be, the couple had three ready places to live: with her sisters at Mattaponi in Virginia, at Frantz's nearby King William land grant, or at the new home in Annapolis.

Two additional pieces of the puzzle become evident when considering marriage customs. First, typically the wedding takes place at or near where the bride lives, often in her church. This would put Frantz and Anna's wedding in Virginia near her home. The small Swiss community to which she belonged may or may not have had clergy or, even less likely, Mennonite clergy. Second, nearby was Reverend Pierre Sabattie, the French Huguenot refugee who Frantz had sailed with to Virginia in 1702, now residing in the colony he had been granted that year beside Michel's King William.

Or the marriage could have been in Annapolis near the new home or in Philadelphia or Germantown, Pennsylvania, by which time Michel had visited. Or anywhere else. But based on custom and friendly clergy, the most likely venue of Anna and Frantz's marriage was her home or church in Virginia.

Wherever they married assuming 1705, Anna and Frantz were both thirty, considered late to be tying the knot in their time.

The Lerber family may have been split over religion. Anna's mother Madlain was a Mennonite religious refugee who had fled Switzerland and its mistreatment of religious minorities and raised four of the couple's daughters with her as Mennonites until she died shortly after arriving in Virginia. It is doubtful that Anna's father, Frantz Ludwig Lerber, could have maintained his official position in government had he been Mennonite. He was most likely Swiss Reformed, the dominant and, in effect, quasi-state religion of Switzerland by that time. If so, Anna's parents had the era's version of a mixed marriage unless perhaps they had separated or divorced, which seems possible given an ocean between them. Or the Protestant father could have been in full sympathy with his wife and the four departed children and been supporting them from afar through his well-paid government position. As it appears that the four sisters had little means of self-support in Virginia, it is not improbable their father continued supporting them.

As Anna herself had settled on Mennonism as her religion, she and Frantz would embark on their own "mixed marriage" in the face of continuing official and societal prejudice. This situation makes clear that theirs was not an arranged marriage nor one of political convenience among social elites, but was based on love, respect, the couple's insistence on religious tolerance, and inherent social risk. Given that Frantz Ludwig Michel was purposely aiding the flight of religious refugees as his calling, he was overtly practicing resistance against religious prejudice as a personal moral purpose. This would have been part of the foundation of his and Anna's marriage and may or may not have set well with his in-laws or his own family.

By all indications, Anna and Frantz had a happy if too brief marriage. After fifteen years together, a hazy record has her dying in in her mid-forties in 1720 but this is one more claim unsupported by proof from an original record.

William Penn's Quaker Refuge

In December of 1702, back home safely from his first trip to the New World, Frantz was surely delighted to again see his mother Ursula, his siblings, his friends, and his castle home at Ralligen. Upon return, he reports to family and friends what he had observed in America. In making his rounds, Michel espouses the concept of founding more colonies in Britain's North American provinces.

While in Berne, Michel meets with his friend—and future relative by marriage—Johann Rudolph Ochs and reports on his Virginia land grant and idea of bringing in Swiss settlers to populate and work it. Michel associate Georg Ritter would have come into the conversation and the three would have begun formulating a detailed plan for settling Swiss religious refugees in America. One can picture the three, perhaps with others, sitting in an early eighteenth-century Bernese coffee house enjoying their reunion as friends and deep into daring visionary discussion of colonizing a new, far-distant continent.

Before being on his way to America the second time, Frantz Ludwig Michel while in London in 1703 had called on William Penn, proprietor of the huge colonial province of Pennsylvania, to learn first-hand of Penn's Quaker philosophy of religious tolerance and of the German refugee settlers that Penn had already welcomed to Pennsylvania. The two men quickly found common cause which led to their discussing the proposition of Michel's Bernese group sending refugees to a new colony to be founded by them in Pennsylvania. Penn was receptive. Discussion centered on settling Swiss colonists, especially Mennonites being persecuted in Switzerland who the Swiss authorities would be only too glad to see go.

Just twenty-two years before, the English King had granted an extraordinarily generous charter to Penn that made Penn, in a stroke, the world's largest private landowner. Anointed as proprietor of his sprawling tract, Penn had sovereign rule over the territory with total power except to declare war. Penn's extraordinary charter of liberties for the domain, which he wrote himself, guaranteed free and fair trial by jury, freedom of religion, freedom from unjust imprisonment, free elections, and to not exploit natives or immigrants. News of the liberality of the new colony spread quickly through Europe, attracting persecuted Huguenots, Mennonites, Amish, Jews and especially Quakers to seek refuge in "Pennsylvania," the name that the King had given the colony. From the Latin, it means "Penn's Forest." Penn, a Quaker himself, sought to create a utopia of personal freedoms, and, far ahead of his time, to a large extent succeeded, going far to plant the seed that would exactly a century later culminate an American revolution along similar lines in 1782. In effect, Penn and his Pennsylvania experiment served as American social prototypes when the new United States Constitution's Bill of Rights would be conceived.

In return for Penn's enormous land grant, it was stipulated that a fifth of all gold and silver mined in Pennsylvania would be remitted to the English Crown. Possibly interested in seeking silver deposits himself and having toured the Virginia governor's (unsuccessful) silver mine explorations, the promise of precious metals may have caught Michel's eye and become part of his negotiations with Penn. In turn, Penn offered to make the Swiss nobleman Pennsylvania's Commissioner of Mines, a position that Michel would take up but not until 1710. Until then, he would be too busy exploring for refugee resettlement sites in Pennsylvania and elsewhere and creating more American refugee colonies.

Michel had wanted to visit Pennsylvania and Philadelphia when in Virginia but had not had time to do so. In October

FIRST EXPLORER

of 1703, Michel left London and sailed for America, this time landing in Annapolis, making good on his previously thwarted effort to visit the Maryland colony. In January of 1704, he wrote Ritter from Anne Arundel County in Maryland of his plans to travel to Philadelphia, so named by William Penn from the Greek "city of brotherly love" to exemplify Penn's vision of his social experiment.

Crossing the Atlantic for the third time after the Maryland expedition, Frantz Ludwig Michel made it to Philadelphia where he came upon an enlightened society unlike any in Europe at the time. Growing rapidly from immigration spurred by Quaker religious tolerance, the Pennsylvania colony's population had grown to 18,000 and Philadelphia's to more than 3,000. Penn's tree plantings begun twenty years earlier now gave form to the green city he had envisioned. Shops were chocked with imports, proving America to be a viable market for English goods. Religious diversity was succeeding, schools were producing a literate populace, and Philadelphia had blossomed into the busy continental leader in science, medicine, social outlook, and style.

As William Penn had moved back to England in 1701 to attend to his affairs there, Michel would have met in Philadelphia with Penn's son, William Penn, Jr., who the senior Penn had put in charge of the colony. Michel might not have been impressed, as the younger Penn had a reputation for overindulgence and poor management.

After the senior Penn's Commissioner of Mines offer, Michel may have explored for silver while in Pennsylvania on this first visit. By 1709 at the latest, we know that he had become aware of Shawnee Indians extracting lead containing traces if silver seventy miles west of Philadelphia at a place in the wilderness that the Shawnee people called Pekowi.

But Michel's main interest in going to Pennsylvania was in observing the German refugee communities that he and Penn had discussed. The first if these that Michel visited was the aptly named Germantown six miles north of Philadelphia. Founded by German, Quaker, and Mennonite families in 1683, the town had quickly become a magnet for Europeans seeking to escape religious persecution. In 1688, Germantown had distinguished itself by becoming the birthplace of the American anti-slavery movement when a group of its residents published a condemnation of slavery and provided it to their Quaker church, the Society of Friends. It took nearly a century, but the 1688 Germantown Quaker Petition Against Slavery resulted in the banning of slavery by the Quaker Church in 1776 and by Pennsylvania in 1780.

Refugee resettlement, freedom of religion, open antipathy toward slavery—into this heady broad-minded atmosphere strode Michel with high approval of what he saw. What he also found in Germantown were the sons of two people he knew from home. Michel wrote to Ochs that he met the son of a Swiss bailiff he knows from Heimbhausen, and Hans Rudolph Bundeli, son of the Bernese rifle maker Johann Rudolph Bundeli.

After his business in Philadelphia, Michel next let loose the explorer in him and trekked westward into Indian country to the colony's Pekowi region for two weeks where he scouted for good land, water, and where to establish a refugee colony, which he would do there in 1710, naming it Pequea. Hans Rudolph Bundeli would become a major figure in Michel's 1710 resettlement of Mennonite refugees to Michel's new colony there.

As it would turn out, being Pennsylvania's Commissioner of Mines in 1705, which surely would have been a comfortable if stodgy sinecure, did not hold Michel's interest more than did being on the move for further exploring. *What's over that next mountain there, and the one beyond that?* He would continue to decline William Penn's offer but in 1710 accept it when it was put forth again.

At the same time, Penn would recommend to the British government that it appoint Michel officially as agent for Mennonite refugees passing through Britain to America. The formality of this dual appointment demonstrates

FIRST EXPLORER

Penn's and Michel's desire to have Michel and his partners funnel refugees to Pennsylvania. Penn's recommendation was acted on, leading in 1710 to Michel's establishing in the wilderness seventy miles west of Philadelphia a Swiss Mennonite refugee colony that would become America's most famous refugee settlement, historically even down to today. We will get to this. The site was where Michel had explored on his first visit to Pennsylvania. Its present-day name of Pequea ("PEK-way") derives from the Shawnee Pekowi ("PEK-oh-wee"), the name of one of the five Shawnee Confederation bands present in the area at the time.

It is likely that before returning home from his Pennsylvania sojourn, he went back to Annapolis where Michel had landed upon arrival. After its designation as the Maryland capital a decade previously, Annapolis, with its comfortable port and springs, had grown in population, amenities, and influence. Its port was already beginning to supplant Port Tobacco's as the province's main port of entry and nautical hub. Annapolis was the place to be in Maryland in 1705 and likely where Michel went after completing his business in Pennsylvania. Annapolis had begun life as the village of Providence in 1649 when it was founded by colonial Governor William Stone.[49]

The British Lords of Trade and Plantations

In March of 1705, Georg Ritter, representing himself, Michel and Ochs, proposed to the Great Council of Berne Canton to settle 400 to 500 emigrants from the canton in Michel's Virginia colony. Relieved to be presented with somewhere to which to expel the Canton's paupers, Mennonites and other Anabaptists, the Council endorsed the plan and submitted it to the British envoy in Berne, who forwarded it to the grandly named Lords of Trade and Plantations in London, the official body that would judge and decide on the proposal. And there the proposal would languish for four years before finally gaining approval after being modified three times.

Here a clarification of "plantations" will help. The term is not used in the adopted American context of slavery, cotton and tobacco, but in its older meaning of a new colony or settlement.

In its original form, the proposal envisioned emigrating the Bernese unwanteds to Michel's lands in Virginia that he had been granted in 1702 and getting a Swiss refugee colony going there, furthering Michel's colonization venture. Also envisioned was rescue of the growing number of German-speaking fugitives fleeing their homes along the Rhine River, the front line of the worsening War of the Spanish Succession raging just north of Switzerland. This consideration, of longer range than the core Virginia settlement proposal, was being actively considered by the Michel-Ritter-Ochs trio as a larger second phase of the project but was not included in the proposal as originally submitted.

It was unusual that the Great Council of Berne would endorse a plan of emigration since, by long-held custom and emigration policy not only of the canton but of most European entities, emigration was taboo and severely restricted or altogether prohibited. Willful emigration was considered as desertion of one's people and subtraction from a country's workforce. Mass emigration was seen as weakening a small country's ability to defend itself. Nevertheless, the Council regarded the presence of its landless and Mennonite populations as bothersome enough to override custom, making the Council anxious to endorse the Ritter-Michel-Ochs resettlement proposal.

After the proposal had been submitted to the Great Council in March, George Ritter escorted a group of Bernese Mennonites to Virginia to see the Shenandoah Valley for himself. In his book on early Virginia explorers, Richard Thornton reports that, "In 1705 George Ritter, a recent immigrant from Bern, Switzerland, led a small party of settlers to the Shenandoah River, immediately north of where the North and South Forks joined. Apparently, the area was still occupied by the Tobacco Indians. The party turned back after discovering that potential settlement sites were claimed by the Indians."⁵⁰ The destination cited is near present-day Riverton, Virginia, where the two river branches meet. Though Ritter respected Indian land claims by removing his colonists, this did not dissuade him and his two Bernese partners from pressing ahead with their resettlement proposal. Another source has Ritter "twice in America."⁵¹

Before Queen Anne's government in London would finally grant approval, the proposal would undergo two major modifications in 1709 and attract an additional two sponsors including one who would all but cause the failure of the colony ultimately settled. The first revision, submitted in 1707, was, instead of at Michel's King William colony, to locate two colonies in Maryland along the banks of the Potomac River at Conoy and Great Falls and a third in Virginia's Shenandoah Valley. The key to approval was the inclusion in the second revision of the trio's proposal of a copy of Michel's 1704 expedition map.

In the summer of 1709 when the British government finally assented to a colonization plan, the Lords of Trade and Plantations approved only a single colony to be situated in the Shenandoah Valley, but then at the last minute switched the permission to Britain's Carolina provinces. Shortly after the switch, the Lords of Trade and Plantations reconsidered the Shenandoah Valley proposal and approved a colony there while continuing its Carolina approval. The site approved in the Shenandoah Valley was at the terminus of Frantz Ludwig Michel's exploration at the southern tip of Massanutten Mountain.

We will get to these twists and turns of fate and their unusual outcome further on. The reader interested in the detail of the application and approval processes may consult the verbatim official records provided in Charles Kemper's 1921 article noted in the bibliography here.⁵²

The year 1709 proved to be the year of full-fledged fruition for the trio's grand plan for transcontinental relocation of refugees. In addition to the two British-approved colonies in the Shenandoah Valley and North Carolina, Frantz Ludwig Michel and William Penn launched a third in Pennsylvania at Pequea Creek, which immediately began resettling European arrivals. As Proprietor of Pennsylvania, Penn did not require permission of the British government to establish refugee colonies and, in fact, had been hosting the one at Germantown near Philadelphia for decades. Of the six refugee colonies that the trio would establish by 1716, the three new colonies approved in 1709—Shenandoah Valley, Pequea, and New Berne, North Carolina—would end up ranking as the most successful and long lasting.

This subchapter, *The British Lords of Trade and Plantations*, has been a necessary laying-out of context of what was to come. What also led up to the three-colony bonanza of 1709 was Michel's second Maryland expedition, which he conducted in 1707.

FIRST EXPLORER

VII. Second Maryland Expedition

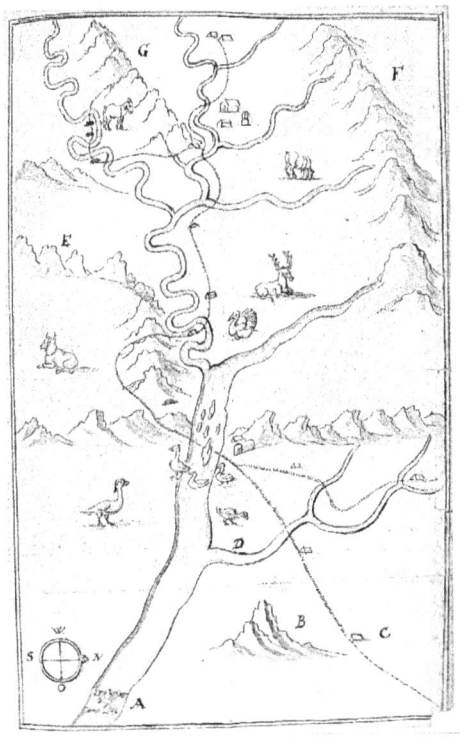

Proving a Vision

By 1707, Frantz Ludwig Michel was ready for yet more exploration. Fresh from being the first European to explore western Maryland and the Shenandoah Valley, Michel's appetite had been whetted as he set about organizing a larger expedition by partly retracing his 1704 Maryland expedition route to establish a presence in the distant wilds that he had been first to explore. His purpose in the second Maryland expedition was to look for economic opportunity in nature that could finance refugee resettlement to prove feasibility of the intercontinental refugee resettlement concept.

Some scholars have debated Michel's purpose in his second Maryland expedition. From the available record alone, little indicates that Michel's motivation in the venture was personal financial gain and much points toward establishing sources of income that his settlers could use to support themselves once arrived. However, beyond the record the distinctions exist that most settlers would definitely need start-up assistance and that Michel appeared to be materially very comfortable at the time and for the rest of his life. If Michel had wanted to better his financial situation, his way to have done it would have been to quit his expensive travel and stay at Ralligen, tending his estate and collecting its rents. Financial motivation also flies in the face of all of the rest of his record of humanitarianism and lifelong financial ease.

In Annapolis, Michel hired a team of sixteen including four Indians and, retracing his 1704 steps through Conoy, led them up the Maryland side of the Potomac River to the mouth of the Shenandoah River where the group stopped. The group included Peter Bezalion, James LeTort, Martin Chartiere, again Mr. Clark from the 1704 expedition, a man named Frank, and two young unnamed French speakers, one from Canada, the other from Virginia.

Two sources have the party stopping at the future site of

Harper's Ferry on the Virginia side of the Potomac but it isn't apparent that Michel had his party cross the river to Virginia. If not, the party stopped near present-day Sandy Hook, Maryland, and the river's White Horse Rapids with its good swimming holes and excellent fishing. On whichever side of the Potomac Michel stopped, what is known is that this is the general area that he chose to establish a base to determine the adequacy natural resources to sustain a sizable new colony. While the weather was still good, the group built cabins for better shelter to endure the coming winter than their camping lean-tos could afford. The faint description of this settlement, if it can even be called that, is more deep-woods outpost than community.

Michel indicated trapping for furs as the experiment of the enterprise, as North American pelts had already become popular in Europe and were fetching good prices. In 1707, North America seemed to have an endless supply. Trapping may well have actually occurred from the outpost but according to a few was a ruse to cover what has been theorized as Michel's true purpose in this latest venture, prospecting for precious metals, silver in particular. The theory may fit with Michel's supposed absence from camp for an undermined period and just as vague reappearance. If this even happened, a plausible explanation could be that Michel hiked back up the Shenandoah Valley to revisit his alleged search for silver ore at the place where he had without explanation lingered in 1704 at three close-together campsites. His purported purpose in secretiveness would have been to keep the location of any ore find to himself.

Though the exact location where he supposedly went has remained a mystery to this day, it soon began to be referred to as Michel's mines, whether or not any actually ever existed or if Michel ever prospected. The main source of doubt that the "Michel's mines" contention bears any credence is that its only proponent was Michel's future settlement project partner, Christoph von Graffenried, who became hateful toward Michel and is well known to have written falsehoods about him. *All* known references to "Michel's mines" trace back to Graffenried's supposition of them. There is no record of any silver ever having been mined in the Shenandoah Valley.

Modern official records show very little silver ever having been mined anywhere in Virginia. An inventory of Virginia silver mines shows several dozen that have existed in the state, but none where Michel is said to have prospected at the southern foot of Massanutten Mountain.[53] Virginia's Division of Geology and Mineral Resources shows no silver production in Virginia until 1885, scant production after that, and none since 1945.[54]

Very little silver has ever been found in Pennsylvania but Michel did find the Shawnee lead diggings at Pequea with their trace silver but made no secret of this.

The reader will meet Christoph von Graffenried shortly.

Meanwhile, Michel's crew had easy success in trapping so the venture appeared to be paying for itself and to have established the economic feasibility settler sustainability.

If the outpost's purpose were to prove a viable economic base for incoming refugees, its fur trapping success alone made the 1707 exploration a winner. This self-sustenance proof was the final piece in the feasibility of the grand master plan conceived by the three Bernese friends. Now all steps from rescue to transport to deliverance to survival had been proven out.

Before Mason and Dixon

Michel's camp had not gone unnoticed by the Conestoga Indians, a tribe that was centered in south central Pennsylvania. Its central village of Paxtang was located on the Susquehanna River where present-day Harrisburg is, and its claimed territory extended out broadly from there into Pennsylvania and parts of western Maryland. Believing that Michel and his party were trespassing, which unwittingly they were, the Conestogas appealed to William

Penn's colonial council to remove the trespassers. Upon investigating, the colonial government meeting in Philadelphia summoned Michel to explain what he and his party were doing so far into Indian territory.

But, as far as Michel was concerned, his camp was in Maryland and he had Maryland's and the Crown's permission to be there. The confusion arose because Pennsylvania considered the camp and the territory where Michel was operating to be in Pennsylvania. The dual claim by the two colonies arose from both having vaguely defined land grants that had the two grant territories overlapping.

Maryland claimed territory as far as fifteen miles *north* of Philadelphia, at that time the colonial capital of Pennsylvania. Pennsylvania's claim would have lopped off a stripe of Maryland from one side of the colony to the other several miles farther south than what would become Baltimore. The overlap of the competing claims comprised a sixty-mile stripe running the entire east-west width of both colonies as in the map here. Also disputed was that both Maryland and Pennsylvania claimed all of Delaware as theirs. Michel's camp was at the map's ✕ symbol.

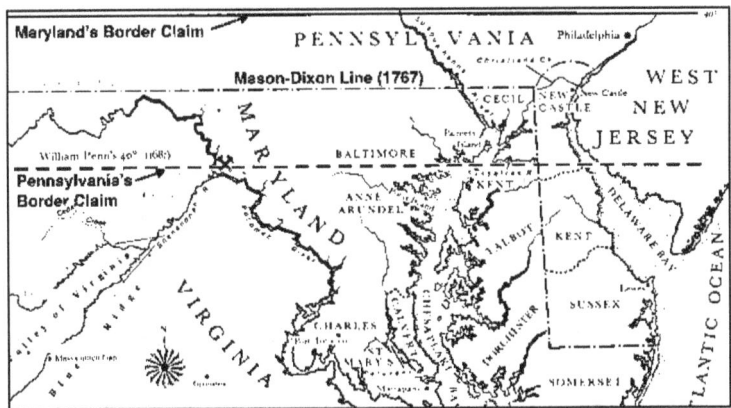

Philadelphians were not inclined to be Marylanders, Baltimoreans not to become Pennsylvanians, and Great Britain's monarchs not to see the squabbling persist. But it would not be until 1767 when Maryland and Pennsylvania, under Crown pressure, had astronomer Charles Mason and surveyor Jeremiah Dixon mark out a border more or less at the midpoint latitude between the two competing claims. Their stone markers, set a mile apart along their line, are mostly still in place along the Mason-Dixon Line.

But in 1707, the overlapping claims were just that and Pennsylvania was enforcing its claim in what would later be deemed to be Maryland. Michel was most likely not even aware of the border dispute but, whether he was or not, he was being called to account so off he went to Philadelphia to answer the complaint. He hadn't much choice if he wasn't to be run out of his camp and perhaps arrested. His defense was simple, that he had thought he was in Maryland and had secured Maryland's consent to be where he was. The Pennsylvania council, headed by the lieutenant governor, heard the case on February 25, 1707, accepted Michel's explanation, and, more or less cordially, gave Michel permission to continue occupying his camp under Pennsylvania's permission. This decision was in direct violation of the treaty between the Conestoga Tribe and the colonial government of Pennsylvania. Under the circumstances, the treaty called for Pennsylvania to expel Michel and his crew. The Conestoga complained to no avail about the lack of enforcement, not the last time that the white man would not deserve to be trusted.

After all of this and wanting to stay in the good graces of both Pennsylvania and Maryland, Michel halted the expedition and returned to Annapolis. It is not known what happened to Michel's outpost but most likely it was simply abandoned, though it might have been that Michel, with other business on two continents, left the outpost to his men for their use.

On April 4, 1708, Frantz Ludwig Michel became a father for the first time when Anna gave birth to the couple's son Christopher. The birth puts Frantz wherever Anna was in America in July of 1707 nine months before, assuming a full-term birth. We know that Frantz was in Annapolis by September 24, 1708, five months after the birth when he writes to Johann Rudolph Ochs and is still there at Christmas when he writes to Georg Ritter. He sails from

Virginia for England on January 6, 1709, takes British citizenship on June 5 and shows up in official records as being in Britain, Switzerland or The Hague as late as May of 1710 when he, Ritter, Graffenried, Petter Isoth and four others form a stock company as their investment in the recently settled New Berne, North Carolina, colony. That June, Michel finally accepts William Penn's offer to be appointed as Pennsylvania Director of Mines and sails for America, aboard the *Maria Hope* which on September 23 lands forty to fifty Mennonite refugees in Philadelphia on their way to Pequea.

This documented series of events sheds light on where the couple and now their child may have lived after the 1705 marriage. We will examine this in depth further on.

Michel's Colonies That Didn't Happen

During his visits to Berne, Michel would meet with Johann Ochs and Georg Ritter who had taken keen interest earlier in Michel's Virginia land grant and were anxious to hear his opinions on opportunities in Maryland. Ritter may have been helping to finance Michel's time in the colonies. New to receiving Michel's reports in late 1707 were Christoph von Graffenried and Petter Isoth, both of Berne Canton, who had been invited by Ritter to sign on as stakeholders with Ritter and Michel in Georg Ritter & Co., the entity which Ritter had founded to act as applicant to the English Crown for permission to found colonies in Virginia or Pennsylvania. Isoth was Ritter's brother-in-law married to Ritter's sister Judith. Ochs was not part of the applicant group but followed its work closely.

Similar to Frantz Ludwig Michel's social status but not exactly, Christoph von Graffenried's father held the title of Lord of Worb ("Vorb"), an area of Berne Canton about a day's horse ride from Ralligen. Christoph von Graffenried was heir apparent to the title. However, Michel's lordship outranked the Graffenried family's social standing by one rank, which made Michel Swiss nobility and Graffenried not, a situation that from the outset vexed the vain Graffenried.[55] For what it was worth, the applicant group now had two lords, not that that would make things easy. See the appendices here for definitions of Swiss title ranks and which families occupied each.

The final piece that Ritter needed for the refugee resettlement project was someone to serve as resident agent in London to shepherd the group's proposal through the bureaucracy and secure official authorization to found one or more colonies in Britain's North American provinces. Ritter recruited Graffenried for the role on the basis of Graffenried having visited London often and become well connected in social and official circles there. Graffenried had studied at universities in Heidelberg and Leyden and then visited England around 1680 where he came to know John Colleton and other Lords Proprietor of Carolina, friendships which he would use to his advantage in 1710.

The arrangement was that Ritter would pay Graffenried a salary on behalf of the resettlement group. Ritter almost certainly did not know that Graffenried was deeply in debt grasping at ways to improve his situation and that his hiring of Graffenried was staving off Graffenried's eventual bankruptcy. As Graffenried would unceasingly demonstrate, he took particular interest in Michel's having mentioned William Penn's "mines" in Pennsylvania.

Ritter had now put together what on the surface would appear to be a team of well-balanced backgrounds that ought to complement one another. Ritter and Isoth had the financial wherewithal and management acumen of the successful international merchants that they were. The lord and the lord-to-be had the social status and connections that go with them that would open most any door. All four had brains and venturesome entrepreneurial outlooks. Michel, though youngest of the group, had already proven himself well-suited temperamentally to his role as explorer and as effective liaison to colonial officialdom. Graffenried's being the oldest of the group at forty-six may have lent him an undeserved edge among the four.

The division of labor among the group was that Ritter would lead and conduct relations with the Bernese government, Michel would conduct the group's relations with colonial governments and continue to explore, and Graffenried would represent the group in dealing with the British government in London. Ritter also acted as financier of the venture. Isoth's role in unclear except to give Ritter a sure vote if he needed it.

Michel's co-applicants wanted his opinion on where in the backcountry of Maryland, Pennsylvania and Virginia that he had explored he thought would be the best sites for which to propose colonies. Michel was able to narrow his choices to three places that he had visited on his 1704 exploration.

The first was Great Falls on the Maryland side of the Potomac River, which offered the possibility of a seagoing port immediately downstream on the Potomac, outstanding scenic beauty, reasonable proximity to the bayside population centers of the colony, a virtually unlimited water supply, and a resolved scene with Indians who had already departed the area.

Michel also recommended the Great Trading Place on the Maryland side of the Potomac where Conoy was soon to be no longer. Here, the advantages were similar to those of Great Falls, less nearness to any community or port, plus excellent farming conditions in the Monocacy Valley.

Michel's third recommendation was "certain Lands on the Southwest Branch of Potomac." Here he is referring to the Shenandoah River which at the time had not yet been named as such. There the main advantage was that both the proprietors of Virginia and the British government were anxious to lift the restriction against settlement beyond the Blue Ridge and open the colony all the way to the Ohio River to cement control over the vast province. And as with Michel's earlier King William land grant, Virginia might well again offer incentives for new settlements farther west. The "certain lands" which Michel specifies were the spot that he had reached at the end of his 1704 explorations at the southern tip pf Massanutten Mountain. This location would be approved by the Lords of Trade and Plantations and in 1731 become the destination of the valley's first group of settlers, a party of European Mennonite refugees.

The decision was made to modify the proposal that Michel and Ritter had submitted to the British Lords of Trade and Plantations to now be permitted to found one of the two Maryland colonies or one in the Shenandoah Valley of Virginia. Isoth and Graffenried signed on as co-applicants of the new proposal with Michel and Ritter, and the group petitioned under its new name, the Society for the Swiss Colony of Virginia. Michel's map from his 1704 expedition was included as part of this proposal, not when it was submitted in 1707, but in its last revision in 1709. Ever since, the map has been in Britain's possession and is filed at the Public Record Office of Great Britain's National Archives in London.

Within days after the map was included, the British Lords of Trade approved the proposal along the lines of what the Society had submitted. Shortly afterward, permission was revised to change colonization permission from the Shenandoah Valley to the Carolinas where the need for colonization was deemed to be stronger. Permission was also eventually granted for a Shenandoah Valley colony. There were never any colonies granted for Great Falls or Conoy.

Probably the strongest influence on the long awaited favorable decision was that in the spring of 1709 London was being flooded with Palatine refugees who were steadily being driven from their homes by the advancing French armies of Louis XIV. The Palatinate was a German duchy near Heidelberg.

It had now been seven years since Michel's first exploration in Virginia. What the Swiss trio had to show for it were the Virginia colony, one now authorized for North Carolina, the Shenandoah Valley proposal under active consideration, and very receptive Pennsylvania and Maryland. Seven years might seem like slow progress but bureaucracies, even friendly ones, are slow and the group's accomplishments required coordination in an era when trans-Atlantic communication took months one way. While progress dragged along, the group was succeeding on a grand-scale with its unprecedented public-private, intercontinental, humanitarian refugee resettlement.

Before moving on, it is necessary to know what happened to Pennsylvania as a prospective destination to resettle refugees. After all, William Penn had been resettling refugees very successfully since he had founded his colony in 1681 and refugee settlements such as Germantown were thriving. Penn was the man who proved the concept of successful intercontinental refugee resettlement, which made Pennsylvania a shining example, so why not continue with Penn and Pennsylvania in applying to the Lords of Trade and Plantations?

Penn the person was controversial in Britain where his radical experiments of religious tolerance and refugee rescue were not always well received in the halls of power. Penn was also preachy in his official dealings and had a reputation as a parvenu who had landed his huge land grant only because of the large amount owed by the Crown to Penn's father. Enough people in the British establishment were standoffish toward Penn and his social experiments to gain him the official cold shoulder so that colonization proposals involving provinces other than Pennsylvania were the ones entertained. Trite but true. Pennsylvania didn't languish because of this but William Penn would.

Pennsylvania Detour

Michel's whereabouts are not easy to track more that 300 years later but are much more likely to appear in what record that remains when he is in America or on the move in Europe negotiating resettlements. Harder to find but for good reason are records of Michel when in Berne where there was no need for him to correspond with Ritter and Ochs.

After Michel's aborted second Maryland expedition, he remains in Maryland or Pennsylvania—it isn't clear which—until at least the beginning of 1709 and then in July begins to appear in several records related to the founding of a North Carolina colony, indicating his presence in London as he and Christoph von Graffenried present Ritter's resettlement group's case to the Lords of Trade and Plantations. Over the next eleven months, Michel turns up in Berne, London, The Hague, Holland and possibly along the Rhine. The last four places appear to have been brief visits involving resettlement with Michel operating from London. The traveler has returned to Europe for nearly two years. His trans-Atlantic voyage to London left Virginia on January 6, 1709, arriving in time for Michel to become a naturalized British citizen on June 5, the apparent reason being to facilitate the trio's colonization application.

During Michel's twenty-one-month London stay, he has a very productive stretch in which he secures British permission to found new colonies in Virginia's Shenandoah Valley and North Carolina and works with William Penn to found a colony at Pequea, Pennsylvania. On June 3, 1710, Michel finally accepts William Penn's offer to serve as Pennsylvania's General Director of Mines. Michel departs London in September aboard the *Maria Hope* and escorts 40 to 50 Mennonite refugees to Philadelphia who go on to Pequea. Michel's being on site in Pennsylvania lets him fill two roles at once, settling incoming European refugees and fulfilling duties as General Director of Mines. In his new civil service role, his duties would have been oversight of existing mines, collection of mining taxes to be remitted to the Crown, and promotion of exploration. Michel the explorer has become Michel the bureaucrat with a much more settled existence wherever he was living.

Assuming that he took up his Mines position for the long term, this raises the question of whether he had brought Anna and their infant son to London or Pennsylvania with him. One would think that the three were together, but the available record does not make this certain.

A side advantage that Michel had in his new position was that he was now ideally placed to facilitate the resettlement of European refugees into the North American colonies, Pennsylvania in particular. In William Penn, Michel has a like-minded humanitarian who had already been sending religious refugees to Pennsylvania since he founded the colony in 1681. In Michel, Penn has someone competent managing the receiving end who is more receptive to refugees and the idea of humanitarian resettlement than Pennsylvania's governors and Penn's son, William, Jr., who Penn had put in nominal charge in Pennsylvania.

So, in parallel with mines, Michel put to good use his time and association with Penn for the purpose of refugee resettlement. In 1710 Georg Ritter assembled a large group of Swiss Mennonite refugees that he delivered to Michel in Britain who on June 29 sent them on to Pennsylvania aboard the *Mary Hope*, which also conveyed Michel. He and Johann Rudolph Bundeli, his Bernese acquaintance who he had met in Germantown, escorted the group from Philadelphia westward to the Pequea location along the aboriginal Conestoga Path that Michel had scouted in 1704-05. The refugee group arrived at Pequea on October 23, 1710, and the first refugee colony beyond Philadelphia was born. William Penn had donated the land for the new colony and Michel had already had 10,000 acres of lots surveyed and laid out by surveyor Jacob Taylor for the refugee arrivals.

This established a flourishing community that grew with shipment after shipment of Mennonite and then Amish, Quaker and other refugees, a humanitarian community that continues to receive foreign newcomers of these faiths to this day.[56]

Beginning with Pequea, other bustling new German and German-speaking Swiss immigrant villages sprouted up nearby on the colony's frontier seventy miles west of Philadelphia in what in 1729 was to become Lancaster County, Pennsylvania. Of the six refugee colonies that Michel, Ritter and Ochs would found, every one of them would be successful but none more so than their Pequea colony. The area, which became mislabeled as Pennsylvania Dutch country, at one time during the eighteenth century comprised nearly half of the population of Pennsylvania. Today it thrives as a lasting heritage subculture of refugee resettlement and freedom of religion and has become a popular tourist destination.

Historian Samuel Wenger of the Mennonite Historical Society of Pennsylvania has reported that "After considering different areas of Europe for settlement, Mennonite leaders decided in February 1717 that Pennsylvania would be the new gathering place for Mennonites. Some started leaving in March of that year to journey to London. By May, some had received certificates that allowed them to receive help from the Dutch Brethren when they arrived in Holland. On August 24, 1717, three ships carrying 363 Mennonites arrived in Philadelphia. It is estimated that by 1732 nearly one-fifth of Mennonites living in the Palatinate emigrated to America."[57]

In the 1720s, the most adventurous from the Pequea area communities would begin migrating westward along Indian trails the eighty-five miles to the Maryland uplands of the Monocacy Valley, with some continuing farther, crossing the upper Potomac River into the northern tip of Virginia. These German-speaking pioneers became the first European settlers of both areas. In the 1750s there was a lull in migration from the Pequea-area German communities as migrants waited out the French and Indian War raging farther west before heading to Maryland's western frontier at the Monocacy Valley to settle.

In 1745 when Irish land developer Daniel Dulaney decided to create a new Maryland town on the Monocacy Plain, to sell the more than 300 lots that he platted he advertised in the German-speaking areas around Pequea and Lancaster County, Pennsylvania, for settlers and found them. Attracted by the stories they had heard from Pennsylvania

FIRST EXPLORER

Germans who had migrated to western Maryland over the previous fifteen years, hundreds more now made the move to Dulaney's new place, which he called Fredericktowne. Business was brisk for Dulaney, so brisk that Fredericktowne became an overnight boom town requiring the Maryland colonial governor in 1748 to charter the huge new Frederick County covering the entire western third of the colony, and to name Fredericktowne as its seat. In fifteen more years, with a virtual flood of German immigrants, Frederick County would be the Maryland colony's most populous and politically influential county.

During the Revolutionary War, few in any counties among the thirteen states had more of a leading role in shaping the outcome of the war. In 1765, the government of Frederick County became the first public body in the thirteen colonies to defy the new British Stamp Act. In 1781, the county sent its state delegate John Hanson to Philadelphia as the president of the original United States government chartered by the Articles of Confederation. In 1776 at the outbreak of war, Hanson had sent the first companies of soldiers to aide General Washington in Boston.

Backing up a few steps, Frantz Ludwig Michel and William Penn spawned Pequea, which spawned the Pennsylvania German country, which spawned Maryland's then largest county, whose leaders spawned a revolution. All of this happened over only two generations from 1709 to 1776 and the initial sparks were Michel and Penn.

FIRST EXPLORER

FIRST EXPLORER

Images and Maps

Michel von Schwertschwendi coat of arms

Michel's front-page family coat of arms
drawing in his 1702 Virginia trip journal

Ralligen Castle exterior and interior today

FIRST EXPLORER

There are no known images of Frantz Ludwig or Anna Michel, nor of any of their sons. Shown here is a charcoal portrait of Andrew Michael II (1783-1851) done in the 1840s. A grandson of Frantz and Anna, Andrew II was the second owner of Cooling Springs. The original portrait survives in possession of descendants of historian Mildred Michael Crewe mentioned in the appendix on family history.

The only known image of Johann Rudolph Ochs, an etching by Johann Rudolph Schellenberg. It is not known where the original exists. The online reference to it is https://www.antiquariat.de/angebote/GID11399179.html.

There are no known images of Georg Ritter.

Top- Johann Rudolph Ochs ancestral home and mill at Wiedlisbach, Bern Canton, Switzerland

Below- Worb Castle at Worb, Bern Canton, Switzerland, ancestral home of Christoph von Graffenried

First Explorer

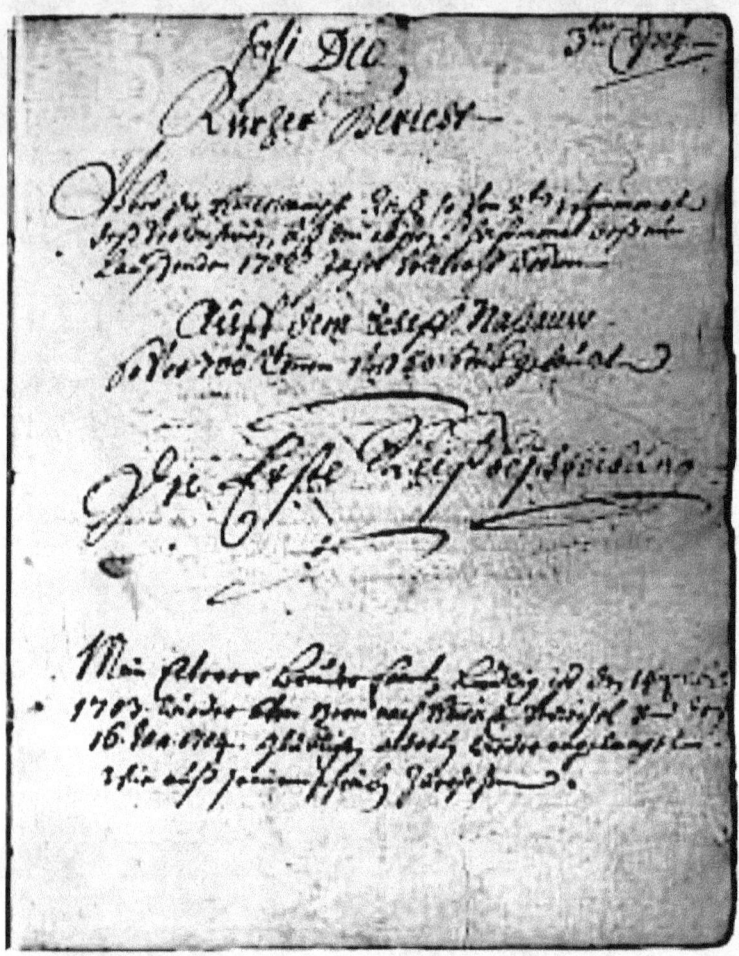

The second page of Frantz Ludwig Michel's 1702 Virginia journal in his own hand. (The first page was his drawing of the Michel von Schwertschwendi family coat of arms.) This entry, the journal's title page, was followed by Michel's first entry on October 31, 1701, in which he records his journey from Switzerland until sailing up the Thames River for London. He wrote the entry aboard the yacht of Lord Galway. His second entry was made on November 4 when he disembarked at London.

FIRST EXPLORER

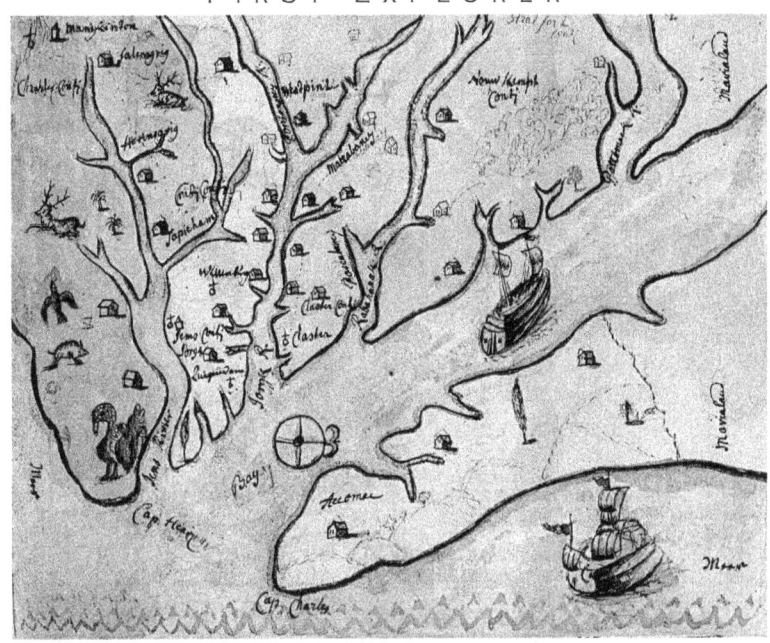

Top
Michel's 1702 journal map of settled areas of Virginia. The map's north points right.

Bottom
Journal drawing of Indians, a village longhouse, and a water spout tornado that Michel had seen at sea.

Michel's drawing of Wren Hall at the College of William and Mary at Williamsburg, Virginia, the oldest existing image of the building. The drawing is used by preservationists today in their restoration work on the old building.

FIRST EXPLORER

The 1725 Courthouse of King William County, Virginia, the nation's oldest. It sits at the center of Frantz Ludwig Michel's land grant.

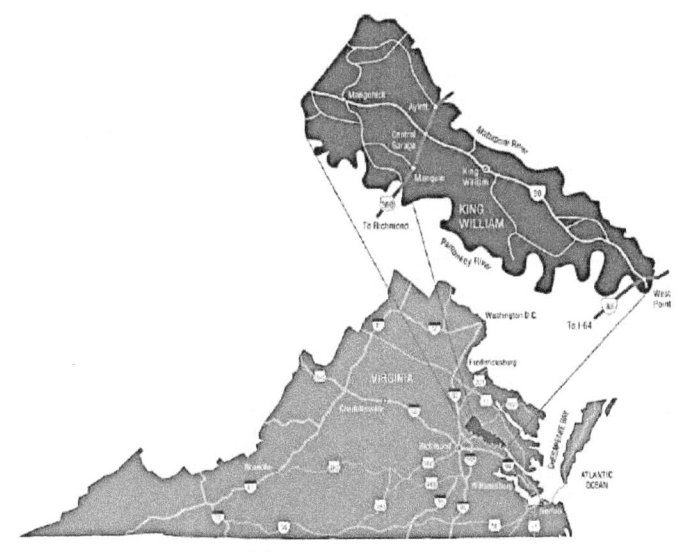

King William County's Virginia location. The county was chartered in 1701, the year before Michel's land grant.

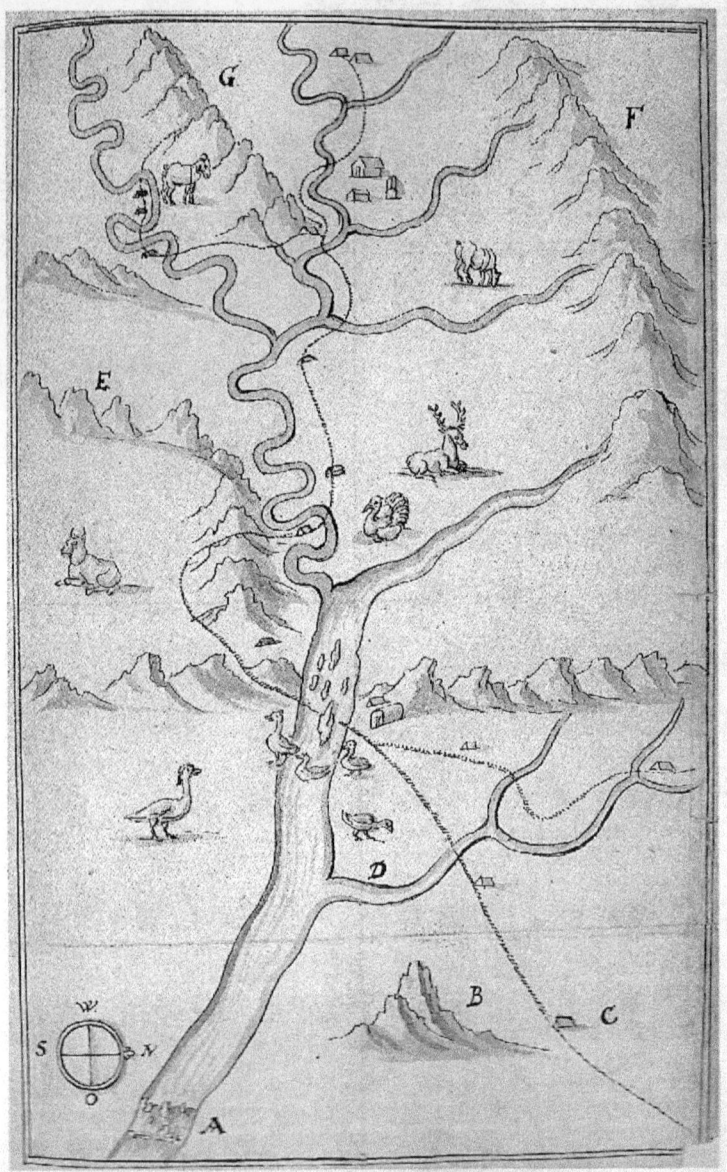

Frantz Ludwig Michel's 1704 exploration map of western Maryland and the Shenandoah Valley as he drew and annotated it. See the appendices for the legend to the map's lettered locations. The dotted lines denote his route and side trip.

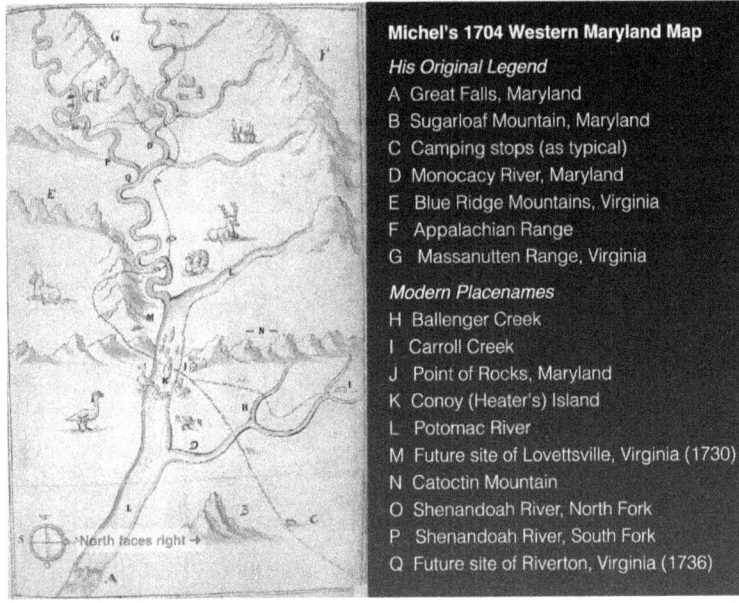

Michel's 1704 route up the Potomac and Shenandoah Rivers and sidetrips. "Pup tent" symbols denote places where Michel camped. These are identified with modern-day place names in an appendix here.

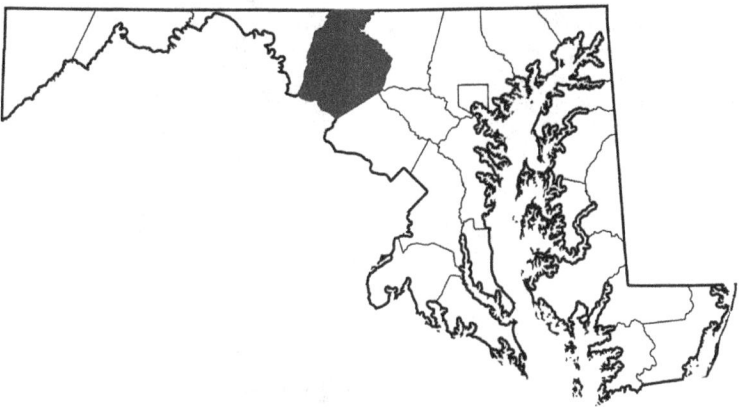

In 1704, the colony of Maryland was settled only within about thirty miles of the Chesapeake Bay. Michel's 1704 exploration of western Maryland was in what would become Frederick County, Maryland, in 1748. It was to there that his sons would resettle in 1762.

Above- Entrance to the Pequea Mine in 1976 at Michel's 1710 Pequea colony. The mine was no longer a working mine by this time but remained open to explorers.

Below- The sealed mine entrance today.

First Explorer

The first map of New Bern, North Carolina drawn in 1710 showing the new colony and its environs. The colony is at the bottom right at the confluence of the Neuse and Trent Rivers. The map's annotations are believed to be those of Christoph von Graffenried.

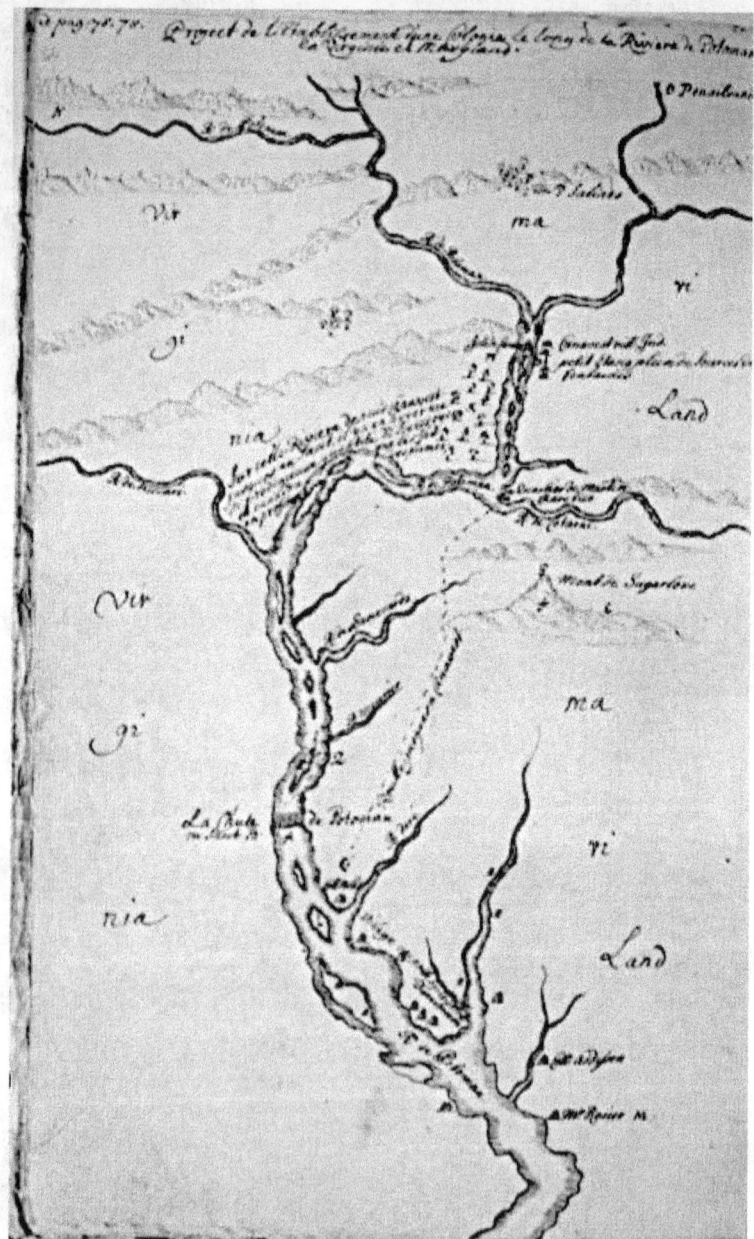

Christoph von Graffenried's 1712 map made when he retraced Michel's 1704 exploration route of western Maryland and the Shenandoah region looking for mines that Graffenried imagined Michel had.

FIRST EXPLORER

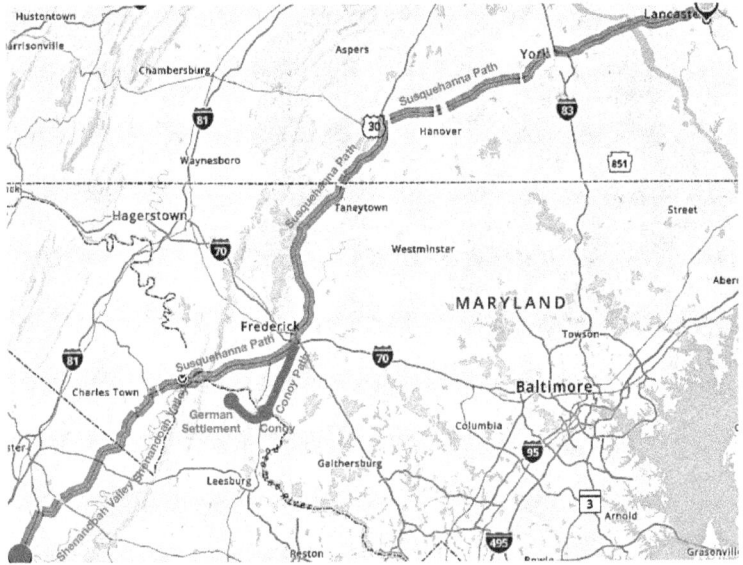

Main German Refugee Settler Routes

The heavy line follows the aboriginal Susquehanna Path running from German communities around Pequea, Pennsylvania, through Frederick, Maryland, ending at the Potomac River at Harper's Ferry, West, Virginia. The route today going south is US 30, Pennsylvania 194, Maryland 194, US 15, US 340. The route through the Shenandoah Valley follows US 11. The map shows Michel's route as far as Massanutten Mountain, Virginia, where he turned around.

The side spur is the route taken by those who migrated to Virginia's German Settlement. From Frederick the route is Ballenger Creek Pike to the Potomac River at Point of Rocks, Maryland, the US 15 bridge across the river, and Lovettsville Road to Lovettsville, Virginia, the modern name of The German Settlement.

This main migration route and spur came into use in the early 1730s in western Maryland and the German Settlement, and from there to the Shenandoah Valley.

First Explorer

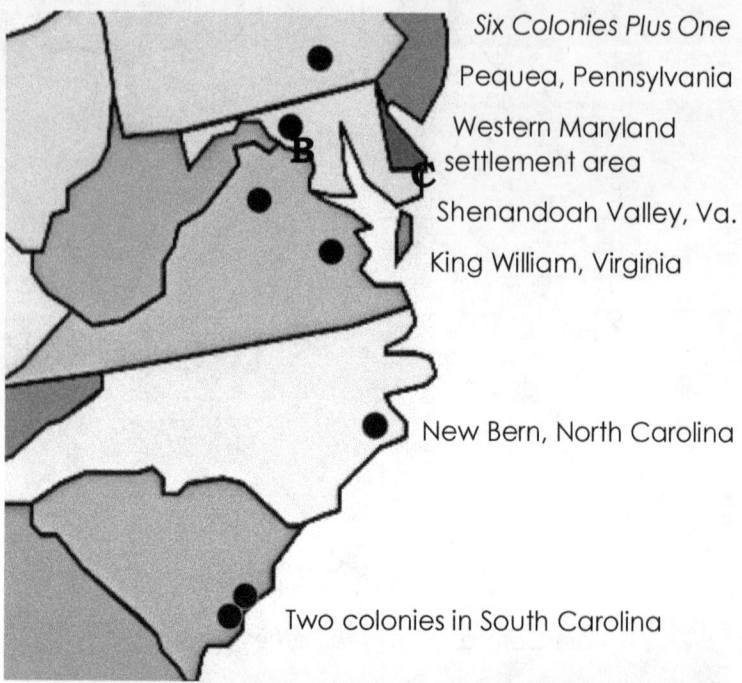

Six Colonies Plus One
Pequea, Pennsylvania
Western Maryland settlement area
Shenandoah Valley, Va.
King William, Virginia

New Bern, North Carolina

Two colonies in South Carolina

William Penn at 22. Quaker humanitarian Penn and his utopian Pennsylvania were the template of his era's religious tolerance. Penn's recruitment of European religious refugees and relocation of them to Pennsylvania proved the feasibility of intercontinental refugee rescue.

First Explorer

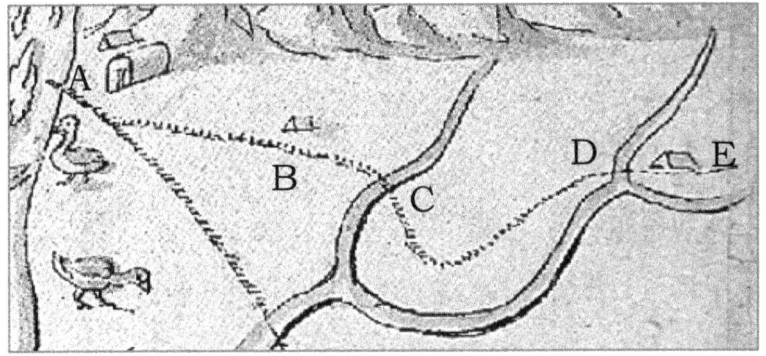

Michel's 1704 Sidetrip

A- Conoy
Michel begins by hiking 2.8 miles to his

B- First camp near the site of the future Cooling Springs founded by Michel's youngest son Andrew in 1768. Michel then continues 7.4 miles to

C- Ballenger Creek, the site of the future Frederick, the county seat founded in 1745. Then he goes 6.5 miles to

D- Carroll Creek also in present-day Frederick. He then crosses Carroll Creek and goes a short distance to his

E- Second camp near the confluence of Carroll Creek and the Monocacy River. He returns using the same route.

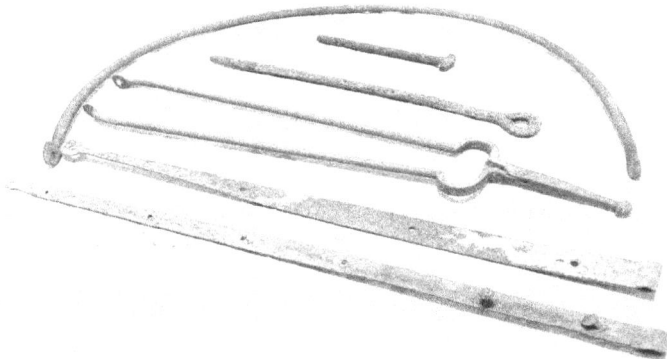

These extant items from Cooling Springs, founded by Andrew Michael after he sold his Michael Foundry in 1768, appear old enough to have come from his foundry. From the top they are a kettle handle, spike, ground hook, fire tongs, and two hasps, the bottom one with rivets.

VIII. Three Carolina Colonies

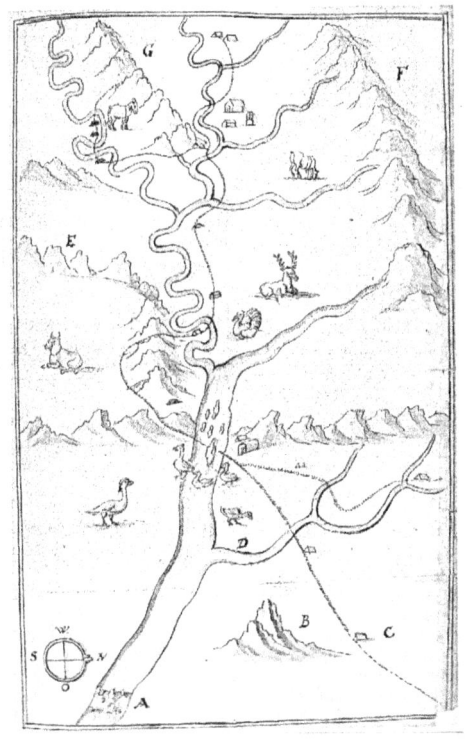

The Trying Founding of New Berne

The year 1709 was the bonanza for the Michel-Ritter-Ochs humanitarian resettlement cause. In addition to what would be the abundantly successful Pequea colony permitted by William Penn, the Lords of Trade and Plantations had finally authorized a colony in the Shenandoah Valley of Virginia and one more in coastal North Carolina. Three of the six colonies that the Michel-Ritter-Ochs trio would found had been authorized within eight months of one another in 1709.

By 1710 as his Pequea colony was beginning to spawn new communities nearby, Michel now had a cushy salaried job as Pennsylvania's Commissioner of Mines, common purpose with Penn, the person he reported to, and flexibility to continue, even accelerate, his life purpose of humanitarian rescue and resettlement. One could say that by 1710 Michel "had it made" and that this ideal situation would be a lot to give up.

But give it up Michel became compelled to do because of circumstances.

What drew Michel to New Berne was the unraveling debacle brought on by Christoph von Graffenried, the alarming news of which by this time had reached other provinces up and down the east coast. A letter from New Berne settler Christen Janson to Michel apprising him of the situation was a plea on behalf of the colony for Michel to try to stabilize New Berne in Michel's capacity as its officially appointed cofounder. Upon arrival at New Berne, Michel found that the continued existence of the colony was tottering, that its surviving settlers had a very uncertain future if the colony foundered, and that the very purpose of the colony—refugee resettlement—could be lost. With that much at stake, Michel made what must have been a much unwanted decision to give up his sweet advantages as Pennsylvania's Commissioner of Mines and try to turn around the ugly situation in North Carolina. And so off

First Explorer

Michel had gone to deal with what had come down upon him.

This unavoidable decision in 1711 would prove to be Michel's life's most trying episode. Try as he might to get control of the bad situation brought on by Graffenried, he would be able to do it only at great personal duress and would suffer at the hands of Graffenried for the rest of his life and even beyond. To see how this came about, we go back two years to 1709-10 in London and to the organizing of the Carolina colony.

British permission to establish a Carolina colony posed a new challenge for the Michel-Ritter-Ochs trio who had not up to that time been faced with having to actually organize a colony after being granted one. The King William colony had been established by Michel on his own in 1702 by proprietor grant and since then was up and running under the management of Michel's hired overseer. Likewise, Michel established the Pequea colony by William Penn's proprietor grant in 1710 and Pequea was smoothly starting to come to life as planned with its first refugee arrivals. In 1710 Britain had recently granted permission for the Shenandoah colony but it would not begin to be settled for another two decades.

In contrast to these three situations, the newly authorized Carolina colony required planning and execution to deal with its realities. Appointments, financing, organizing, spelling out contractual obligations, and arranging the first arrivals of refugees to the colony would all need to take place and did in 1709 and 1710.

After the Carolina proprietors had appointed Michel and Graffenried as co-founders and operators of Bernburg, as the colony was first named, Georg Ritter drew up a contract to establish an operating entity of the colony, name its investors, set the venture's capitalization, and spell out fiduciary practices. Georg Ritter & Cie. was formed as the legal entity through which the contract took force. The parties to the contract were the proprietor-appointed colony operators—Michel and Graffenried—in contract with the other investors including Ritter, his brother-in-law Petter Isoth, and four others apparently recruited by Ritter.[58]

It is notable that Johann Rudolph Ochs was not an investor in the new company nor signatory of the contract. However, he, Michel and Ritter would continue their close coordination of refugee resettlement unabated.

The physical assets of the company consisted of 17,500 acres at the colony site in North Carolina comprising the 5,000 acres that Graffenried had bought for himself, 2,500 that Michel promises to buy, and 10,000 that Ritter purchases on behalf of Ritter & Cie.

The liquid assets of the company are to consist of paid-in startup capital of 7,200 pounds sterling, quite a large amount in those days, allocated as twenty-four stock shares at 300 pounds apiece. Each of the eight investors is issued and charged for one share initially, leaving sixteen shares available for future investment by others.

The contract stipulates that Graffenried shall be granted one share immediately for his 5,000-acre land purchase put into the company, Ritter one share "for the expenses he has incurred," and Michel one share "for his labor and for the mine contributed to the benefit of the company." This arrangement shows that the contract also serves as a prospectus to attract additional investors. As Michel, Ritter and Graffenried are all given credit for their shares of paid-in capital, this leaves it to Isoth and the four silent investors to pay in their total of £1,500 to provide all of the company's start-up liquidity. No found record shows whether or not this was ever actually paid in.

As for the mine that Michel is expected to contribute, this is a very long bet as "the mine" does not yet seem to exist according to the contract wording which states, "Mr. Michel reserves this to himself, because he contributes the mines in Pennsylvania to the good of the Society, that the first three years, when these mines *shall be open and begin* to produce the profits, shall come to him in advance." (Emphasis added.)

A lead mine showing traces of silver had been operating in Pennsylvania since aboriginal times and conspicuously it was located at Pequea. Records of the Pennsylvania Bureau of Topographic and Geologic Survey and scholarly historical articles refer to a Pequea Silver Mine.

In 1643, Roger Williams, who would found the colony of Rhode Island, wrote *A Key Into the Languages of America*, an early anthropological piece in which he describes mines at Pequea being worked by Indians. Williams wrote that Indians there had developed an art of casting pewter and brass into "very neat" smoking pipes and that they had long been doing so.[59]

The mine's primary ore was lead but its white-vein quartz medium also contained traces of silver which could be smelted out into the single metal. Assays of the mine's ore around the time of the Civil War showed that when Pequea ore was smelted a marginal amount of ten to sixteen ounces of silver per ton could be had.

These yields make this mainly a lead mine but also at best a marginal side producer of silver. One of the Pequea Mine's main uses was as a producer of lead shot for Union rifles during the Civil War. Whenever it was that Michel got the Pequea Mine going, apparently it was a viable if marginal silver producer. We are left to wonder whether in 1710, when the New Berne investors pledged their pocketbooks, the Pequea Mine was unfounded hope or ore-proven mine. This is the oldest silver-producing mine of record in Pennsylvania and perhaps in America. Pictures of its entrance are provided in the pictorial pages here. Pequea Mine has been long idle and today is the main attraction of a state park. Little silver was ever found in Pennsylvania, and none is mined in the state today.

The contract speaks of "mines" in the plural. But the investors when they signed knew either of only one working mine or none, so all that they had to go was Michel's hope of finding good silver ore at Pequea. There was only this one mine in the vicinity of Pequea but over time it did end up with multiple entrances.

The contract awarded "To every participant . . . a piece of land in an acceptable place at the building up of the city [New Berne], as well as a free estate of five hundred acres in Virginia." The contract does not specify whether the 500-acre manors are to come from the King William colony, the recently approved Shenandoah colony, or elsewhere. There is no known record that any of these allotments was ever made.

The remainder of the contract is devoted to obligations, prohibitions, and administration, and concludes with the appointment of two London fiduciaries charged with the group's banking and accounting. Dated May 18, 1710, the contract took effect immediately. It is provided as an appendix here.

The contract amounted to more than that by also serving as what today would be called a start-up plan. But what the contract/plan conspicuously lacked was an operating plan or explicit recognition of any internal weaknesses or external threats that needed to be corrected. Two glaring problems from the outset dealt with colony leadership.

The first was the two-headed chief executive position, a sure-fire organizational pitfall stemming from the Carolina proprietors designating both Michel and Graffenried as colony co-founders to run New Berne.

The second and nearly fatal gap was adequately assessing—what today is background checking—of Christoph von Graffenried. Unknown to his seven contract partners when they transacted the contract was that Graffenried was deep into personal financial binds, and that he was mentally unbalanced and unfit to lead. We will get to the sad consequences of Graffenried's condition shortly.

With the signing of the contract, the Carolina colony startup had its Crown and provincial permissions, land, financing plan, and operating personnel in place, all of which then joined the one remaining element to realize the colony's mission of resettling refugees, the refugees themselves who had already begun arriving. In the fall of 1709,

150 families consisting of 650 Palatine refugees rescued by Ritter and Ochs had been delivered to North Carolina to first populate New Berne. Their arrival preceded the contract by months, and, in fact, it was the problems that the settlers encountered that led to the contract as a corrective measure.

These first arrivals did not have pleasant passage. The refugee settlers had been attacked in the Atlantic by French privateers who robbed them of most of their belongings. A full third of the passengers, malnourished by war or sickened aboard, died during passage. To get by when they arrived, the settlers sold much of the little they had left as they labored to make a home at New Berne late in the season as cold weather approached.

A second shipment of 250 passengers including Swiss Mennonites arriving soon after had been savaged just off the Carolina coast by pirates after experiencing similar mortality in transit.

The survivors of these two groups, already long suffering from religious persecution and war in their homelands, arrived forlorn and malnourished but somehow still hopeful. After all of this and planting late in the season, the crops that the settlers were able to get into the ground would prove insufficient to get them through the winter without hunger. During this first settling of the colony, co-founder Michel is still in Pennsylvania arranging refugee resettlements there and it is colony co-founder Graffenried who is in sole charge of New Berne. Graffenried had made insufficient provision to feed the settlers after their late fall arrival. Of the 900 souls full of hope who had boarded ships bound for the New World, only a third would still be alive by the summer of 1710 and they were in bad shape.

The situation would only deepen as Graffenried seemed unable to steer a constructive course for the settlers or receive much assistance from the proprietors. It didn't help that Graffenried was dismissive of his Palatine charges as when he referred to them, in comparison to his Swiss settlers, as "the worst people I ever saw."[60] How the new colony devolved to this sorry stage is rooted in its strange origin, the convoluted Crown permission to found it in 1709.

Hijacked

Stepping back in time once more, we recall that the Lords of Trade and Plantations had not gotten around to deciding on the Bernese group's 1705 proposal until 1709 and, when they did, rejected the group's petition to establish colonies in Pennsylvania or Maryland but did permit the applicants to submit a revised proposal for a Shenandoah Valley, Virginia, colony with stronger language protecting British rights and interests. With Christoph von Graffenried then having been hired by Georg Ritter on behalf of the trio to represent the group in London, a revised proposal had been submitted jointly by him and Michel that, among other new features, promised that any immigrants the group brought over from Europe would not become public charges and that the colony would conform to the same "ecclesiastical, civil and military affairs" as expected of "all other faithful subjects of Your Majesty." The proposal was for 100 acres for each of a planned 600 settlers, a territory about seven miles square.

On August 22, 1709, the group's revised petition was finally approved by the Lords of Trade and on September 19 Queen Anne granted permission to proceed. The published decision ordered the Governor of Virginia to "allot unto them certain Lands on the Southwest Branch of Potomac" (the Shenandoah River). Five years after Frantz Ludwig Michel had become the first European to explore the Shenandoah Valley, his vision of being permitted to provide lands there for refugees had now been realized.

Or so it seemed.

Soon after the approval, several moves occurred involving Graffenried and to his advantage, resulting in the rescinding of permission for the Shenandoah colony and instead authorizing a North Carolina colony. This switch came about from a competing proposal from Graffenried to found a North Carolina colony. As the Lords of Trade wanted for the time being only one new colony of non-British subjects in Britain's North American provinces, permission was transferred from the Shenandoah Valley to North Carolina.

As it turned out, Graffenried's win had come from intense behind-the-scenes lobbying, little if any of it above boards or with the interests of his Bernese colleagues in mind. It would appear that the Michel-Ritter-Ochs trio may have had no way of knowing that Graffenried had submitted a separate proposal in the trio's name for a Carolina colony, and that they were therefore in competition with it.

Even while their proposal was being considered by the British, Graffenried was prowling the halls of the bureaucracy for other opportunities. In his rounds, he met John Lawson, Surveyor General of the Carolinas, who was in London at the time to recruit settlers to relocate to the Carolinas to begin populating the two provinces. Lawson had his eye on the thousands of German refugees having recently fled to London from the Palatinate because of religious discrimination and continuing war in their area. Learning of the Swiss group's application to found a colony in the Shenandoah Valley, Lawson kept a close eye on the matter, hoping that the Crown would approve the Swiss proposal. When the proposal was approved, Lawson was ready with one of his own, which he broached to Graffenried.

Lawson's and Graffenried's interests coincided. By the trio's having received its permission, Graffenried as their agent could now send hundreds of settlers to America. Lawson would be able to meet his charge from the Carolina proprietors to find settlers to grow their colonies if he could find a way to divert the trio's colonists to North Carolina.

However, neither Graffenried nor the Michel-Ritter-Ochs trio had any apparent reason to make what appeared to be a complicated and unnecessary switch, so why bother?

Lawson must have been a shrewd reader of character as he found the perfect hook to entice the self-impressed Graffenried. Lawson had the North Carolina proprietors sweeten the proposition by throwing in the offer to have them grant a title of either Landgrave or Baron to Graffenried if Graffenried would purchase 5,000 acres of land from them and use his position as London spokesman for his Swiss colleagues to throw the colonization deal to North Carolina. Graffenried bit hard despite his very recently having left Switzerland under a cloud for being heavily in debt. On August 4 of 1709, Graffenried paid fifty pounds sterling, a handsome sum in those days, for 5,000 acres of land in North Carolina.

And for the titles.

Later mis-readings of the switch had Michel being in cahoots with Graffenried but as things played out there is no evidence to make one think that Michel would have had any reason to want the switch or to partner with Graffenried at the expense of Ritter and Ochs.

Graffenried then lobbied Lawson to have *both* titles and got them: Landgrave and Baron of Bernberg, the proprietors' name of the Carolina settlement-to-be before it was changed to New Berne. Landgrave is a European nobility title denoting a regional jurisdiction held by someone with at least the rank of Count. The Landgrave title was at the time held by some German royalty as high as princes. In the European hierarchy of titles, Baron is one rank higher than Lord so now "Baron" Graffenried," according to him, outranked his co-founder, Frantz Ludwig Michel, the mere Lord of Ralligen. Henceforth, Graffenried unilaterally asserted this titular one-upmanship and would act on it, brushing aside that legally he and Michel were listed as co-founders of New Berne. By 1711, Graffenried had self-inflated his title to Landgrave of Carolina—all of it—a fiction to which the Carolina proprietors lent no credence but no correction either.

The absurdities of Graffenried's exalted new titles were that they had no meaning in America, none of whose colonies and then states ever legally established any form of nobility, and that the titles would be ridiculed in Europe as wholly illegitimate because Graffenried had no noble blood and his titles had been granted by no one of nobility in a position to grant them. Glaringly worse was that Graffenried had purchased the titles. In the Swiss hierarchy of titles, Graffenried's two procured ones were null and did not elevate him an *iota*: he remained *vest*, "dependable," not *edelvest*, "noble and dependable," as was Michel. All but Graffenried would recognize this in practice. See the table in the appendices here for the full listing of Swiss title ranks with their definitions.

The sleazy irony of Graffenried's new titles is that all involved—the Carolina proprietors who bestowed them, Michel, Lawson, anyone else close to the situation, and, deep down, Graffenried himself—understood the deception of the titles and that the reason that the absurd transaction had taken place at all was that the proprietors saw that Graffenried's overriding vanity could be taken advantage of to their own ends. "Baron" Graffenried strutted and preened while others laughed up their sleeves at him. In the operation of the New Berne colony, Michel ignored Graffenried's purchased halo as much as he could but found no way to countermand Graffenried's usurpations of control because Graffenried continued to have the complicity of the North Carolina proprietors who had sold him the titles in the first place. The proprietors themselves had gotten trapped in Graffenried's ego ruse nearly as deeply as had their make-believe count.

In May of 1709, shortly after Ritter had hired him, Graffenried, heavily in debt in Switzerland, had departed Berne suddenly, stiffing his creditors and abandoning his wife and thirteen children. All the while as Graffenried was conniving the colony transfer and wangling his titles, his family in Berne was on a path toward destitution. By August, Graffenried's wife Regina watched as the family's situation deteriorated to the extent that she became desperate enough to apply to the Great Council of Berne for help in paying her husband's creditors.

So *all in the same month,* Graffenried swings the trio's colony permission from Virginia to the Carolinas behind the backs of his ostensible venture partners, pays handsomely for his two ersatz titles, skips out on his creditors at home, leaves his wife and family in dire financial condition, and deceives the group he represents about all of this. But he couldn't hide it for long. Directly because of him, much worse was yet to come for Christoph von Graffenried, his family, and the North Carolina colony.

During this same time, Frantz Ludwig Michel on June 5, 1709, had become a British citizen as did Graffenried the following month. The apparent reason was to facilitate their colonization application. Given that they would both continue to be deeply involved in Swiss matters, Michel and Graffenried may have maintained dual Swiss and British citizenship.

What is clear is that when Georg Ritter hired Graffenried in early 1709 as the trio's London agent, Ritter could not have been aware of Graffenried's financial woes or inability to manage money, or he would never have hired Graffenried. What explains Ritter's seeming gullibility was a slick convincing glibness that Graffenried became known for that had already slipped him far into the upper reaches of London social circles. Where those traits came from will be addressed shortly.

What is not clear is where someone who couldn't pay his bills got fifty pounds, a large sum at the time, to make a major land purchase of 5,000 acres, nearly eight square miles. That much land situated at the New Berne colony location today is worth about $50,750,000.[61] It is doubtful that Graffenried had any collateral to put up unless it was just the land itself. It is unclear who the lenders were unless the Carolina proprietors themselves, the eight Englishmen to whom King Charles II had granted joint ownership of North Carolina in 1665. Each of these men either had remained loyal to the Crown or had aided in Charles's restoration to the English throne. North Carolina was the King's reward to them.

If the proprietors were the lenders, they simply took back the 5,000 acres when Graffenried later defaulted on payment. If others were the creditors, they were left in the lurch unless the land was put up as collateral to them and the proprietors permitted them to take title and repay the loan themselves. As to how Graffenried expected to repay the loan, his salary from Ritter would not have been nearly enough. The only other apparent source in his indebted situation would have come from net revenues of the operation of the New Berne colony, a long bet on a yet unsure thing. Furthermore, how net revenue would be used was not Graffenried's decision alone but that of Georg Ritter & Cie. and its eight investors. The investment partners would have had no interest in using their shares of the colony's dividends to help Graffenried pay his personal debts. Graffenried would have been free to use his own share, but would that be enough to service his large debt?

At this point, Graffenried may or may not have become aware that his father, the Lord of Worb back in Switzerland, had had his son declared bankrupt and removed from his position on the Great Council of Berne. Christoph von Graffenried was now hanging by the thread of the continuing good will of his investment partners and the salary being paid to him by Georg Ritter.

Above all, what Graffenried needed to do when Michel arrived in New Berne to straighten things out was to cultivate a good relationship with Michel whose evaluation of Graffenried was now Graffenried's lifeline. But when the "Count" used his "title" to insist on deference from Michel, who would have had no difficulty in grasping the situation's unmanageable pathology, Graffenried had spent the last shred of goodwill that he had anywhere. It would soon be game over for Christoph von Graffenried.

Imaginary Silver

After hearing of the Spanish stealing rich lodes of native gold and silver artifacts in Mexico and South America and hauling galleons of it back to Spain since the 1500s, some in Britain's North American colonies became fascinated with the prospect of finding the precious metals in their own lands. Those who had prospected for gold or silver in Britain's American colonies had had scant luck, but the common assumption was that that was only because there was much prospecting left to do.

In his explorations Frantz Ludwig Michel probably did not have silver in mind. During his first time in Virginia he had heard of the unsuccessful exploration for silver by Governor Francis Nicholson. On Michel's extensive 1704 exploration of western Maryland and Virginia's Shenandoah Valley, he was primarily interested in scouting for good sites for colonies but is said to have also kept an eye out for likely places where silver or gold might be found. However, this speculation was Graffenried's alone which casts doubt that Michel did look for ores on this exploration. Early on before Michel had explored Pequea and come across the Shawnee diggings, Graffenried took a close interest and seized upon his own notion of Michel's supposedly having found silver in 1704 in the Shenandoah Valley.

In researching *First Explorer*, the author came upon nothing to indicate that, up to the time of the contract, Michel had ever suggested that any places he had explored might actually make good prospecting sites, much less that he had identified any place he had been as having silver. The impression Michel left was a fair one that he may have paid a measure of attention to identifying promising prospecting sites and found none but felt that more assiduous prospecting could possibly turn up something. And there he left it.

Then when Michel explored around Pequea he did find silver at the Shawnee Indians' lead diggings but not much of it. It is not clear just when Michel found silver there. It could have been in late 1704 when he scouted west of Philadelphia in the Pequea area. Or perhaps in early 1707 when he was back in Pennsylvania traveling the colony with Governor Evans. Whenever it was that Michel may have come across the Indian diggings at Pequea, there was a Pequea mine precisely where Michel was known to have been. What no one including Michel could have known then was that this wasn't much of a mine if one was looking for silver. This was a lead mine.

The contract that Michel and Graffenried signed with Ritter, Isoth and the others explicitly mentions "Michel's mines in Pennsylvania." It is conspicuous that sixteen days after the contract signing Michel accepts William Penn's offer to become Pennsylvania's Director of Mines. The timing would seem to indicate that Michel wants to try to make good on his new contractual obligations with his investment partners regarding mines.

By the time the contract was signed, the other three knew of Graffenried's financial situation, how colony permission had been switched to Carolina, Graffenried's false titles, and that Graffenried isn't to be trusted. So why would Michel go ahead and enter into a contact with the likes of Graffenried?

The Pequea Mine was far from a good producer (and never would be) and may or may not have been Michel's to contribute in the first place. Then there is the matter that under Pennsylvania's royal charter a fifth of all silver mined in Pennsylvania is owed to the British Crown. The plural "mines" of the contract are future hopes that may or may not be realized. (They weren't.) Michel, safe in that he can't lose what he never had or can afford to lose what there isn't much of, signs. His purpose, and that of Ritter and Isoth, is to attempt to get better control over their faltering Carolina investment by using the contract as a tighter job description on Graffenried. The contract also re-emphasizes Michel's and Graffenried's co-equal status as the colony's executives but that would prove to be of no avail.

For Graffenried, he now seemingly has an employment contract extension with Ritter & Co., partial claim to Michel's silver, and expectation of cash flow from "Michel's mines" back to the Society that can fund Graffenried's salary and dividends. But what won't work for Graffenried is what Michel is to pay back from mines if there is little or no silver. The risk is almost entirely Graffenried's, and the onus of the contract is now squarely on Graffenried's ability to manage the New Berne settlement more competently. The contract's effects on Michel personally are close to nil.

So, the motivation that Michel, Ritter and Isoth had to sign a contract with a suspect character was to use it to regain more control over the New Berne venture without unacceptable risk to themselves. This appears to be a situation in which the three had close discussions to parse out risks, gains, features, and wording of the contract. Under the contract, the only real risk to the three was project failure, which did happen. However, Graffenried had everything to lose and did, but he didn't seem to grasp how, under the contract's features, that could happen to him. When Graffenried continued to mismanage the New Berne colony, cause an Indian War, and lose the loyalty of the colonizers, his three partners lost patience and simply dissolved Ritter & Cie., owner of the contract, costing Graffenried his salary, which was his last remaining means of support. His employer would be dissolved out from under him.

On May 6, 1711, Graffenried writes to Ritter acknowledging the end of the employment contract between the two. Then on the same day there is the very odd letter that Graffenried sends to friends in Berne. He writes:

"There came up to me from the sea a little old Englishman, to sell me oysters. He inquired for F. Michel, but since he was not present anymore and understanding that we were good friends he wanted to show me something that probably would be acceptable to me. He said he had, sometime ago, traveled with F. Michel and the Governor of Virginia, to look for mines; but he knew of a better and richer one, and in that connection, he could tell me all the circumstances of F. Michel's trip. It agreed well with what I already knew very well. Although before this I had entirely discounted Squire Michel's affairs, I saw by this there were nevertheless realities. Now according to this report, I have some hope. This mine, the little man indicated to me is a gold mine in Virginia, while F. Michel's is a silver mine in Pennsylvania; and this gold mine is said by report to be eight days out from here, while the other is more than fourteen days from Philadelphia. At the discovery of this nearer and better mine F. Michel was not present, but Governor Nicholson of Virginia was. In the matter of the gold, the Governor would let neither him nor anyone else know and also forbade him to tell anyone of it."

However, official records show that, "The earliest recording of gold mining activity in Virginia began about 1804 as placer mining, followed quickly by lode mining. Mining continued unabated until the onset of the California Gold Rush, at which point most serious speculators moved west. Production continued at a low level until the Civil War, when it virtually ground to a halt."[62]

In his previous letters and journal entries mentioning mines or Michel, Graffenried makes no mention of what he has to say above. Then suddenly out of the ether comes his "little old Englishmen" letter that, were it to be believed, makes out Michel as a liar and attempts to shift suspicion to him for Graffenried's failures. Given that no gold would be mined in Virginia for nearly a century after Graffenried's letter, it appears to be a work of fiction.

To recapitulate, all on the same day—May 6, 1711— Graffenried acknowledges having been fired, writes what may be a delusional letter, and begins a campaign of invective against Michel that he will continue for the rest of Graffenried's life.

In his mind, Graffenried needed to cling to the belief that there was silver or gold to be found, since his purpose of being in America from the start was to strike it rich to be able to pay off his mounting debts in Europe and America. A colony or two should do the trick over time but a mine, oh, so much faster. Suspicious that for years Michel had been holding back on him, Graffenried in 1712 went looking himself for silver and "Michel's mines" by tramping the very route that Michel had explored in 1704 as far as the Shenandoah Valley. The only thing new that Graffenried found was that French trapper Martin Chartier had set up a trading post at the mouth of the Monocacy River. Graffenried drew an annotated map of his explorations shown in the illustration pages here on which he notes a location where he thinks "Michel's mines" are. Denoted by "N" in the upper left corner, this location is somewhere in Virginia's Massanutten Range. There has never been silver found in this area. It wasn't until 1860 when the nation's first successful silver mine began operation in Nevada.

The five lines of script in the map's midst are located where Graffenried proposes a colony. The location is four miles west of Canoy along the Carolina Path approximately where the village of Lucketts, Virginia, is today. The area wasn't settled until the late 1700s.

One author assumes that when Christoph von Graffenried retraced Michel's 1704 exploration in 1712, Michel went along, which wouldn't explain why Graffenried hired a guide. Michel, in South Carolina by this time, certainly abhorred this folly.

In 1710 when Graffenried, Michel, Georg Ritter and Petter Isoth had conceived the idea of recruiting experienced German miners to come to Virginia and start digging, mining engineer Johann Justus Albrecht from the mining region around Siegerland, Germany, was identified to do the recruiting of skilled miners. Accounts vary as to whether Albrecht had been contracted by Graffenried, Michel or Georg Ritter. Eventually from this, forty-two miners and their families were transported from London to Virginia but not until 1714 by which time both Michel and Graffenried had departed New Berne, Graffenried to Switzerland, Michel to King William. The miners never discovered any silver in the area but did end up manning an ironworks that Virginia Governor Alexander Spotswood developed. Spotswood named the German mining settlement Germanna. The mining experiment would fail even after Frantz Ludwig Michel's attempted turnaround of it twenty years later. Today the Germanna location is a Virginia State historic site.

The Rogue

As author John Blankenbaker has reported, "So uncertain were the plans of the North Carolina proprietors, on the date that Graffenried purchased his land, [that] the proprietors had not obtained the Crown's approval for assistance in transporting the Germans to North Carolina. So Graffenried had invested his fifty pounds in an enterprise which was not yet approved. With the purchase of the land (and the titles), Graffenried became the most important man in the 'Swiss Colonization Society.' Also, from this time forward, it becomes hard to distinguish Graffenried's actions on his own personal behalf from the actions on behalf of the 'Society.' Over the course of September, the proprietors sold 2,500 hundred acres to Michel and 10,000 acres to the Society. They also issued an option for 100,000 acres to Graffenried and his heirs, but this land was intended for the Society. Thereafter, Graffenried starts referring to the 17,500 acres (his 5,000, Michel's 2,500 acres, and the Society's 10,000 acres) as 'his'." [63]

Michel, Ritter and Isoth hadn't much choice but to acknowledge the *fait accompli* of usurpation of the colony and of the titles that Graffenried had wangled, as he had left them no other options but cashing out and quitting. One wonders why they didn't do this earlier than they did but the likely reasons were that they had put in years to get this far and that they were now, in fact, part owners of another New World colony, their objective all along. Their long-term goal had been met, but hardly as smoothly or profitably as they had planned, and their newest partner had managed to put himself in charge and ignore them.

All this left Michel in a second-fiddle position. Michel's association with Graffenried would further deteriorate and dash Michel's ability in continuing with the New Berne colony. Further along, Graffenried's unending intrigues would lead to his own utter ruination. This was the beginning of the end of the relationship between the two men and perhaps between their families who had moved in the same high Swiss social circles for generations and lived only thirty-five miles apart in Berne Canton. There had even been intermarriage when Dorothea Michel von Schwertschwendi in 1536 had married Niklaus von Graffenried.

In early 1711 when Georg Ritter & Cie. is dissolved, Michel departs the New Berne colony. On July 17, 1711, John Urmston, a North Carolina colonial official, reports on receiving notification that, ". . . the Baron had no credit in England, nor had he any money anywhere, through ill usage in their way hither & since their arrival 900 Palatines there are but 300 now alive."[64] Graffenried's squandering and mismanagement had led to the deaths of 600 hopeful refugees.

Fiasco

By 1712, the New Berne colony would be in shambles.

From the outset, the Carolina colony was plagued by Graffenried's leadership, such as it was, his absences, and his overt undermining of Michel who the colonists liked and trusted. But the colony also was subject to serious setbacks from the outside which it had no way to avoid, and from Graffenried's blunders in dealing with neighboring Indians.

The community's first season of crops was insufficient to ward off hunger the following winter. New Berne was unwittingly planted where the Tuscarora village of Chattoka had been and an Indian graveyard still existed, offending the tribe. Further harming relations with the area's original residents, Graffenried summarily evicted Tuscarora families from their nearby lands without payment. This was an invitation for retaliation by the Tuscarora who were superior in number, resulting in the deaths of 130 settlers and damage to the New Berne town when the village was attacked.

During September of 1711 when Graffenried and John Lawson, the Carolina Surveyor General who had arranged for Graffenried's titles, ventured up the Neuse River looking for native grapes to start a vineyard, the Tuscarora captured them and put them on trial for the New Berne colony's disdainful treatment of its Indian neighbors. Both were found guilty. When Lawson continued his rude attitude even as a captive, the natives tried and executed him after ritual torture. Remaining in character even as Lawson lay screaming, Graffenried persuaded his captors to release him. One account says that he did so by impersonated his way out of captivity by convincing his captors that he was the Governor of Carolina, but in his memoir Graffenried claims that he was let go by convincing his captors that he *wasn't* the governor.[65] Whichever it was, when getting back to New Berne he found it torched with more settlers dead and many of the rest having fled for their lives. The incident triggered the Tuscarora War against New Berne that would last off and on into 1720.

After Michel, Ritter and Isoth severed their relationships with Graffenried and halted their support to the colony as long as Graffenried remained in charge, Graffenried in desperation left the colony and went to Virginia to scout for a location to which to transplant the entire New Berne community. In his absence, Michel, who had gone back north, returned, took charge of the colony, and worked with the surviving settlers to set a viable plan for the colony based on making peace with the Tuscarora to permit full attention to the colony's development.

When Graffenried returned to New Berne, he announced that the community would be picking up and moving to a spot on the Virginia side of the Potomac River where, by the way, he was sure that silver could be found. The place he intended for them was the one near Canoy that he had proposed for a colony on his wild goose chase exploration looking for "Michel's mines."

At this point, the New Berne settlers had had enough of Graffenried and, to the last person, refused to move. Seeing that it was now Michel who had the allegiance of the community, Graffenried took to bad-mouthing him among the residents and in his writings, simply ignored the wishes of the community and, with the blessing of the North Carolina proprietors, reasserted control.

Having no way to pry leadership away from "Baron" Graffenried or to tamp down Graffenried's erratic judgment, Frantz Ludwig Michel no longer had any future for himself in the colony other than to resign himself to being Graffenried's subservient lieutenant which he wasn't about to do. It was at this juncture with his own future at stake, that Michel had little recourse but to quit the New Berne experiment a second time, which he did.

Out of spite one supposes, Graffenried years later tried to claim that Michel had "died among the Indians"[66] in 1720. Note that the wording doesn't say that Michel was killed, but instead casts the impression of desertion and dissipation. Graffenried's claim of Michel's demise was never put forth formally but was found scrawled in the margin of one of Graffenried's memoirs years after it had been written and has deceived researchers up to the present. There is no other reference anywhere found saying that Frantz Ludwig Michel died this way. If he had, it would have shown up in official colonial records long ago and in verifiable accounts of him today. What does appear consistently in genealogical accounts is that Michel died in 1720 but none of the accounts supports this date with primary documentation. In fact, Frantz Ludwig Michel lived in Virginia until at least 1746.

When the people of New Berne as a group more and more loudly refused to follow Graffenried any longer, he abandoned them in late summer of 1714, leaving them to their own devices, which quickly became their and New Berne's salvation. His other motivation for leaving was that Christoph von Graffenried was broke. When Graffenried had joined Georg Ritter's colonization association in 1707, Ritter hired Graffenried on salary. When Ritter shut down the association, Graffenried's last source of income was cut off. Having exhausted his credit on both continents and with no other gigs going, Graffenried needed to get home as fast as possible if he could scrape together enough to do even that.

After having to sneak through Virginia and Maryland, both of which where he was forbidden to leave because of his debts, and slipping quietly out of New York, Graffenried was now a wanted fugitive on the run as he headed back to Switzerland for the last time. Fearing correctly that his American creditors would have debt collectors waiting for him at major ports, Graffenried used an obscure route to cross the English Channel. Traveling under a false identity and not daring to use his own passport, he boarded a ship in London and had the captain let him off temporarily to bypass English customs inspection. The scheme backfired. As customs inspectors went through his chest, the worried Graffenried put on a good face, spoke French to the inspector, slipped him a half sovereign, and asked the inspector not to disturb his nicely folded coats. Brazen enough to put this into his memoirs, Graffenried wrote that the ruse worked to conceal the contraband that he was smuggling illegally in his chest.

Crossing the English Channel turned out to be more difficult than crossing the Atlantic had been as Graffenried was now having difficulty paying even for food and lodging. When the French delayed him for lack of a passport, he was able to argue that he was Swiss and was allowed to go on. By his own account, when stopped further along he was able to summon enough fast talk to keep moving. Christoph von Graffenried finally straggled home to his father's Worb Castle in Berne Canton on November 11, 1714, St. Martin's Day in olden times. The broken man, now fifty-three, had shambled back to his family forlorn and not being sure what awaited him next. His years of erratic judgement had caught up with Christoph von Graffenried.

The reception Graffenried received from family and friends was cold. Recall that in August of 1709, Graffenried's wife Regina had had to apply to the Great Council of Berne for assistance in paying her husband's creditors. Hoping to find help to re-establish his position at New Berne, Graffenried was now spurned by prospective investors. Though St. Martin's Day observes the ending of autumn toil and the opening of hiring fairs for those between jobs, the Day had no relief in store for the make-believe baron. His father Anton von Graffenried, Lord of Worb, had had his son declared bankrupt, had him removed from his seat on the Great Council of Berne, and had stripped him of hereditary right to inherit the title of Lord. Just as embarrassed as the father must have been Christoph's brother, Emanuel von Graffenried, the Schultheiss (Mayor) of Berne.[67] Perhaps it was because of Christoph's scandal that Emanuel stepped down as mayor after having served for fourteen years.[68]

Christoph von Graffenried was down and out for good, now with no one to hire or comfort him.

Last Colonies

After Frantz Ludwig Michel ended his time at New Berne in the spring of 1711, there is a year's gap in the record as to his whereabouts. Absent any record during this time, the best assumption is that he is at home wherever he is living in America using his respite to correspond with Ritter and Ochs in Berne to sort out the New Berne debacle and move on with their refugee resettlement work. The record shows that their project continued on with Ritter and Ochs personally recruiting large numbers of refugees and escorting them to Holland or London, and Michel making arrangements for their getting settled at the trio's colonies at King William, Pequea and New Berne after Graffenried departed.

By March of 1712 we know that Michel is in South Carolina, when he has his purchase of 2,500 acres there record-

FIRST EXPLORER

ed in provincial land records. Michel shows up in the historical record on March 12, 1712, when he is praised by the South Carolina colony's military commander, John Barnwell, for Michel's success in negotiating peace with the Tuscarora tribe. On March 19 when Barnwell is too ill to attend a scheduled meeting with Tuscarora Chief Hancock, Barnwell sends Michel in his place, referring to him as Captain Louis Mitchell, Anglicizing the name. This might not have been in error as, when Michel had taken British citizenship in May of 1709, he may also have undergone a formal name change or have informally take up the English name. The other motivation that he may have had was tiring of hearing English speakers mispronounce the name as French.

On his assignment, Michel arrives at the meeting place but is stood up by Chief Hancock who mistrusts Barnwell with good reason. Barnwell then orders that the Tuscarora fort where Chief Hancock lives be taken and puts Michel, now Colonel Mitchell in Barnwell's log, in charge of the campaign. The fort is constructed of log palisades and is sturdy enough against other tribes or rifles but not against anything heavier. We recall that as a young man having just completed his higher education, Michel had served a stint as a military officer. Requesting North Carolina's assistance, South Carolina receives a squadron from, of all sources, Christoph von Graffenried, which he dispatches as "50 men from *my* colony" who, in sweet irony, Barnwell promptly places under Michel's command.[69] Graffenried himself doesn't accompany his men.

Michel rolls light cannon into place, surrounds the fort with his troops, and gives the order to batter down the fort's front gate. His men then march into the fort with fifes and trumpets blaring. At this point, Michel has the chief and all of his warriors at his mercy but instead of killing them and subjugating the survivors as was already the practice of the British, Michel, on his own, orders a parley between him and Chief Hancock for the purpose of negotiating a peace treaty that over the next few hours is hammered out on a small table brought along for the purpose. Michel then orders his troops to retreat back to the coast, no lives are lost, and the Tuscarora uprising is quelled peacefully for the time being.

Here we see not so much Michel the military veteran as, once again, Michel the humanitarian in what might have been Frantz Ludwig Michel's finest moment. Barnwell's praise of Michel is effusive, calling him "my bosom friend." Nevertheless, the peace borne of the treaty would be short-lived.

The next mention we see of Michel in the colonies on this his sixth exploration is his presence at the battle of the Tuscarora War on March 22, 1713, when the tribe's last stronghold, Fort Nuheruka, North Carolina, was overrun by a colonial army from South Carolina commanded by Colonel James Moore and made up mainly of Yamasee, Apalachee, Catawba, and Cherokee Indians willing to exact various grudges against the Tuscarora. In this we see the sad spectacle to be repeated of European invaders turning native against native. Casualties include hundreds burned to death in the fort, 170 more killed outside, and 400 taken to South Carolina where they are sold into slavery. This was one of the worst one-day slaughters of natives on either of the American continents in history. Michel's role that day is unclear but there is no known record of his engaging in battle.

The defeat of the Tuscarora, the most powerful of North Carolina tribes, opened the colony's interior to European settlement. Shattered forever, the few remnants of the Carolina Tuscaroras began moving north to live among the Iroquois in New York who accepted the Tuscarora as the sixth nation of the Iroquois Six Nations Confederation. Tuscarora is an Iroquoian language. The Confederation continues to exist today. Its constituent nations are the Mohawk, Oneida, Onondaga, Cayuga, Seneca, and Tuscarora.

English colonial powers in America would have done well to have taken a lesson or two from the Iroquois. The Iroquois ("People of the Longhouse") Confederacy is one of the world's oldest participatory democracies. Benjamin Franklin was so impressed by the Confederacy's makeup and balance-of-power provisions of its Constitution, the *Great Law of Peace*, that he brought these aspects of Iroquois governance to the table at the Constitutional Convention in 1787. The Confederacy's governing body, the Great Council of fifty peace chief sachems, continues to meet regularly in a revered longhouse.

Perhaps because he was disillusioned by the massacre, on October 19, 1713, Michel appointed William Price of South Carolina as his power of attorney in preparation for his departure. There are fleeting references to Michel in South Carolina later, matters which Price can tend to, but none confirming Michel's continued presence. Then Frantz Ludwig Michel again vanishes from the written record until 1715 when he becomes a father for the second time. This means that he was with his family or at least was nine months beforehand presumably but where?

In 1716, Michel is briefly back in South Carolina to put forth a proposal that the South Carolina proprietors establish a second colony for refugees. This is accepted and the next day, August 4, 1716, "Colonel Lewis Mitchell" is paid fifty pounds. After King William, the Shenandoah Valley, Pequea, New Berne, and the first South Carolina colony, this makes the sixth and last colony that Michel will found to receive European refugees.

Later in the month, he explores the area he proposed for the settlers "before returning northward"[70] and leaving South Carolina. He is now forty-one. Where he goes has not made it into the record, but a best guess is Michel's King William colony in Virginia. Late in writing *First Explorer*, one of the author's contracted researchers uncovered two obscure land transactions involving Michel's King William colony dated 1718 and 1722. Michel may also have gone on to his Annapolis house, Philadelphia, Pequea or all of them.

Here we exhaust all but a shred of the known record on Frantz Ludwig Michel until 1728 and enter into analysis and speculation in trying to divine where he was and what he was doing until then. There are glimpses that we will get to but no certain record of where Frantz and Anna Michel lived out the rest of their lives or, with one exception, how Frantz occupied himself after founding his last colony. The weight of evidence and analysis points to the couple making America their home but there are also reasonable arguments why they might have chosen to live in Switzerland or settle in London.

IX. Searching for Frantz Ludwig Michel

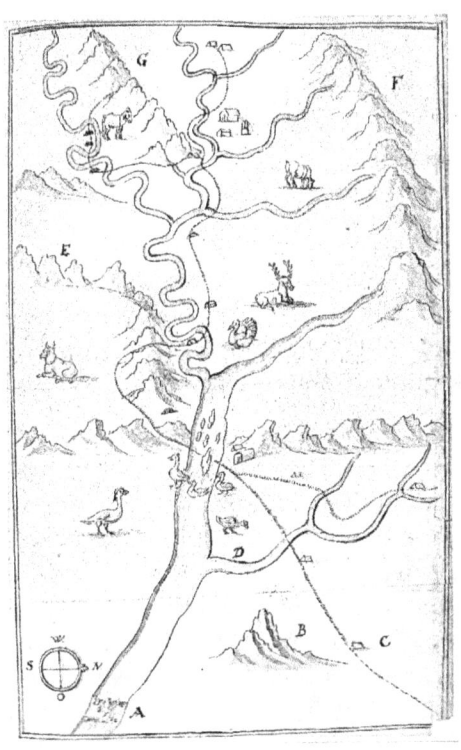

The Case for Returning to Switzerland

Based on Frantz's life up to 1713, it might be that this man who had led such an extraordinarily useful life up to this point would want to continue doing so and would therefore have chosen the place that would best offer continued engagement. This argument, taken alone, points to Europe rather than America. By 1713, Michel's two Virginia colonies were refugee realities with cooperative backing of the colonial government. Maryland and Pennsylvania were warmly receptive to refugee newcomers who were being sent there regularly by the trio. So were the Carolinas officially receptive despite the troubles of New Berne that were soon to be mending. The main work to be done now was in Europe moving people westward.

If not in America, Frantz Ludwig Michel had to live somewhere during his remaining years but where? In Europe he had the choices of Great Britain where he had lived for two years and in 1709 become a naturalized British citizen, or back home in Switzerland at Ralligen or Berne.

A clue pointing toward Europe is we know from what record is available that Michel's correspondence stops when he is in Switzerland or unaccounted for. Virtually all of his surviving correspondence was written from America or London, with nearly all of it going to Ritter or Ochs concerning the trio's resettlement project. There was no need for correspondence among the three when Michel was in Switzerland. There is no known correspondence among them after 1713 but it is known that from that year on their resettlement enterprise continued unabated for the rest of their lives and beyond. If Michel had chosen to live in London, his correspondence with Ritter would have continued and this may well have happened but there is no extant record of it. However, if Michel had settled in London, there would have been none necessary between him and Ochs from 1717 on as Ochs, by then a British citizen, moved permanently to London that year.

While it is a distinct possibility that Frantz and Anna chose to reside in London, more signs point to Switzerland if the choice made was Europe rather than America.

One more influence leaning toward Michel returning to Switzerland is that by 1713 the War of the Spanish Succession was ending. After thirteen years and an estimated 400,000 combat deaths and an additional 300,000 to 950,000 having perished from disease, the Treaty of Utrecht in July of 1713 mostly ended fighting among the combatants. The Treaties of Rastatt and Baden in March of 1714 ended it completely. Europe, and especially the areas along the Rhine that had experienced the worst of the war, could now begin recovering in peace. As the relieved situation made resettlement to America much less complicated, it increased the volume of refugees who could now leave without fear of being caught up in war. This was especially true of religious refugees who were being persecuted as much as ever in the absence of war.

So, if the choice was London or Switzerland and not America, Frantz Ludwig Michel more likely would have come home to his Lord's life with its castle, relatives, friends, humanitarian partners close by, and the familiarity of the beautiful European city of Berne with its libraries, concert hall, teashops and gardens. Or he could have gone home to Switzerland simply to decide on which continent to live, which could have been just what Michel did. What had to be on his mind were Anna and Christopher who he longed to be with if they had not been with him in America. A logical calculus would have been to go home to his family for welcome respite to think about the future if his mind had not been made up already.

Leaning further in favor of the couple living in Switzerland in their approaching middle age is that both had family and deep roots there, but neither is there any record of them settling in Switzerland. Frantz's humanitarian partners were close at hand in Berne where he could remain as effective as ever in his refugee resettlement work at the source of people needing to escape as on the American end of the pipeline. In America, Michel, Ritter and Ochs had by 1710 secured British rights to resettle refugees in Virginia, Maryland, Pennsylvania, and North Carolina, and had been successfully doing so. The pipeline was flowing freely on the receiving end.

But what of the prospect of Mennonite Anna again living in Berne Canton, seat of Switzerland's religious prejudices? Recall the exemption for Mennonite wives of Protestant or Catholic men, Frantz's nobility social standing, and Anna's father's official position in Berne's government, Anna would have been a special case and accorded a good degree of latitude, if not complete exemption from prejudice. But refugee Anna had made her choice when she fled Switzerland for Virginia at the turn of the century. There she enjoyed the religious freedom denied her at home so what would make her want to take the plunge back into a world of ugly ostracism?

There was one last reason that Frantz Ludwig Michel may have wanted to be home in his later years and that was to protect his reputation against the vilifications that Graffenried was spreading about him after Graffenried's own return home and the publication of his memoirs. On the other hand, that might well have been the very reason for the couple *not* to have chosen to live in Switzerland.

A certified Swiss genealogist contracted in writing *First Explorer* searched for traces of Frantz and Anna in Switzerland and found only records showing their baptisms in 1675 and questionable death references. There was no marriage or burial record found for either of them in Switzerland's generally very complete church and civil records, nor any Swiss record of children by them. However, there is the possibility that, being Mennonite, Anna may not have believed in civil registrations, hence the absence of records. Also contributing to the absence of records is that, in their zeal to persecute Switzerland's Mennonites, Swiss authorities would burn Mennonite churches and church records.

Frantz's single remaining journal has him domiciled in

Switzerland only as late as February 14, 1703, when he departs Berne for the second time for London where he meets William Penn and begins conferring with him. The journal ends in early 1704 in Annapolis. There is no further existing record that suggests that Frantz Ludwig Michel ever resided in Switzerland again. There is a visit to Berne on March 31, 1710, to meet with local Mennonites who Georg Ritter the following month will escort to Holland where Michel meets them. Michel then returns to London, soon accepts William Penn's appointment as Pennsylvania's Director of Mines and escorts a group of Mennonite refugees from Britain to Pennsylvania. After fifteen months in Europe, Michel is back in America, perhaps for good.

The Case for Cosmopolitan London

We recall that in his first stay in London in 1703 Michel had conferred with William Penn when the two honed their ideas of transcontinental refugee rescue. During Michel's second London stay in 1709-10, he worked on polishing the trio's colonization proposal to the Lords of Trade and Plantations. Michel had enjoyed success at nearly every turn during his stints in London and no doubt had explored the burgeoning city's charms. With the end of the War of the Spanish Succession in 1714, Great Britain had supplanted The Netherlands as Europe's leading commercial power and was now the world's foremost military and naval power as well. Britain's arts, architecture and science were all flourishing like never before, much of it centered in London. In many ways, London was the place to be in 1713.

But a deep search in 2022 by a well-credentialed British genealogy researcher turned up no confirmable trace of the couple having resided in London. Other than the history trail left behind by Frantz in his dealings with William Penn and officially with the Lords of Trade and Plantations, there is no indication of Michel being in London for any other reason including family.

The researcher did turn up two London burial records from Bunhill Fields Cemetery in London showing a couple who could possibly have been Frantz and Anna Michel, a Mr. Michell (with two ells) of Aldermanbury buried in a vault on January 11, 1725, and a Mrs. Michel, also of Aldermanbury, buried in the vault November 9, 1733. Vault burials are generally those of wealthier people, which our couple were. As Michell and Mitchell are common English surnames for a naturalized British citizen as Frantz Ludwig Michel was, it would not have been unusual for him to have Anglicized his name to Michell. What may have made this more likely is that the German pronunciation of Michel (mee-KEL) is not known to most English speakers who will then mispronounce the name in the French as mee-SHEL. Endless corrections become tiring.

However, the burial records for Mr. Michell and Mrs. Michel lack their first names so this couple has odds against being the Frantz and Anna we are looking for. But this Mrs. Michel's surname *is* what we are looking for, this is a woman of comfortable circumstances as was Anna, and the time frame and place are right.[71] A thorough search of church records, including those of the small Mennonite community in Britain at the time, turned up no trace of Anna either by married or maiden name.

Found: Francis Michael, Virginian

With genealogical and records research having all but eliminated Frantz and Anna residing in Switzerland or Britain, the focus shifts to America to see if any research or reasoning presents a convincing case that America is where the couple lived out their lives. The examination of an America scenario, while still leaving open some perplexing questions, has presented a realistic case that Frantz and Anna made their permanent home in America, regarding King William as their base.

Though it is not entirely conclusive when looking at America as where to find the couple, there are not the brick walls met when considering Switzerland or London. However, while there is much more of a convincing case that it was America, not Switzerland or London, where the couple chose to live, including discovery of conclusive evidence, at the same time a few contradictory signs arise.

When he departed South Carolina the first time in 1713, Frantz Ludwig Michel, now thirty-eight, did not lack for pleasant options from which to choose to spend the next stage of his life if America was his choice. He could have settled at his King William, Virginia, colony, which by this time was increasingly well suited under the supervision of the competent overseer Michel had put in charge. There he, Anna and son Christopher could have built a life for the family that in not too many years would likely have included a handsome manor house, high position in Virginia social and political circles, friendly rather than warring relations with Indian neighbors, and tranquility.

Or choosing Philadelphia, the eastern seaboard's most vibrant place, was an attractive option. Or the family could settle at Pequea or in one of the other nearby Germanspeaking refugee communities of Pennsylvania where Anna would have been especially comfortable among Mennonite neighbors. Or the family could have settled into the home that Frantz had built at Annapolis, Maryland, the year before they married. He wouldn't know that within a year Graffenried would desert New Berne making it a welcoming place again, so there, too, would have been an option.

Until looking more deeply, there seemed to be little in the thin extant record that leans toward Michel ending up at one location over another among the places where he traveled in America, not even the two places that he owned, King William and his Maryland home.

A careful cataloguing of Michel's whereabouts from year to year shows him in Annapolis for fifteen months from August 1703 when he begins preparing for his first Maryland expedition through at least December of 1704. In May of 1704, he wrote to Johann Rudolph Ochs of having had a home built in *Arundel Conti* (Anne Arundel County), Maryland. Michel doesn't say that the home is in Annapolis, the county seat and colonial capital, but most likely it is or is nearby as his letters to Ochs and Ritter tell of his meetings and preparations for his two Maryland expeditions occurring in Annapolis. Michel already has a home at King William or good places to build one there so his having built a home at Annapolis speaks of the seriousness of his Maryland disposition. There could have been another motivation: if Michel is ready to propose to Anna, it would be better to be able to have a home to offer her other than the inns where he stays. The year after he has his Annapolis home built, he does propose. Given that he had just built the home, it may well be that he had done so for marriage.

After 1704, the record goes blank on Michel for two years until 1707 *when he is again—or still—in Annapolis* now preparing for his second Maryland expedition. We know that during 1705 is when he marries Anna, probably at her home at Mattaponi in Virginia as would have been the custom. We don't know where they are during the 1705-06 blank period but do know that on either end of the period Frantz is at his Annapolis home. So, he quite probably marries in America and brings his bride to Annapolis where they set up married life in the new home. If so, this could mean that Frantz had not yet build a home at King William.

But there was time enough during the 1705-06 blank period of Michel's whereabouts that the courtship and marriage could have taken place in Switzerland. Or wherever.

Assuming either marriage scenario—America or Switzerland—the couple would have lived wherever they were until January of 1709 when we know that Frantz departs Annapolis for London for twenty-one months where he takes British citizenship and secures permission for three more American colonies before sailing to Philadelphia as Pennsylvania's new Commissioner of Mines in the fall of 1710. We don't know whether Anna had accompanied Frantz to London or stayed in America.

FIRST EXPLORER

After returning to America, Michel appears to be first in Pennsylvania as its Commissioner of Mines, then on record in the Carolinas, which he departs early in 1713. Now the record goes blank on him again until he briefly reappears in South Carolina in 1716 after the birth of his second child. He doesn't spend long in South Carolina, as he needs to get back to his growing family. But where was he during the 1713-16 gap?

Following is a timetable in months of where Frantz Ludwig Michel resided—or when his location in unknown—from the first time he departed Switzerland in 1701. Shaded bands are when he was known to be in America. *Italicized* bands are when the record on Michel is blank or vague.

With this, Frantz and Anna Michel's lives become clearer. In the thirteen years after quitting Switzerland in 1703, Michel chose to live in America interrupted only by the twenty-one-month stint in London when he made international refugee resettlement a working reality, his career purpose. During his London period, Michel became a British citizen of the new variety called American. During his unaccounted-for periods, married and in his thirties, he lives a conventional family life as would be expected.

PERIOD	MICHEL AT	DURING THIS	MOS.
July 24, 1675 October 7, 1701	Ralligen, Switzerland	His early life	—
October 8, 1701 November 30, 1702	Virginia (55 days)	King William grant Visits Anna	14
December 1, 1702 August 28, 1703	Switzerland	Confers with Ochs and Ritter	9
August 29, 1703 Late 1704	Annapolis	First Maryland expedition. Builds Annapolis home.	15
Late 1704 Early 1707	*Probably America*	*Marries Anna von Lerber in 1705*	≈26
Early 1707 January 5, 1709	Annapolis	Second Maryland expedition. First child born.	≈24

FIRST EXPLORER

January 6, 1709 September 22, 1710	London	Founds colonies, rescues refugees, becomes British	21
September 23, 1710 October 19, 1713	Pennsylvania N. Carolina	Gets three new colonies running	37
October 20, 1713 August 2, 1716	Probably America	Homelife wherever home was	33
August 3, 1716 Later in 1716	S. Carolina	Last colony, then "headed north"	≈1
1716 – 17??	Doubtless America	Homelife wherever home was	?

For those unfamiliar with it, the "≈" symbol means approximately.

Anna's not showing up in either Swiss or London records following her emigration to America raises the supposition that, after her family supply purchases were made in London in 1702, she returned home to Virginia as planned and then stayed put in America with the possible exception of accompanying her husband during his twenty-one-month stay in London. She, too, may have become a naturalized British citizen. As there is no record of her having done so in Britain, her naturalization would have occurred in America. Whether or not she did, Anna appears to have lived as an American and come to consider herself as one.

Expert historical research in Maryland commissioned for *First Explorer* turned up no trace of Frantz Ludwig Michel in Maryland other than his well-documented explorations of 1704 and 1707 and his 1704 letters to Ritter and Ochs. A deep search of official land documents produced no evidence of the home we know from his own extant record that Michel had had built and occupied in Anne Arundel County, Maryland. This begs the question of what circumstances might account for Michel's home not showing up in Maryland land records. Failure to register it? Squatting? Lax recording requirements? Someone else as the landowner? An entity as owner?

The researcher's suspicion is that Michel "may have been

FIRST EXPLORER

granted the land provisionally" where he had his home built. As a Swiss nobleman and Lord of Ralligen, Frantz Ludwig Michel met open doors wherever he went in the colonies or abroad. Upon arrival in Virginia in 1702, he went straight to the governor, presented his papers, introduced himself, and within fifteen days was granted a tract that became much or all of a new county. Upon arrival in Maryland, the same embrace was encountered, with quick permission to be the first to explore the entire uncharted province and to establish refugee settlements wherever he chose. So, with these kinds of welcomes, it is not improbable that this privileged adventurer may have been awarded some manner of special auspices for his Maryland living arrangement. Whatever the case, we know from his own record that he built a home and occupied it in Maryland.

Further expert historical research in Virginia next commissioned for *First Explorer* turned up 1718 and 1722 land records for one "Francis Michael" within King William County along the Mattaponi River. The later record shows a tract being sold, with neither seller nor buyer as Michael, between two identified parties who reside in King and Queen County directly across the Mattaponi River from King William County. Michel's adjacent land is mentioned as part of the boundary description of the tract being sold. This discovered record shows Michel's 1702 land grant as adjoining the sold tract, which may have included the home of the Lerber sisters who lived along the Mattaponi River. As the researcher notes, "Land deeds and conveyances often used descriptions that included the property lines of neighbors as a way to help locate the property. While it's not always full proof, most often land deeds would also specify whether the neighbors were alive or deceased."[72] This deed does not specify but the default assumption is a living owner.

As for "Francis Michael," here again we have the multiplicity of names by which Frantz Ludwig Michel was identified. In official documents (so far) we have Frantz and Francis; Ludwig, Louis and Luys; and Michel, Michell,

Mitchell and now Michael. There will be yet more name variants to come, which doesn't make researching the holder of the names easy. The Virginia, Maryland, London and Switzerland record searches conducted for *First Explorer* all employed multiple name variants.

The discovery of the 1722 land transaction extends by six years further than any other source the suspected whereabouts of Michel, however the nature of the deed implies but doesn't prove that Michel was alive in 1718 or 1722. Nor does the transaction tell us precisely where Frantz and Anna were living at the time, but it is conspicuous that these are records of a place directly amidst the known Michel and Lerber lands.

Given that the King William search did not turn up Michel under his birth name but did find Francis Michael precisely where we would have expected Michel, we can be encouraged that we may have found our man. This hypothesis is bolstered by Michel having taken British citizenship in 1709 and being known by an English name in South Carolina in 1713 and 1716. Had Frantz Ludwig Michel become a Brit to the extent of Anglicizing his name?

The 1718 and 1722 records involving Michel's King William grant appear to tell us where Frantz Ludwig Michel went after leaving South Carolina in 1716 to "head northward" as the surviving official South Carolina record states. Six years later, Frantz Ludwig Michel and presumably Anna appear to be at King William where in 1702 Michel had gotten his American start and visited the woman he would marry. After all of the intercontinental sleuthing to learn where Frantz and Anna were in their later years, King William may well have been the most expected outcome from the start.

What greatly complicates researching the couple at this time and place is that in 1885 a courthouse fire destroyed most of King William County's civil records.

While circumstances above are not absolute proof positive that Francis Michael is Frantz Ludwig Michel, taken together they clearly become the most convincing lead. With

FIRST EXPLORER

a second round of Virginia research findings, no doubt is left that we have found Frantz Ludwig Michel, now Francis Michael, up through at least 1731 when he is fifty-six.

Late in the writing of *First Explorer* just when the trail seemed to run cold, research was expanded to counties contiguous to King William plus one ring of counties beyond that. This revealed a motherlode of official records again in the name of a "Francis Michael" and this man's conspicuous connections to Virginia Governor Alexander Spotswood who Frantz Ludwig Michel knew well.

The first among Francis Michael's twenty-six mentions from this expanded research is his being awarded a tract of 400 acres directly adjacent to Governor Spotswood's estate in Spotsylvania County, Virginia. The two adjoining domains are at Germanna, the German-staffed mining project that Michel, Christoph von Graffenried and Georg Ritter had established in 1714. Among the more than two dozen records found on Francis Michael in this county are seven involving his court appointments as what today would be called an expert witness, his twice serving as an estate appraiser or trustee for the court, his taking an oath as a local militia officer, and his appointment as a grand juror. These official county records on Francis Michael show him variously as Michael, Mical, Micall and Mycall but it is clear from the entries that this is one man. Michael's grand juror and expert witness appointments indicate a person of high status in that era, befitting of the Frantz Ludwig Michel we know.

The clincher that this Francis Michael is the elusive Frantz Ludwig Michel comes from the recorded property description of the 400-acre tract that he was awarded, which reads, "On 28 September 1728, the colony issued to Francis Michael a tract of 400 acres of new land in Spotsylvania County, in St. George's Parish, on the great fork of the Rappahannock River, at the head of Michael's Branch."[73] The "great fork of the Rappahannock River" is where the Rapidan River, the Rappahannock's largest tributary, flows in. What is located precisely at this confluence is Germanna, the colony of miners that Michel had sent to Virginia fourteen years earlier. Germanna is also only nine miles from the Mattaponi River that forms one boundary of nearby King William County. So, Francis Michael's decision of where to situate his 400 awarded acres is made on the basis of a place that he well knew. "New land" in the property description means that the tract had been owned by the colonial proprietors up until then. "Awarded" means that this was not a purchase but that the colonial government gave the tract to Francis Michael outright. Then Francis Michael even had the local creek named after him. It would not have been coincidental that Michael's Germanna grant was located directly adjacent to the Germanna estate and stone mansion of Governor Spotswood.

Perhaps the likely a reason for his being awarded the 400 acres was unfinished business: by 1728 the Germanna mining project was faltering badly and needed to be restored to health, as Governor Spotswood's mismanagement had caused most of the miners to move on, crippling operations. It may have been that the recently retired governor specifically recruited the project's founder to turn the operation around and sweetened the request by arranging the award of Francis Michael's 400 free acres. Being free to him, this latest land grant amounted to a sizable bequest redeemable whenever Michael might choose to sell it, which he would.

Further corroborating that we have found the right man is the close fit between what we now see him doing versus Frantz Ludwig Michel's upbringing. This inheritor of a lordship was steeped in generations of his family managing lands, enterprises, people and money, adjudicating others' disputes, and being in charge, all of which he was unsurprisingly now doing. Francis Michael had to have been regarded as a good hire by Alexander Spotswood's Spotsylvania County.

After three years of trying, the Germanna mining turnaround attempt wouldn't work. Later in the century, Germanna would entirely depopulate and the Spotswood Mansion would fall into disrepair and be torn down. Today, the remnants of one of the colony's foremost plantation dwellings and gardens are owned by the Commonwealth of Virginia and managed by the University of Mary Washington. The Germanna site, now fields and forest, is listed on the National Register of Historic Places.

On and on the Spotsylvania County record goes on Francis Michael, concluding on September 5, 1731, with the recordation of his sale of this same 400 acres to Samuel Wright for fifteen pounds sterling.[74] This is the last of the known Francis Michael records in Spotsylvania County.

We note that Francis Michael's twenty-six recorded events in Spotsylvania County take place over only three years. Then—yes, once again—the record goes blank on Frantz Ludwig Michel/Francis Michael. What he appears to have done next was because of what was at the time rapidly unfolding in the Shenandoah Valley.

Michael may have been aware that in 1727 German Mennonite refugee Adam Mueller had migrated from near Pequea to become first European settler of the Shenandoah Valley. He would have learned that in 1730 Swiss immigrant Jacob Stover had been awarded a 5,000-acre grant at Massanutten Mountain, near the location of the colony that the Michel-Ritter-Ochs trio had gained permission for in 1709. Now in 1731, the first Mennonite settlers had begun arriving at the Shenandoah Valley colony that the trio had created for them, finally making the colony a reality. It is not far-fetched to think that Francis Michael would have gone there to receive and help them settle in. After all, they were his charges.

What jumps out nearly as much from the Spotsylvania findings is Michael's—let us now call him Michael for events from 1728 on—proximity to Alexander Spotswood, as their Germanna tracts adjoin.

Spotswood was appointed Governor of Virginia in June of 1710, the same month that Michel was appointed by William Penn as Pennsylvania's Director of Mines. Both men immediately set off from London to take up their new assignments. Spotswood and Michel had probably met in London and Spotswood certainly knew of Michel's securing permission the previous year for his Shenandoah Valley refugee colony in Virginia. Before his arrival in Virginia, the governor was aware of the group of German miners who Michel, Graffenried and Ritter intended to recruit to the place where they were to begin mining, which with their coming in 1714 would become the westernmost reach of European habitation in Virginia. Upon his arrival in Virginia, Spotswood would take great interest in the arrival of these miners, eventually employ them himself, and name their new community Germanna. The name derives from German and Queen Anne.

In 1716, Spotswood became an explorer himself when he led his "knights of the golden horseshoe"[75] expedition over a newly discovered pass through the Virginia Blue Ridge into the Shenandoah Valley, the first visit by a Virginia official to the valley and apparently the third overall after Michel's 1704 exploration and Ritter's 1705 visit.[76]

It isn't clear how frequent was the personal contact between the two men before Michael shows up in Spotsylvania, but it is certain that Governor Spotswood is the one with whom Michael dealt concerning Michael's official relations in Virginia from 1710 on. Spotswood served as governor until 1722 when he left office and retired to his newly constructed estate at Germanna in the recently formed Spotsylvania County named in his honor.

As much as whatever official dealings they shared, the two men had much else in common. Born seventeen months apart into privilege, both had served as young army officers, shared the outlook of the same generation of well-placed Europeans, reveled in exploration, had enlightened attitudes toward Indians, were entrepreneurial, married late, and were visionaries. Socially, both claimed illustrious lineage, noble in Michel's case, baronial in Spotswood's. What would have bonded the two men as strongly as anything was that they shared the triumph of being the earliest explorers beyond Virginia's Atlantic piedmont. And Spotswood knew who had been there first.

With so much in common, it would not have been unlikely that the two enjoyed each other's company and became friends. Other than his inborn wanderlust and new land grant, it isn't clear what might have convinced Francis Michael to uproot himself from King William and go forty miles deeper into the wilds to Germanna. Possibly, there may have been no move at all as Spotsylvania County was created in part by annexing the northern reaches of King William County. Perhaps the attraction was that Spotswood offered a vision of what his new domain was to become that was attractive enough to entice Francis Michael. Then, too, there are some who *yearn* to move about.[77] Michel/Michael certainly fits the type.

Another reason that Francis Michael may have decided to take up new duties in Spotsylvania County was widowerhood. A 1731 record shows Francis Michael married to "Mary of St. Mark's Parish, Spotsylvania County." This leaves us more unclear than ever about the fate of Anna Barbara von Lerber Michel, the Swiss Mennonite religious refugee who, to find her freedom, fled to Virginia to gain it and found much more. If Internet accounts are to be believed, she lived until at least 1720 when she gave birth to the couple's last child, Andrew Michael. She was forty-four or forty-five at the time. Anna may have died in childbirth, an all too common fate until the twentieth century.

Alexander Spotswood lived on in the county named for him until June 7, 1740, when he died at sixty-three while on official business in, ironically, Annapolis. He is believed to be buried there but this is uncertain. In 1730, he had been appointed Postmaster General of North America and the West Indies in which position he served until 1739. In 1737, Spotswood appointed as Postmaster of Philadelphia a young protégé of his, Benjamin Franklin.

The conclusion after a year's worth of three-country sleuthing is that we still are not entirely certain where the couple spent their marriage or where they are buried. But the weight of evidence now points overwhelmingly to America as where the couple lived all along.

We now know definitely that Frantz lived in Annapolis, then London, then King William County, then perhaps Spotsylvania County, and that when he disappeared from the record again in 1731, he was fifty-six.

We now know that Anna lived at Mattaponi before marriage, then perhaps Annapolis after marrying, then perhaps in London with Frantz, then apparently at King William, and then possibly at Spotsylvania County. Given that Frantz spent twenty-one months in London in 1709-10, it seems more likely than not that Anna and first son Christopher accompanied him. Joining the pieces of the location puzzle, the most likely picture that emerges is the most predictable one that the family stuck together wherever the father's work took him, with King William their base all along. There Anna had the company of her sisters and Mennonite community and Frantz the countryside that he had chosen all the way back in 1702.

That we know so much more about Frantz than Anna reflects the repressed status of the women of her era, typically disregarded in records of their time. Anna Michael was the author's fifth-great-grandmother, now recognized and honored 300 years later.

Deep searches have not turned up grave sites for either of them.

After Francis Michael's latest vanishing in 1731, we come back to his perpetual attendant question of where did he go this time.

He is now fifty-six. His oldest son, Christopher, now twenty-three, may have made Francis a grandfather by now. As a widower, he is raising teenage William and eleven-year-old Andrew, with the help of his second wife. Apparently, Francis is now also a step-father. By 1731, the eventual total demise of the Germanna colony mining experiment may have become obvious, making it time for Francis to move on to other endeavors. If that were the case, it is probable that it would have been he who recommended to Spotswood to wind down the mining project even though Germanna was the county seat at the time. This was also the opportunity before property values declined for Francis to sell the 400 acres he had been given and make his tidy profit.

It isn't clear from 1728 to 1731 in his Spotsylvania years that Francis Michael actually resided at his land at Germanna, which would have entailed moving his sons there or being away from them periodically. There is no indication that he owned a home there. As Germanna was only about seventy miles from King William, a day-long carriage ride, he may have remained at home and made visits as necessary to Germanna for his court appearances. This seems the more likely 1728-31 scenario for Francis Michael.

The only other high-feasibility prospect as to what Francis Michael did when he cashed out of his Spotsylvania County land grant in 1731 is that he went up to his Shenandoah colony which had just begun receiving the Mennonite refugees that Johann Ochs was sending on. The responsible Francis Michael probably did make this visit, but it isn't likely that he moved his family there. So, what Michael almost certainly did was to get his latest consignment of refugees comfortably settled at his Shenandoah colony, then return home to King William if he hadn't been there all along. King William is his home base and had been for at least the twenty years since 1711. This also makes King William highly likely where Francis Michael lived out the rest of his life and is buried but this we don't know. Here again we encounter the 1885 fire that destroyed most King William County official records.

From 1731 when last appearing in Spotsylvania County records until 1734, the record on Francis Michael again goes blank but, based on his habits up to this time, we are most likely to find him at home at King William. At this point, the author recommissioned his Virginia genealogy investigator to expand the search for Francis Michael farther west into Virginia with a third round of Virginia research, resulting in this very skilled researcher turning up another trove of official records on Francis Michael, this time in Orange County, Virginia. However, no move to there appeared to have been necessary on Michael's part as Orange County was created in August of 1734 by carving off the western part of Spotsylvania County. Germanna was no longer in Spotsylvania County whose new seat became the village of Spotsylvania Courthouse, today's county seat. Originally, Germanna was part of the new Orange County and served as its county seat but in a later reconfiguring of the Virginia county map was included in Culpepper County. So, if Michael was residing at Germanna, he simply woke up one morning in a new county with no move at all.

With the usual varying of the spelling of his last name again blurring the scene, Francis Michael appears in Orange County official records nineteen times from May of 1735 until March of 1746. He is serving in several court-appointed capacities as land transaction witness, lease recipient, bondsman, and in official appointments as roads commissioner, county appraiser, county surveyor, and estate surety, similar to the kinds of official appointments in which he had served in Spotsylvania County.

One Orange County official entry appears to explain where Michael and his family may have lived while Francis was working in Orange County. "On 15 July 1735, William Beverley of Essex County, Virginia, leased to Francis Mycall of Orange County, Virginia, planter, for the lives of said Francis, his wife Marey, and son George, 100 acres of land, part of Stockwell in St. Mark's Parish, Orange County, saving always liberty 'of making a path thro' the said land where it shall be necessary for and desired by one or more tenants of William Beverley'." The record goes on to say that "Francis was to pay rent annually on November 26 and in 1740, £730 of tobacco at any convenient place on the south side of the Rappahannock and every year afterwards, £365 tobacco. Francis agreed to plant 64 apple trees and 100 peach trees, the apple trees to be planted 24 feet asunder, the peach trees 18 feet asunder."[78] Now the adventurous Francis is an orchardist though he may not have resided at the orchard.

Mention of the Rappahannock River lets us know that this property lies in the northeast extreme of the county near Germanna. In the Orange County records found on Francis, sons John and George are mentioned, presumably his stepsons through Mary (the Marey above). We will get to the four sons often ascribed to Francis and Anna shortly.

Some skepticism may warranted about whether the Orange County Francis Michael found is the same Francis Michael of King William County and Spotsylvania County confirmed to be Frantz Ludwig Michel. Doubt stems from the multiple spellings of the subject's last name and from his signature. Regarding name spellings, the variations found in Orange County are virtually the same as those found in Spotsylvania County where there is no doubt that the man found there with various last name spellings is indeed our man. Furthermore, the names, whatever their spelling, are on official records of services performed that are of the nature that we know Michael specialized in.

In some of the Orange County records, Michael's name appears where a signature is required but the last name is misspelled suggesting that someone else wrote it. Between first  and last names in some cases appears a styled F for Francis replete with serifs as shown here. This image is taken from an actual 1735 record in which "Francis Michell" served as witness to a land transaction involving Governor Spotswood. Ordinarily in that era, those signing with only a single letter, usually an X, were illiterate. There is no ready explanation why Michael's *F* would appear as part of his signature. From his astutely composed journals and letters, we know that Francis Michael was anything but illiterate. Further, it is highly unlikely that an illiterate person would have been chosen to serve as witness to important official documents. Perhaps Francis Michael used his *F* mark as a manner of distinction or just personal style. At any rate, the Orange County documents he was party to were precisely of the types that the known and quite literate Francis Michael had been involved with for years.

In a fourth round of research, Francis Michael was not found in Augusta County or Frederick County after those counties were created from the western reaches of Orange County in December of 1738. This tells us that Francis stayed in or around Germanna, which remained the county seat until 1749. With his last found Orange County record of 1746, the trail on Francis Michael appears to have run out for good as he then vanishes for the last time. He is still only a day's ride from King William where he is most likely to have gone, or been all along, if still living.

By 1746 when we once again lose sight of Francis Michael, he is now seventy, well into old age for his era. Up to this point, he has the vigor and mental acuity of a younger man, having kept on for nearly two decades with his high-level professional work on behalf of the counties where he has worked. By this advancing autumn of his life, Francis has piled up a rich store of accomplishments and memories.

Francis Michael would have become aware that in the late 1720s German-speakers from the Pequea area had begun settling along the route of his 1704 sidetrip in western Maryland, concentrating themselves at the twin creeks he found at the end of that exploration. He likely heard in 1732 that in that year another group of German-speakers was creating a settlement across the Potomac River from Canoy. In time, he would learn the names of these new villages, Fredericktowne and the German Settlement. He would have known that in 1729 enough European refugees had settled around Pequea to create the new Lancaster County, Pennsylvania. He took pleasure in knowing that in the seventeen years since New Berne was freed of Christoph von Graffenried the community had stabilized and begun thriving.

Francis Michael would have seen a handsome new courthouse go up in 1725, perhaps in view from his home, as King William County had gained enough settlers to need a county seat and government. The courthouse, still in use today and wonderfully cared for, is the nation's oldest. It is shown in the center pictorial pages here. With a population of only 250 today, the county seat of King William is one of the nation's smallest.

Now elderly by his era's standards, the young Swiss nobleman Frantz Ludwig Michel von Schwertschwendi, the Lord of Ralligen, who had become the graying American everyman Francis Michael, could look back in what must have been profound satisfaction at the good that he had wrought. The audacious vision of the young explorer in his twenties had panned out into spectacular success by his forties and fifties. In 1746, now in his seventies, the hundreds of refugees he had earlier rescued to America had swelled into the thousands. The year before, the town of Frederick, Maryland had been platted and begun being settled by migrants from Pequea. Lancaster County, Pennsylvania, where he had created its first settlement at Pequea, was booming as the church-designated destination of European Mennonite refugees. New Berne had survived its terrible beginning and was now growing to the extent that it would become the state capital eventually. Francis's Shenandoah Valley colony had been receiving and comfortably settling Mennonite refugees and others for fifteen years.

One would think that, now beginning his eighth decade, Francis Michael saw that his visionary humanitarianism had bent the arc of history and far for the better. What he had accomplished could not have escaped notice on two continents. What must his friends and neighbors have thought of the aging humanitarian legend among them who had conceived of unprecedented, large-scale, intercontinental refugee rescue and then pulled it off so spectacularly? The province of Virginia awarded him land. The counties where he lived minded over him with comfortable sinecures. His children would follow in his footsteps with their inherited ethic of philanthropy. One hopes that a slower, mellow and contented Francis Michael would have eased into his twilight unburdened.

Our not knowing when he died actually points to his having lived out his life at King William. For a person of Francis Michael's social standing, there would have been a probate record of his estate but none could be found in a multiple county search. If he had died in Spotsylvania County or Orange County where he worked in his later years, there would be a probate record but not if he died in King William County which had almost all of its official records destroyed in the courthouse fire of 1885.

The Trio Passes On

Francis Michael may have died in 1746 when the obtainable record runs out on him. Whenever he may have passed on, let us also remember his humanitarian partners Georg Ritter and Johann Rudolph Ochs who never stopped shuttling European refugees to America. We now look at the passings of the three.

After leaving New Berne in early 1711 Michel goes back to King William and is home again. In 1715 as Michel turns forty, his second child, William, arrives. Michel is now middle-aged and slowing. He might be just as curious as ever to know what lies over that next mountain but is less inclined toward the strenuousness of exploration. He is more likely to be fond of a settled domestic life with wife, home, growing family, and local community.

In the research for *First Explorer*, no record turned up of Michel cultivating a lively civic life as his father had. But now from the four walls of home, he could bask in his role of family man and become active with an influential circle of friends, which we have seen that he did. His New World explorations and humanitarian colony foundings would likely have lain celebrity status upon him, welcome or not. It is not unlikely that the salons of Williamsburg came calling.

The available record is less than complete regarding whether Frantz did or didn't actively continue his refugee resettlement work after 1716 in South Carolina but circumstances suggest that he did. With Ritter and Ochs as hard at work as ever, there isn't much reason to think that humanitarian-by-choice Michel did not do the same, which he had been doing continuously since 1702. After all, he had created six refugee colonies in America and personally delivered Mennonite and other families across the ocean to great effect. His was an epoch-making success so why stop now? We know that by 1718 and perhaps earlier, Frantz Ludwig Michel had become Francis Michael, putting a fine point on his Americanization.

It is known that Georg Ritter continued resettling people regularly after he dissolved Ritter & Cie. in 1711. After that, Ritter continually shuttled from Berne to places along the Rhine gathering religious and war refugees, escorting refugee parties down the Rhine to safety in The Netherlands, and dispatching them on to Ochs in London for their resettlement in America. The exemplary humanitarian Georg Ritter kept this up until he died in 1723 at fifty-six.

As the probable last survivor of the trio, Johann Rudolph Ochs continued enrolling and resettling refugees until he died in 1749 at seventy-six by which time the trio's resettlement mission had taken on a permanent expanded life of its own.

By 1717 when Ochs resettled in London, the trio would thenceforth be scattered. But certainly, old friends Michel, Ritter, Ochs and Isoth would correspond and relate more than their social lives. It is also known that well into the eighteenth century the Great Council of Berne had remained determined to go on expelling the canton's Mennonite believers, giving the four men as much reason as ever to continue their resettlement work and little incentive to let up. The Great Council also continued to be dependent on the key assistance of the trio in the council's Mennonite removal.

Exasperation with the persecuting authorities was surely present among the four but so was the men's moral imperative that had driven them so far in the first place. One more powerful incentive to continue, even strengthen, the group's resettlement work was that in 1714, after thirteen long and very bloody years of conflict, the War of the Spanish Succession had finally drawn to a close, making the logistics of resettling people far easier.

Much of the knowledge of the group's work up to Michel's letters from Annapolis in 1704 comes from the surviving international correspondence among Michel, Ritter, and Ochs. But by 1711 with Michel settled in Virginia as no longer the shuttler between continents, there would now be only correspondence lost into the mists of time. The strongest element in concluding that the four went right on resettling refugees is that their finely honed consciences would not have tolerated just dropping their project, which there was no reason to do. Humanitarian refugee resettlement was their chosen lives' work, and it was under-pinned with moral imperative.

Two key personnel changes occurred after Michel's 1716 return from his quick visit to South Carolina.

In 1718, William Penn died after long lingering from incapacitating strokes suffered in 1712. Afterward, Pennsylvania was in the hands of its governors and would continue in its Penn-established ecumenical ways welcoming European religious refugees, a practice which continues to this day. In William Penn's passing, the world lost a great humanitarian and the innovator of mass transcontinental refugee rescue, a stupendous conceptual and logistical feat for any era. William Penn has never received adequate credit for the moral example that he and his Pennsylvania experiment set.

The other major personnel change was that in 1717 Johann Rudolph Ochs moved permanently to London where he took on frequent engraving work for the Royal Mint, reporting to Mint director Sir Isaac Newton. For several years, Ochs's work for the Mint was done on a contractual basis, one assignment at a time. Ochs encountered difficulty in getting paid for his work by the elderly and faltering Newton. After entirely upending Aristotelian physics *at the age of nineteen* while self-quarantined during the 1665 plague of London, Newton suffered mental collapse, depression, and paranoia by age fifty. To keep the idolized Newton from descending into poverty, he was awarded the directorship of the Royal Mint where the great scientist proved unfit. He held the position until he died in 1727 at eighty-four after failing to pay Ochs for several years' work causing Ochs great distress including a bankruptcy in Switzerland.

When Newton's successor took office, Ochs was hired full-time and worked at the Mint as Engraver for the rest of his career. Being based in London allowed Ochs to fill the role that Graffenried had had as the trio's on-site liaison to the British government on refugee resettlement. Ochs's now being based in London for his work at the Mint ideally positioned him for the resettlement role. Ochs would remain with the Mint for twenty years, retiring at sixty-six. He would continue relocating refugees to America until he died at seventy-six in 1749. Ochs's son, John Ralph Ochs, succeeded his father as Engraver at the Mint, serving in the position until 1787. Both father and son retired on comfortable pensions.

Once home from London, Michel had resumed his interrupted household life at King William. His and Anna's first child, Christopher, had been born in 1708 when Michel and Anna were either at Annapolis after his second Maryland expedition or back home at King William. As husband and wife appear to have been together continuously after Frantz's departure from North Carolina in 1711, this makes feasible the timing of the births of the three children who were born after Christopher. William came along in 1715 and Andrew in 1720. Nicholas, if indeed the couple had a child of this name, arrived at an unknown date but, given the birth dates of William and Andrew, probably between the two, though it is possible that Nicholas was a twin of either of them or not the progeny of Anna and

Frantz at all.

One envisions the couple now at last content with being together at home for good. Anna is glad about her longed-for more settled life as she and her husband enjoy mixing in the local social scene and being near her sisters. By 1715, Christopher is seven and a schoolboy. Baby Wilhelm arrives that year and before long the couple will have another child on the way. The couple uses their home to entertain. Christmases are celebrated as a family perhaps in traditional old Swiss style around the hearth. They gather by the fireside in winter. As they stroll their gardens in summer, they gaze across their tranquil domain into the far Virginia distance where Frantz had explored in his twenties. He teaches his boys to ride and swim. He reads to and tutors them. He lunches with friends and discusses the things that men talk about. He stays busy finding homes in the New World for freedom-hungry religious refugees. In their lost letters, Michel and Ochs fret about the plight of their Mennonite in-laws and friends.

A growing family, holidays at home, acclaimed exploration and humanitarianism, social life once again, perhaps a favorite hiking trail. A tranquil domestic life had been realized for the couple and their growing brood. And staying close to home did not have to crimp Frantz's ability to aid refugees as he went right on getting them resettled until we lose sight of him finally in 1746 when he is in his seventies. It isn't hard to imagine that the aging explorer scouts out local hiking trails, straps on the relic of his 1704 knapsack, and heads out. *What's over that far hill there, and up the Rapidan River?* Heading through middle age, tranquility had arrived for Frantz and Anna Michel and their family.

But it wouldn't last. Anna died sometime after her last child was born in 1720, perhaps in childbirth. By 1731, we know that Francis Michael has remarried. We know where he is after that but not where or when he died.

X. The Lasting Sway of Michael's Nemesis

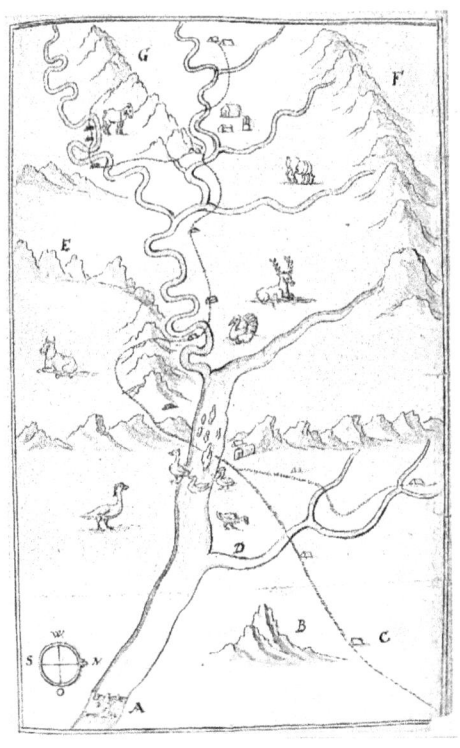

The Curse and Demise of Christoph von Graffenried

Whichever country Michel settled in, it would be surprising if he had not had to spend time fending off Christoph von Graffenried's continuing enmity. In November of 1714, Graffenried had made it back to Switzerland, returning to Worb, his family's ancestral seat, only to learn that his embarrassed father had had him declared bankrupt, resigned him from his position on the Great Council of Berne, and made Christoph's son Ludwig heir to the title of Lord, displacing Christoph as inheritor. It isn't clear how Graffenried's father had handled the situation resulting from Christoph's abandonment of his wife Regina and their children.

Clearly unhinged at this point, Graffenried said no matter to his cold reception as he was now a baron, two ranks higher than his father, and insisted that he be addressed as such, using the bogus title he had finagled in North Carolina. Christoph von Graffenried's stunningly narcissistic posing as a higher social rank than he was could never be recognized in Switzerland or the rest of Europe and was mocked as the purchased embellishment that it was. Graffenried didn't seem to comprehend this, convincing himself that it must be the world that was askew, and would persist in the fantasy for the rest of his life: he was a full-fledged baron and everyone else was wrong to say that he wasn't.

Sociopathicly narcissistic, Graffenried would be unrelenting in maintaining the fictional narratives of his "baroncy," his "great achievements" in the colonies, and how any failings there could only have been the fault of others who, by the way, were maltreating him. This should sound familiar to Americans of the 2020s. Graffenried wrote that the "fatal blow" from his father was the cause of his, Christoph's, "total ruin."

As there was much residue to sort out from the aftermath of the breakup of the North Carolina experiment, one hopes that Michel found ways to put distance between himself and Graffenried and that he gained a decent measure of peace in what were to be his remaining years. Anna would resent that Graffenried's unending fabrications needed be countered and that her husband was weighed down by being the target of an irrational mind. Dealing with Graffenried's self-serving distortion of history that he would never stop spinning would have been more of an ongoing plague for Michel had it not been for Graffenried's public preposterousness. But it would put a crimp in how history would remember Frantz Ludwig Michel that Graffenried nearly outlived him and had three decades after he fled New Berne to push his fabricated rendition of the association between the two.

The remainder of Graffenried's life as it unfolded left no doubt about the man. In Christoph's mind, his father's replacing him as heir with Christoph's son Ludwig estranged Christoph from his son. As revenge on his own son, as soon as the grandfather died in 1730 Christoph connived a way to force son Ludwig to give up his designation as heir so Christoph could wrangle back the estate. Finding means to circumvent his own father, Ludwig was able to have a new castle of his own built by 1737, which then served as the Graffenried family seat until Christoph died.

Citing continuing financial profligacy and delusional superiority, Christoph von Graffenried's family in 1740 had him legally declared mentally incompetent and committed him as a ward of the state. He was utterly dependent on the family for his upkeep until he died at eighty-two in 1743, having lived the last thirty years of his life in the fog of his imaginary barony. Even then, the worst was yet to come for Christoph von Graffenried.

Graffenried's Ghost

In an effort to defend himself from critics once back home at Worb, Christoph von Graffenried set about writing a memoir entitled *Relation of My American Project* presenting his version of events in America. First publishing the 42,000-word memoir in French in 1717, Graffenried kept at it year after year, writing at least two more versions, one in German and a revision in French. His manuscripts were later translated into English, are easily accessed in all three languages, and by default became the go-to reference concerning the founding of New Berne.

There is no known memoir by Frantz Ludwig Michel and little written by him that is still available other than what has been cited here and in the bibliography. His fullest first-hand account is the highly informative journal that he kept in 1701-02 of his journey to Virginia and back and his early time in Annapolis in 1704 but those two periods cover only twenty-three months of his life. So Graffenried produced a comprehensive version of his time in America and Michel didn't, leaving researchers up to today more reliant on what Graffenried had to say.

Michel probably intended to record for posterity, especially if he knew as of 1717 that Graffenried had gotten his memoir's first version of events before the public. Michel might well have had occasion to hear of Graffenried's memoir from his brother Hans or from Georg Ritter once it had been published but, if so, perhaps too quickly discounted it as the fanciful concoction of a disgraced chronic dissembler. Whether or not Michel had writing his memoirs in mind, death caught up with him and there would be no Frantz Ludwig Michel memoirs, at least none known to have survived. Meanwhile, Graffenried would live into his eighties pushing out his take on events version after embellished version.

After a two-century lull in attention to when and why colonization finally began extending westward from the Atlantic seaboard, a trickle of interest began with William Hinke's curiosity about Frantz Ludwig Michel resulting in Hinke's 1916 translation and publication of Michel's journal. This triggered curiosity about the interesting story of America's first explorer of the eastern hinterland and in Michel's later founding of New Bern, which introduced readers to Graffenried. Those digging a little deeper would come to Graffenried's memoir. Beginning in the early twentieth century, it was the lengthy memoir that won out over Michel's much briefer journal and for a century became much of the believed history of the two men's colonization work. Scholars today agree that the memoir was largely self-serving and caution against its use.

A good example would be the adulation that today is conferred on Graffenried in the state of North Carolina and its town of New Bern. Near the center of the charming old town are a bust and plaque proclaiming Christoph von Graffenried as the sole founder of New Bern. The town's website echoes, "New Bern was settled in 1710 by Swiss and Palatine immigrants led by Christoph von Graffenried," never mind that the government of the colony in 1710 had officially declared Michel and Graffenried as co-founders or that it was Graffenried who deserted New Bern. How the rewriting of this history happened was that Graffenried's memoir painted a rosy picture that misled the state and the town. One recent local column characterized Michel, newly discovered by its author, as Graffenried's "sidekick."

Knowing the actual history now, it becomes obvious that Graffenried's main purpose in writing his memoir was self-rehabilitation in the eyes of history and to try to recast himself in favorable light. For the most part, it worked and, while he was at it, Graffenried was unsparing in his denigration of Michel, his life mirror-opposite and perceived nemesis. The subtitle of Graffenried's memoir gives away the memoir's slant: *Written on account of certain persons who complained that I had undertaken this colony imprudently, to the disadvantage and ruin of many people–a charge which is easily cleared up.* Until near the end of the twentieth century, Graffenried's redacted account worked.

It was Michel who *didn't* desert wife and children, *didn't* embarrass his family, *didn't* stiff his creditors, *didn't* drive New Berne into near ruin, *didn't* concoct a deceptive fantasy and call it a memoir, and *didn't* live in ignominy the rest of his life. What Christoph von Graffenried needed the absolute least in his make-believe baroncy at New Berne was anyone present who knew the difference between real and counterfeit nobility but there was Michel, authentic Swiss nobility in the flesh, as constant physical reminder. Graffenried's sham posturing and preening left no way for Michel to respect Graffenried, and both men knew it whether or not either ever bothered to say so to the other. But until the twentieth century, long life would give Graffenried and his memoir the last word, deceiving some researchers even today.

His *Relation of My American Project* isn't so much historical account as self-idolizing auto-hagiography of an idealized account of events. In it, Graffenried is the Baron, the Landgrave, even the inflated "Landgrave of the Carolinas" of which there was never any such thing. He is never the cause of problems, only the long-suffering victim as problems are caused by others. He dismisses the colonial government having memorialized Frantz Ludwig Michel as co-founder of New Berne and writes of him as Mr. M., his ostensible subordinate. Graffenried can do no wrong, taking credit for anything that goes right and blaming others for what goes awry even when he was the cause. His ever-mounting debts couldn't be the result of his own profligacy but come from the small-mindedness of others who fail to recognize the brilliance of his schemes. His illegal smuggling of contraband as he flees for home isn't seen as shameful but as something to boast of publicly in his memoir. His total and abject undoing upon returning home is his much-embarrassed father's fault.

Graffenried's overconfidence, exalted self-image, negligence with others' assets and his own, inability to predict how his behavior would bring his downfall, guiltless manipulation of others, refusal to accept responsibility, and idealizing *his* "American project" as memoir are all characteristics of narcissistic sociopathy. Often glib, polished, and initially persuasive, sociopaths can wreak havoc on those around them and on organizations and communities large and small. New Berne recovered, then finally thrived

FIRST EXPLORER

only after Graffenried left, and late in the eighteenth century even served as the state capital for a time. Characteristically of sociopathy, when Graffenried fled back home he had no followers or friends on either continent, not even his family. Though in abject ruin and with the most important of people around him telling him so, Graffenried's mind could not accept his downfall or any version of life in which he was not paramount. He would persist publicly in the fairytale that he was the baron, the landgrave, the one in charge, the oracle to be heeded, even after being committed as a ward of the state, even until death.

Sociopathy is not a term to be thrown around blithely. The condition's clinical definition is "Sociopath: A person who has a personality disorder characterized by shallow emotions, reduced fear, stress tolerance, lack of empathy or guilt, cold-heartedness, egocentricity, superficiality, manipulativeness, irresponsibility, impulsiveness, antisocial behavior such as parasitic lifestyle, and criminality."[79] The terms sociopath and psychopath are now considered synonymous.

Analysis done by Oxford psychologist Kevin Dutton, author of *The Wisdom of Psychopaths: What Saints, Spies, and Serial Killers Can Teach Us About Success*, produced an occupational ranking showing that large-company CEOs, lawyers and media personalities top the list of professions chosen by the sociopath.[80] Dutton's work builds on Robert Hare's *Without Conscience: The Disturbing World of the Sociopaths Among Us* and on Hare's long work on occupational sociopathy. Hare also authored the bluntly titled *Snakes in Suits: When Sociopaths Go to Work*. Dutton's and Hare's books have become widely discussed and generally accepted. Dutton was careful to point out that the CEOs of which he wrote were not CEOs in general but those of major organizations in particular, predominantly in the private sector but not entirely.

In the early 1700s, the term chief executive officer did not exist but certain positions of responsibility and power at that time were the close equivalent. Overseeing a major novel land grant in a large colony that at the time was expanding settlement equates to what today is considered a major chief executive position. Though the North Carolina administration titled Michel and Graffenried as co-founders of New Bern, in Graffenried's mind he acted as if being solely in charge.

As Hare and Dutton found, there is an impetus among sociopaths who are bright enough to aspire to power that impels them toward it and, if they can get so far, all the way to the top, the larger the organization, the better as far as they are concerned. The sociopath has the advantage by understanding and taking advantage of how the healthy mind works, while the balanced person is vulnerable unless understanding the sociopathic mind.

Christoph von Graffenried reserved the worst of his self-serving invective for his checkmate nemesis, Michel. When Michel defends himself in a fistfight in Pennsylvania, Graffenried makes out Michel to be a drunken lout. When Michel relaxes in the evening with friends aboard the sloop that he bought for New Berne, Graffenried inflates this into late-night decadence. Years after he wrote it, Graffenried goes back to his memoir and scrawls in the margin that Michel had deserted his South Carolina colonies to "live among the Indians," today a discredited debunked claim.[81] If Michel had never left South Carolina, why had he appointed a power of attorney to look after his residual affairs there? Why does the official record state that Michel departed to "head northward"? How then did Michel outlive Graffenried?

As for the sloop, at one time Graffenried carelessly left the boat lying on its side on the banks of the Neuse River. By his own account, the sloop's demise came when Graffenried failed to keep an eye on the galley stove he was using which caught fire. When Graffenried abandoned the boat in a canoe, the sloop was destroyed when the fire reached a powder keg that exploded, blowing the boat apart.[82] In writing of the incident in his memoir, Graffenried assumes no responsibility for the boat's destruction.

After William Hinke's 1916 article on Michel, another century would pass before a definitive examination of the two New Berne founders would be published by Andreas Mielke and Sandra Yelton in 2011, their twelve masterfully researched articles comprising an entire issue of the journal *Pennsylvania Mennonite Heritage*. Toward the end of the issue, Mielke and Yelton assess memoirist Graffenried as "anything but an objective reporter of events." In the eighty-page journal, Mielke and Yelton do a skilled scholarly job of setting the record straight on both Michel and Graffenried.

As we have seen here with Graffenried, sociopathy (which the author has written on)[83] is a debilitating, life-altering mental condition that, by its nature, is seldom able to elicit sympathy from others. Science now believes that sociopathy is a genetic disorder that people are born with, and that it is amenable to therapy. A sociopathic blind spot is lack of empathy, making it difficult or impossible to appreciate that the negative reactions of others will eventually isolate or, as in Graffenried's case, take down the sociopath. Despite the repulsive treatment of others often exhibited by sociopaths, they still deserve pity for being victims of such an insidious condition not of their own making. Said a modern descendant of Christoph von Graffenried, "It is said that with great strength often comes great weakness, and Christopher's weaknesses led him to a sad end."[84]

We are left to believe that Christoph von Graffenried persisted in playing his character role of mock baron even beyond 1740 when his brother Ludwig and the family had Christoph declared a ward of the state. Graffenried died in 1743 at eighty-two pitied and shunned but still living the fantasy of the Baron and the Landgrave of New Berne, in his made-up world where he could do no wrong. Once in his grave, the greatest indignity, entirely undeserved, was yet to come for Christoph von Graffenried.

So, the story of Frantz Ludwig Michel became more than

that of a man born to privilege who realized unprecedented humanitarian and exploratory accomplishments as his chosen path in life. Michel's legacy also became a case study of the abuse that one influential person with serious mental illness is able with enough determination to inflict on the innocents around him. But the damage that Graffenried's memoirs and his tongue did to Michel's legacy as Michel appears in the historical record today is far from unique in the annals of harm wreaked by sociopathic people on others. Such harm can occur any day anywhere and does.

As in *First Explorer*'s foreword, much credit is due Christoph von Graffenried's distinguished family, which from at least the 1500s has provided generations of public servants to the benefit of Switzerland. Christoph's grandfather, father and brother all served in responsible positions as mayors, members of the Great Council of Berne, Lords and in other high posts. Christoph's brother served as mayor of Berne and, as of this writing more than 300 years later, Alec Graffenried is mayor of the city. One of Christoph von Graffenried's sons emigrated to America and produced a distinguished line there. This is a family with a half millennium of ongoing public service that fully deserves to be recognized for that, not for a single wrongdoer long ago.

FIRST EXPLORER

XI. Francis Michael Remembered

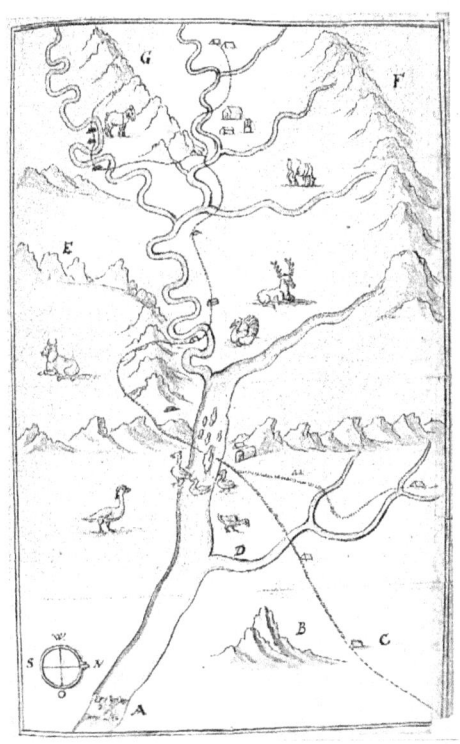

Refugee Resettlement Bends History

In 1700, England's twelve North American colonies (Georgia was not established until 1732) had a non-native population of an estimated quarter million, nearly all of whom were English immigrants or their descendants. By the time of the Revolutionary War, the colonies' Indian population had dropped significantly, the non-native population had grown tenfold, and only one in twelve recent immigrants was an English speaker from England, Scotland, Ireland or Wales. Researcher Aaron Fogelman has shown that, of all European immigrant groups coming to America during the 1700-1769 period, German-speaking immigrants (Germans, Swiss and Alsatians) outnumbered all other European immigrant groups. From the decade of the 1700s through the 1760s, German speakers averaged about forty percent of all European immigrants to America. Next in rank order were northern Irish, English, southern Irish, Scots and Welsh. All other European countries accounted for barely one percent of the total.[85] It is no coincidence that this abundance of German-speaking immigrants benefitted from a friendly organized resettlement effort working specifically on their behalf to get them to America, the transcontinental humanitarian venture created by Michel, Ritter and Ochs.

The ranking above covers only European immigrants, leading to the question as to the largest group of people to come to America in the eighteenth century. In every decade through the 1770s and quite probably through the end of the century, the number of Africans brought into the thirteen colonies—yes, all thirteen—far exceeded the number of Germans, English-speakers, or any other group. In fact, African immigrants alone accounted for nearly a majority of all immigration to America during the 1700-1769 period, forty-eight percent to be precise. This sad statistic predicts the story of much of what followed that reverberates down to the present in what was to become the United States.

FIRST EXPLORER

It has not proven possible to measure precisely, but it is certain that Michel's Bernese trio had a major impact on emigration to America and accounted for some substantial portion of German, Swiss and Alsatian immigration. In the first place, it is strikingly unusual that the two largest immigrant groups to English colonies would not be English speakers themselves. Today, German surnames rank as second most frequent among Americans. In the 1990 United States census, nearly a quarter of Americans identified their ethnic origin as German and that does not include other German-speaking origins such as Switzerland and Alsace.

The clearest evidence of Francis Michael's specific impact on what would become the United States would be to know to what extent German-speaking immigrants settled in the areas that Michel explored and opened as colonies to settlement for refugees. The map here from the research of Aaron Fogelman answers definitively where German-speaking immigrants were concentrated as of 1760.

Proceeding southward, we come to settlement area A in the Hudson, Mohawk and Schoharie Valleys of New York where 3,000 to 4,000 German refugees were settled in 1710 when sponsored by British Queen Anne. Starting in 1723, many of these had begun relocating to near Reading, Pennsylvania, in the Tulpehocken Valley and by 1732 on down to northern Virginia's German Settlement to form a new German community there.[86]

Area B is southeastern Pennsylvania where Germans and Swiss settled in Philadelphia and nearby Germantown before 1710 when Michel founded his most successful colony at Pequea west of there in area B.

Area C is western Maryland and northern Virginia including its German Settlement, D is the Shenandoah Valley, and E is Michel's King William colony. Areas C and D are precisely those that Michel's explorations opened to settlement a quarter century before Germans, Swiss and Alsatians began pouring in. Michel's King William colony began receiving immigrants earliest of all.

Of the estimated 64,800 German-speaking immigrants to America up to 1760, nearly all but the minority who settled in New York went to the hatched areas shown on the map in Pennsylvania, Maryland and Virginia. These were precisely the areas settled by German, Swiss and Alsatian refugees.

The map of Francis Michael's colony locations and the map of where German-speaking refugees had settled fifty years later are clear-cut overlays of each another.

Michael's resettlement plan that he launched as a twenty-seven-year-old in 1702 in Virginia had evolved into a highly successful, innovative, public-private partnership that by 1760 had drawn tens of thousands to the very lands that he, Ritter and Ochs had opened for them. The public-private partnership involving the Swiss and British governments on the one hand in concert with the Michel-Ritter-Ochs humanitarian venture on the other had worked. This organized, subsidized, large-scale, public-private resettlement of refugees—across an ocean no less—appears to have been a world first.

Frantz Ludwig Michael, George Ritter and Johann Rudolf Ochs conceived of and brought to life nothing less than a humanitarian triumph larger and bolder than any other of their time.

Like None Before Him: Francis Michael's Legacy

As a young man having just completed his studies and

military service, Frantz Ludwig Michel's pondering of his future took a path of lofty ambition not along conventional lines of wealth, power or fame but something much higher drawn from his own sensibilities: doing as much good in the world as he could during his allotted time. The young nobleman chose a life as humanitarian over easy lordship. By age twenty-six, he was on his way to Virginia where during his whirlwind fifty-five-day stay he founded his first colony according to the plan that he, Ritter, and Ochs had dreamed. Fourteen years later, then forty-one, Michel would dash down to South Carolina to launch his sixth and last refugee colony.

Owing to several obstacles, it is difficult to estimate the number of refugees who have settled in the United States until well into the twentieth century when official counts were begun. It has also been difficult to estimate the number of refugees that the Michel-Ritter-Ochs venture resettled but with the six colonies that they founded plus the number of immigrants they sent to Maryland the total would be well into the thousands. Then there were refugees who emigrated to these sites on their own, not through the trio's pipeline but from having heard about it. Ochs and Ritter did their parts in keeping the pipeline flowing until they died and Michael did the same well into old age from Virginia until at least 1746. The trio's pipeline did not die with Francis Michael as evidenced twenty-one years later when his son Andrew delivered 500 more souls to Pennsylvania.

What had started with a relative trickle of refugees to England's North American colonies at the turn of the eighteenth century became a steady flow by mid-century and then a torrent by the 1800s. Author A. B. Faust estimates that by the 1734-44 decade when Francis Michael and Ochs was still at work, annual emigration from Berne Canton alone had reached 3,000 and for all of Switzerland, 12,000. Owing to Switzerland's onerous prohibitions against emigrating, a significant proportion of these Swiss emigrants would have been religious refugees who Switzerland was still pushing out. With the Swiss government's sanction, Ochs would continue making the arrangements for the refugees' safe passage. By 1883, United States immigration records show annual Swiss immigration still at 12,000.[87] By that time the recently-formed Swiss Federation had eased freedom of religion and emigration.

Michael's humanitarian instincts extended to his relations with Indians. When he set up his King William colony, he did not chase off the Mattaponi and Pamunkey peoples whose land it had been for centuries but instead included them peacefully into his fold. His taking this path effectively insulated the two tribes against the depredations suffered by virtually all other Virginia tribes and certainly had much to do with the Mattaponi and Pamunkey being the only two federally recognized tribes in Virginia today.

When Michael lingered at Conoy for the better part of a week, perhaps longer, he and the Conoy were comfortable enough with one another for his stay. On his sidetrip from Conoy, he probably had a Conoy guide and may have had the sidetrip's attractive destination suggested by his hosts.

In his second Maryland exploration in 1708, four of the people he hired were Indian.

Most tellingly, when "Colonel Mitchell" took Fort Hancock, the Tuscarora stronghold in the Carolinas and a slaughter would have been expected if other commanders had been in charge, he deployed humanitarianism instead and forged a peace treaty preserving the lives of the Tuscaroras for the time being.

If Francis Michael was first an exceptional humanitarian, he was second an exceptional explorer, and it was a close second. When Michael went on his acclaimed 500-mile outing to explore the wilds up the Potomac River in Maryland and the Shenandoah River in Virginia, he was not only the first European to conduct more than a survey that far inland in these two colonies but in *any* of England's colonies along the Atlantic seaboard.[88] After a century of English presence, its settlers still clung close to navigable waters downstream from the east coast fall line of rivers flowing to the Atlantic. There were reasons why colonists had not ventured farther inland—Indians upset with settlers, lush resources where they were already, time away from maintaining survival, expense—but lack of curiosity was present as much as any other reason.

In Maryland in 1704, little European settlement extended beyond twenty to thirty miles inland west of the Chesapeake Bay. In Pennsylvania, German colonies only sixty miles from Philadelphia would not come about until Michael and Penn's Pequea colony was founded in 1710. When Michael arrived in North Carolina that year as a New Berne founder, Bath, the single European settlement in the province, was fifteen miles from salt water. New Berne extended that only to thirty-five miles. There were a few exceptions such as Albany, New York, founded in 1614 by the Dutch and well inland but Albany was Dutch, not coast-hugging English.

Lying aback at varying distances behind the entire string of Atlantic coast colonies loomed the Appalachian Range posing falsely in the minds of English settlers as a block to exploration. The range's closest proximity to the Atlantic Ocean or to the Chesapeake Bay just happens to be where the range bends in eastward in western Maryland and southeastern Pennsylvania. Michel wasn't likely to have had any way of knowing it but his route from Annapolis to Conoy where the Appalachians begin at Catoctin Mountain was the shortest route to reach the mountains that he could have taken anywhere along the entire eastern seaboard. What serendipity.

What Francis Michael revealed in his breakthrough 1704 Maryland exploration was that there was attractive territory in the farther reaches of the Atlantic piedmont and into the Appalachians where valley after beautiful valley lay tucked between the long ridges of the range. His 1704 map and reports of his exploration were firsts, caught the attention of others, and opened the way for settlement beyond the Atlantic coast. The young explorer had been the first to unlock the way from the east into the interior of the giant continent.

His lifting the veil from the deeper interior would in a few years lead to new settlements where European refugees, among others, would go. The earliest German settlers began coming down the Susquehanna Path from Pequea and eastern Pennsylvania into western Maryland in the late 1720s. Western Maryland's oldest surviving dwelling, the Beatty-Cramer House near Frederick, went up in 1732.[89] The town would be platted thirteen years later.

Some of these German settlers kept on going through western Maryland, crossing the Potomac River at Conoy and in 1732 settling what became known as the German Settlement five miles along Michel's path from Conoy to the Shenandoah River. The community thrives today as Lovettsville, Virginia, still with plenty of old German names.

Others went farther, settling places up and down the 200 miles of the Shenandoah Valley. After reports of Michel's exploration of the valley reached England, Lord Fairfax, proprietor of the vast Virginia colony (the western boundary of which was 200 miles beyond the Pacific coast), ordered his governor of Virginia, Alexander Spotswood, to ride to the valley and claim it. Spotswood was the third European after Michel and Ritter to enter the Shenandoah Valley. However, two monuments commemorating his visit mistakenly proclaim him as the first European there.

In 1730 when Virginia opened the Shenandoah Valley for settlement, the first settlers who came the following year were Mennonite refugees. The virgin territory of the Shenandoah Valley saw its first written account by a settler in 1741 when Jost Hite of Philadelphia County, Pennsylvania, moved in during the fall of that year well down the valley near today's Staunton, Virginia. As the website of the genealogical organization First Settlers of the Shenandoah Valley states, "Adventurous Europeans, mostly of German and Scots-Irish heritage were lured by the excellent farmland of the Shenandoah Valley and began to settle and fence their claims. Immigration into the valley, and trade from the valley back to market centers, was connected first with Pennsylvania Germans. Because of the physical barrier of the Allegheny Front on the west, the settlers were steered south into Virginia. The Blue Ridge Mountains to the east and the slow population growth in the Virginia piedmont deterred the English from moving into the Shenandoah Valley."[90]

So, German-speaking people including Michael's refugees did. In short order, four new Virginia counties had been created in the valley.

Michael the humanitarian, with the steady energies of Ritter and Ochs, had established the means of getting large numbers of European refugees to America, and Michael the explorer had founded six colonies and opened the lands where those refugees could prosper. What these three men wrought would be permanent, developing into custom, then institution, and then after independence into policy and federal sponsorship. It was the youngest member of the trio who did *all* the spectacularly successful exploration and settlement work on the receiving end.

What Michael, Ritter and Ochs had wrought was America's first organized multi-colony refugee resettlement program, a huge-hearted humanitarian venture which continues to this day, now deeply institutionalized as part of the federal government.

Francis Michael had his other accomplishments—his first-of-their-kind drawings of Williamsburg, his 1702 Virginia journal, and his 1704 exploration map—all of which usefully survive. He also left sons who were Americans including one who would continue his father's European refugee rescues.

The overarching legacy of the foresighted adventurer is his opening a new continent, joining it to an older one, and moving thousands from one to the other, delivering them unto opportunity, religious freedom, and peace that they had not had where they were coming from. Realizing this took a grand vision as broad as anyone's of his era, superior execution to pull it off, and the heart of a great humanitarian to drive it all. Vision, ability to deliver, and heart Francis Michael all had in large measure. He would be first to say that Georg Ritter and Johann Rudolph Ochs deserve as much credit as he, and in that he would be right.

He did all that they did *and* was eastern America's first great explorer.

Halfway through his life, Frantz Ludwig Michel took British citizenship and shortly after that the English name Francis Michael. The immigrant Lord of Ralligen had chosen to become an American even to Anglicizing his name, making his transition to Citizen Michael complete. Now middle-aged with his exploring and colony founding behind him, he spent the remainder of his life witnessing the colonies he had founded thrive on behalf of other immigrants and using his talents for the benefit of the people in the Virginia counties that he served in his official roles. After a late start, Francis Michael was also husband to two wives, father, step-father, and grandfather.

Today there is barely any memory of Frantz Ludwig Michel in the lands that he explored or Francis Michael in the Virginia that he served or even among the descendants of those he saved. There are no known images of Francis or Anna Michael. As far as is known, their lives ended without either writing a memoir. Their burial places are unknown.

XII. The Family in America

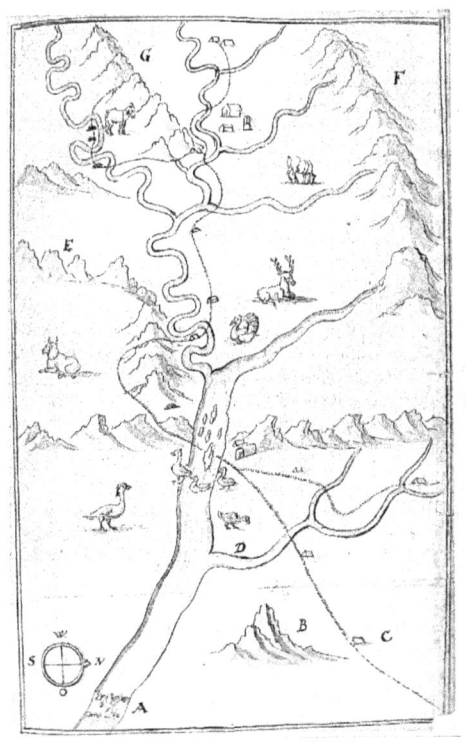

The Sons

Here based on conflicting surviving records, we encounter two competing lines of reasoning as to the fates of Frantz and Anna Michel and who their children may have been, and a third line of reasoning that seems most explanatory.

The Sons Were Not Orphans of Francis and Anna

One scenario is based on the scant but consistent Internet and genealogical record that has some tragedy, or perhaps multiple tragedies, striking the family in 1720 when both parents are said to have died at age of forty-four or forty-five depending on when in the year they died. This is the year that the last child attributed to them, Andrew, was born so possibly Anna died in childbirth, a common tragedy that befell women all too frequently until the twentieth century. If this scenario were true, more likely the couple succumbed to one of the diseases that few die of anymore but that in the early eighteenth century routinely battered places anywhere. Dying in 1720 in Berne on December 19 was Anna's father, Frantz Ludwig von Lerber.

This scenario supposes that the couple died in Europe, their four sons had been born there, and as orphans they emigrated to Pequea or nearby in the 1750s. At first glance, this scenario seems consistent with Mildred Michael Crewe's research done in the 1950s, Internet accounts, and some of the oral tradition handed down in the author's family. However, the expert genealogical searches performed in 2022 for *First Explorer* turned up nothing on the couple's children having been born in Europe. Nor did they turn up anything on Anna Michel in Switzerland or London after she fled Switzerland in 1699 or 1700.

The Sons as Virginians

The competing line of reasoning stems from discoveries made in researching *First Explorer* in Virginia records from 1718 to 1746 showing that Frantz was living at or near his King William colony during this period, and the definitive discovery of him serving Virginia's Spotsylvania and Orange Counties as late as age seventy.

This second scenario is based on Frantz Ludwig Michel's confirmed presence in Virginia as late as 1746 when first-scenario accounts say he was no longer living. This second scenario indicates Michel's being in America continuously from late 1710 when he completed his London work. In this case, the last three children attributed to Frantz and Anna, and probably their first child as well, would have been born in America, casting doubt on their arriving from Europe in the 1750s.

These two scenarios would appear to be in direct conflict with one another, with both containing caveats inviting conjecture.

The strongest caveat of the European case is that genealogical searches were commissioned only for Bern Canton, Switzerland and for London, but the children's births could have occurred elsewhere in Switzerland, Britain or Europe and may not have been recorded because the children's Mennonite mother appears to have followed her church's practice of opposing civil involvement.

A caveat of the America case is that Frantz showing up as property owner Francis Michael at King William as late as 1722 is likely but not absolute proof that he was still alive at that time. As the researcher put it, "[S]ince Michael is identified as a neighbor in 1722, it does not give a status - it does not identify whether Michael was deceased or not, so he could have been alive at the time, he may not have been. At the very least, the land was still in Michael's name as of 1722 (even if he were deceased)."

But this same diligent researcher's subsequent research confirmed Michel, by then Francis Michael, as alive in counties neighboring King William as late as 1746. This shows that the quite consistent Internet date of 1720 for the death Frantz is incorrect, though it may be correct for Anna. Again, no primary record could be found backing up any of the Internet claims of the 1720 date.

Based on the confirmed finding of Michel/Michael alive as late as 1746, the competing death date of 1720 is considered disproven. This also shows that the four sons were not orphaned as would have been the case with the 1720 death dates for Francis and Anna. If the sons were alive in 1746, their ages were thirty-eight (Christopher), thirty-one (William), twenty-six (Andrew), and uncertain (Nicholas).

With these caveats, we are again back in the mists of time three hundred years ago confronted with the predictable challenge of doing our best to identify the most probable conclusion. The clearest material on which to proceed lies in the consistency of Francis's appearances in Virginia land, civil, and church records well beyond 1720, suggestive genealogy in generations after Francis and Anna, and the historical tie-ins between Francis and at least one son attributed to him that are too closely parallel to be coincidental. Of the two cases above—Europe versus America—we will proceed where far more evidence has been found but no Internet mention, the American conjecture in which Francis and Anna called Virginia home.

The American scenario is thoroughly at odds with the four brothers emigrating from Europe to America in the 1750s. If they had been born in America, why would all four end up in Europe only to head back to America? Here we examine the root reference to the brothers emigrating, the research commissioned by Mildred Michael Crewe sometime before 1952. In Maryland colonial records, Crewe's researcher found seven men living in Frederick County, Maryland, in the 1750s and 1760s with the last name Michel or Michael including four with birth dates of 1720 or earlier. Neither Michel nor Michael is a common a German surname. Screening for language, gender, age, surname and decade in a county of a few thousand and coming up with four hits stretches the laws of probability unless there is an explanatory factor at work. Here there may be: the four are purported to be brothers.

Crewe's researcher then found four men with the same names in Library of Congress ship passenger logs all landing at Annapolis over a span of several years, ostensibly ending up in Frederick after several more years. Their supposed delay to reach Frederick dovetailed with Michael family oral history of the brothers arriving in Frederick after waiting out the French and Indian War around Pequea. But if the four brothers were not the immigrants found in the ship logs but were Frantz and Anna's offspring born in Virginia, why would the four move to Pennsylvania rather than going straight to Maryland where they ended up?

There are also no known birth or baptism records available showing Frantz and Anna as the parents of any of the four (or of any other) children. Again, this could be due to civil registration being anathema to Mennonites, official destruction of Mennonite records, or loss through the passage of time. Relying on what circumstantial evidence is available about the brothers individually including that uncovered in researching *First Explorer*, we can come to broad estimates as to the likelihood of each of the four being a child of Frantz and Anna.

In addition to the indications in the following table, all four arrived in Frederick with money as evidenced by each making heavy real estate purchases, all became naturalized British citizens within months of each other, and Frederick was where Frantz Ludwig Michel had explored on his 1704 sidetrip.

CHILD	FRANTZ & ANNA PARENT SIGNS	SON OR NOT
Christopher	Bought large rural tract Same denomination as Frantz Anna's grandchild has her name Andreas as sibling oral tradition	Likely
William	Bought two Frederick properties Church donation with Andreas Likely helped build foundry	Possibly
Andrew	Bought four Frederick properties Refugee rescue of 500 in 1767 Bought tract at Frantz campsite Christopher sibling oral tradition	Convincing

Nicholas   Arrived years before other three   Can't tell
             Frederick record ends early

Another possibility is that none of these men was the child of Frantz and Anna, a theory that one sees in one or two places on the Internet. What is to explain the four emigrating from Switzerland or nearby assuming that that actually happened? While in the absence of birth or baptismal records there is some small probability that this could be the case, there is too much in parallel between Frantz's life and the sons' lives to be coincidental, particularly how closely Andrew, the youngest son, followed literally in Frantz's footsteps to Frederick, then to Cooling Springs, with his own refugee rescue delivery to Pequea along the way.

A distant possibility is that the four were not European immigrants at all but American returnees escorting refugees. Supporting this theory is that, according to handed-down oral tradition, upon landing in Annapolis all four first went to Frantz Ludwig Michel's Pennsylvania colony. If they were delivering immigrants, it could have been for payment which would have provided each with a grubstake. And what better mentor could they have had for conducting trans-Atlantic refugee rescue than their own father. The Library of Congress ship logs showing the arrival of the four to Annapolis have all four embarking from points along the Rhine River or nearby where emigration to America was heaviest. However, though feasible, the four leaving Virginia for Maryland via Europe and Pequea seems vanishingly improbable.

We are left with no birth or baptismal records for the four, in keeping with Anna's Mennonite practices, making it not possible to know their origins and leaving us with their mystery. But we are also left to ponder the deep corroborative oral tradition, their arrival in Frederick with well financed, and the close life-shadowing of the explorer by his reputed youngest son, Andrew.

In the 1728-1746 Virginia records found, two men named John and George Michael are referred to as Francis Michael's sons. These names appear nowhere else in research done for *First Explorer*. John and George appear to be Francis's stepsons by Mary, his second wife.

The Sons' Arrival in Frederick

A third scenario that now arises is that the four found in Frederick church and land records were not the same four found in the ship logs. In fact, in the fragment of Crewe's record available, *nothing ties the four European immigrants of the ship logs to Frederick except supposition.* This leaves open a scenario of the four arriving to Frederick not from Europe but from their home 150 miles away in Virginia. This, too, so far is unproven but, everything else considered, is the simplest and most plausible scenario. But here again we run into a conundrum as this is at odds with the four becoming naturalized British citizens within a few months of each other after arriving in Frederick *unless* to correct the lack of registration of their births if that were the case, which is probable given their mother's aversion to civil participation.

There was good reason why in middle age the brothers would pick up and move from Virginia to Frederick. In 1760s Virginia, counties where they may have been living were growing but not developing beyond farm land with small sleepy county seats as evidenced up to today. This part of Virginia permanently stagnated economically (but in doing so was able to preserve its natural beauty).

At the same time, Frederick was booming and Frederick County was well on its way by 1770 to becoming Maryland's most populous and politically influential county. In many ways, Frederick County was the place to be in the mid-Atlantic in 1762 when the brothers arrived. Why not pick up and move to better one's economic opportunities *and* feel right at home where the sons' father had explored?

In the end, it has not been possible to pin down without at least some doubt who the descendants of Francis and Anna Michael may have been but this third scenario of the brothers' short move for good reason is the most convincing.

There would appear to be another factor at play. We note that the author has lived on five continents in seven countries, visited fifty-one more, and driven across North America at least a dozen times just *to see what's over that next mountain there*. The author's father worked on four continents in his career and would go overseas as often as his employer was willing to send him. And the author's son is a professional geographer and map maker. Now where might all of this wanderlust have come from?

Lives Refashioned on the 1760s Frontier

As we see from the variable record thus far, it isn't certain where Frantz and Anna spent the early years of their marriage or even if they were always together. Frantz was highly mobile, moving among six colonies from Pennsylvania to South Carolina, and shuttling back and forth across the Atlantic. Did Anna accompany the peripatetic Frantz? Did she remain in Virginia seeing her husband only when he found time to get home? Or, if they were usually together, had the couple maintained some semblance of regular residence in Virginia at Mattaponi with her sisters or at King William on Frantz's land grant? When he was in Europe, Frantz spent periods in London so did the couple live there off and on?

The research commissioned for *First Explorer* has not been able to answer many of these 300-year-old questions definitively but has by process of elimination revealed the strong likelihood that, at least after Frantz returned from Europe in early 1711, the couple resided in King William County, Virginia, the original American home for both of them. Except for the London stint, King William is also the most probable base for the couple from their 1705 marriage on, though possibly there were times spent temporarily in Annapolis or Pennsylvania when Frantz was exploring or working in those places.

If it is difficult to trace Frantz's movements more than 300 years later, it has proven much harder to trace Anna's. Nearly all we know about when they were together is based on when their children were born. Knowing that the last three were born from 1715 to 1720 tells when the parents were together but not definitively where they were.

While there are few clues as to where the couple may have resided early in their marriage, there are more as to where they spent the years after Frantz departed Europe in 1711. As late as 1717 there are faint references to Michel from the Carolinas, not to his presence there but to others mentioning him in one context or another.[91]

We have only scant indication as to what occupations the four sons took up, but we know that they had a privileged upbringing, and it has been easy to deduce that they arrived in Frederick in the 1760s[92] well off financially. We will see that William was experienced in large stone building construction, that Andrew was inclined toward iron-making and refugee recruitment and resettlement. We know that the two at the same time made very generous donations to their church's building fund.

Wherever they migrated from—Virginia or Europe—oral tradition among their descendants is that the four waited to move to Frederick until the French and Indian War (called the Seven Years War in Europe) abated. During the war, which lasted from 1756 to 1763, raids into western Maryland savaged communities, slaughtered settlers, and largely halted western migration beyond Fredericktowne. Many settlers living in pioneer areas west of Frederick abandoned their homes and farms and retreated to Fredericktowne if they were not massacred first. An attractive destination for new settlement only a few years before, Frederick County had become one of the most dangerous places in North America. The handed-down story is that the brothers delayed moving to Frederick County until it became safe to do so, but from where?

During the last year of the war, the British and their American colonist allies were able to make enough headway to begin clearing the area west of Frederick of enemies and make Frederick County safer once more for settlers. Finally, with signing the Treaty of Paris in 1763, the war was over and peaceful life began to be restored in western Maryland. In the year just before this as the war was cooling, the brothers would make their move to Fredericktown as it was then known, quickly make major investments in properties and commerce, and take their places high in local civic life. They were that new breed the world was beginning to talk about, people who called themselves Americans.[93]

But why by 1762 would the Michel brothers have traded the established comforts of the Pennsylvania German or Virginia communities—we don't know which—where they had lived long enough to make friends and sink roots for a rough frontier town in the making with the embers of war still smoldering not far away? The only answers that seem plausible are that the brothers had made it a goal to settle where their father's famous map showed his sidetrip and to move for better economic opportunity So, for them perhaps it had to be Frederick all along. The place they made their way to in the early 1760s was precisely the same spot that their father had gotten to on his sidetrip from Conoy that day in 1704, the two large creeks that drain into the Monocacy River at what later had become Fredericktowne.

After being in Frederick not long, the four wasted no time in becoming naturalized once they reached Frederick. William led the way in 1761. Nicholas became naturalized as a British citizen on September 21, 1763, and six days later Christopher did the same. The youngest brother, Andrew, was naturalized a few months later on April 11, 1764. All four would become American citizens on August 2, 1776, the day that the Declaration of Independence was ratified by the last of the thirteen colonies, which, by that last signature, became thirteen independent nation-states, but not yet united into a single country. That wouldn't come until 1781 with Frederick County playing a central role.

Early on after arriving in Frederick, the brothers made their marks in property acquisition, industrial development, church support and useful citizenship.

The brothers quickly began establishing their civic lives in the town. In those days and long after, much of one's social life meant church life. Sunday was the day when people would saddle up or hitch the wagon and get to see friends at church. At least two of the brothers belonged to the Evangelical Lutheran Church in Frederick. Church records show William and Andrew Michael teaming up in 1763 to donate one pound sterling to the church building fund. To put this into the context of currency value at the time, one pound sterling would purchase twenty acres of good farmland.[94] Twenty acres of good farmland in Frederick County in 2022 would be worth approximately $240,000. Theirs was a generous donation for its time.

The church, the oldest still in operation in western Maryland, had been founded in 1736 in a log building as the earliest settlers were beginning to arrive. What the brothers were donating to was a new masonry church building, which itself was replaced in 1854 with the church of today, a tall steepled landmark that in 2021 completed its most major renovation since the 1880s. The church is located—where else—on Church Street in Frederick.

Andrew Michael married Maria Barbel "Barbara" Sinn in the Evangelical Lutheran Church in 1761. She had been baptized in the church in December of 1743. When they married, Barbara was eighteen, making her twenty-three years younger than her husband, then forty-one.

Christopher Michael arrived in Frederick with his wife Anna Thankbonder whom he had married in 1753.

Property records show that almost immediately after they arrived the brothers made heavy property investments.

Nicholas had migrated to Frederick in 1758 during the war and that year bought forty-six acres of Stony Hall from Ulrich Erb.

Christopher bought from Luke Barnard 250 acres of the

tract "The Sun Is Down and the Moon Is Up" located across Catoctin Mountain from Fredericktowne in the Catoctin Valley near what in 1833 would become Middletown, Maryland. Christopher deeded the property to his son Petter Michael in 1771.

In 1762, Andrew bought part of Tasker's Chance, the original large Crown grant in which Fredericktowne was built. On May 6, 1762, he also purchased lots ("dolts") numbers one and two of the town layout that Daniel Dulaney had platted in 1745. These lots are at the northwest corner of South Carroll Street and East All Saints Street in Frederick's Historic District. The same year that he bought these two lots, Andrew bought from Casper Myer two more lots in Frederick "on the road from Fredericktowne toward Conococheague" that lay within original founding Crown grants of Long Acre and Tasker's Chance. These lots are believed to be those of today's 254 and 256 West Patrick Street in Frederick in the town's Historic District. In 1803 during the Jefferson administration, this road became the first trans-Appalachian and first federally sponsored highway, the National Road. It is today's US Route 40 and, in the west, Interstate 80.

In 1764 William bought lot 279 and another Frederick property from Daniel Dulany. The first lot is near the corner of today's East Street and East Seventh Street. William purchased a third Frederick property from Conrad Shawn in 1766.

The brothers' quick extensive investments in centrally located lots and buildings in Fredericktowne indicate that they had arrived with money and plenty of it. These weren't the German-speaking farmers and tradesmen fleeing poverty, war, and persecution in the old country who came and built log homes, but transplanted European gentry who could afford to make their marks as soon as they arrived and did. The mindset that they brought with them was inbred from generations of lordships, provincial domains, assumed privilege, and their family being in charge. In the social flux of the 1760s, large land acquisitions with names like Tasker's Chance, The Sun is Down and the Moon is Up, Stony Hall, and Cooling Springs were not so much farms as estates or manors. That three of the four settled in the county seat tells us that these were people whose habits were genteel and of towns rather than farms.

The most public evidence of the brothers' economic status was the foundry which Andrew built on his first two Frederick lots in 1762 apparently with his brother Wilhelm's help as construction overseer of the large stone building. Andrew's brothers may have gone in with him financially on this major investment but no evidence of that was encountered in researching *First Explorer* and title was held in Andrew's name. The two-and-a-half-story stone building would have been one of the largest in the county up to that time, a landmark for much of its existence, and, being the region's first foundry, a major boon to local economic development. Theretofore, larger forged iron pieces had to be transported overland from the port of Annapolis but now they were being cast in and for the local market at western Maryland's first foundry. Building it was bold foresight by Andrew.

The author is in possession of several inherited iron implements believed to have been forged by the foundry during Andrew's ownership. See the center pictorial pages here. Today, 260 years later as of this writing, the Michael Foundry still stands, now serving as Sky Stage, a performing arts venue.[95]

If Andrew Michael wanted to make his mark economically in Frederick, he had multiple large-scale entrepreneurial opportunities from which to choose including land development, dry goods provisioning, European goods importation or founding a bank, to name a few. With such attractive options, why was creating a foundry Andrew's choice?

We recall that Andrew's father Francis established the Germanna mining operation in 1714 and in 1728 was brought in by Governor Spotswood try to turn around the faltering operation. Spotswood initially had had his miners search for precious metals but when none was found had them dig local iron ore which Spotswood smelted in the foundry that he built at Germanna. Andrew's father was apparently at or involved with Germanna and its foundry through 1746 when we lose last sight of him. By this time, Andrew is twenty-six and had taken in the operations of the foundry since his childhood at his father's side. When he moves to Frederick at forty-two, Andrew chooses to do what he would appear to know best, smelting iron and benefitting his new community with the implements that he is able to turn out.

This hypothesized linkage between Francis the iron maker father and Andrew the iron maker son is one more strong clue to a father-son relationship between the two.

On November 23, 1767, showing both the humanitarian instincts and the energy of his father Francis, Andrew Michael delivered to the burgeoning German communities around Pequea, Pennsylvania, 500 refugees and other settlers who he escorted from German-speaking lands along the Rhine where he had gathered them.[96] Andrew may have benefitted financially in this if he was working in effect as personal relocator. Whether or not he did, it took vision and daring to dash off from his successful foundry and new home comforts on a mission of humanitarianism. It is no mystery as to where the example that had been handed down to him came from.

The same day that Andrew was delivering his charges in Pennsylvania, a surveyor in Maryland began marking off for Andrew a 340-acre tract named Cooley Springs, so called for the four springs on the property. In March of 1768, Andreas sold his foundry to Samuel Barrance, who in July of 1776 sold it to the county's representative in the colonial legislature, Delegate John Hanson, who then used the foundry to manufacture weapons and munitions during the Revolutionary War. On November 5, 1781, Frederick's John Hanson would be elected as the first president of the United States under its original government chartered by the Articles of Confederation.[97, 98] With the formation of its first government and election of its first head of state, this nearly forgotten date is when the United States legally came into being as a nation, its actual birthdate, now all but forgotten.

Receiving his land patent from provincial governor Horatio Sharpe for his tract on July 12, 1768, Andrew completed the purchase from Ignatius Sims. Later that year, Andrew moved his family there, took up the life of large landholder directly in the footsteps of his Swiss ancestors, and renamed his new home Cooling Springs, the property's name today. Andrew's new tract was part of the 10,000-acre Carrollton Manor, an original land grant from King George of England to Lord Baltimore and his agent in America, Charles Carroll, father of Charles Carroll of Carrollton, a signer of the Declaration of Independence.

In 1786 Andrew purchased the adjacent 107-acre Flag Pond tract from Thomas and Sara Duckett, bringing the Cooling Springs holdings to 447 acres. Cooling Springs' size made it one of the Maryland colony's largest properties for a number of years. As of this writing, the eighth American generation of the family lives at Cooling Springs, making it one of only a few properties in the United States owned as long in one family's possession. In 2012, Cooling Springs celebrated its 250th anniversary with a front-page spread in the county's daily newspaper.

Andrew, flush from his foundry sale, had his pick of properties anywhere in the colony's largest county or elsewhere. Why this particular property? It is entirely possible that Andrew chose Cooling Springs because it was a better match to his purchase criteria than anything else he may have looked at. The two creeks, four freshwater springs, near view of Catoctin Mountain, good soil and picturesque rolling land would have been attractive. But there were other properties available with similar qualities in the still thinly populated county.

This property happened to be on the exact route that his father had walked on that day in 1704 on his sidetrip from Conoy to what would become Frederick. Had Frantz sung the praises to his children about the beautiful spot with the good water that he had passed twice on his sidetrip? Did he take a closer look on the way back to Conoy? Did Frantz tell the sons of one of his favorite places and how to find it? Maybe and we will never know for certain, but it is conspicuous that, of all the properties he could have chosen, Andrew bought a particularly nice one in the immediate vicinity of where his father's campsite had been as on his father's 1704 map. The sidetrip's first campsite shown on his map is along the aboriginal path from Conoy, today's Ballenger Creek Pike, where Cooling Springs is located.

Andrew's story of Cooling Springs, Frederick, refugee rescue, philanthropy, and his own vision founding a major industry in western Maryland is so suggestive of Francis Michael as to put to rest suggestion of coincidence. These parallels are perhaps stronger evidence of a father-son relationship than all of the more concrete evidence that we have seen here.

In 1796, Andrew Michael, voted in the United States presidential election held November 9 to 12 that year. Also voting were his sons Andrew, Jr., William and Jacob, and Andrew's nephews Ludwick and Christopher.[99] Did the clan prefer Adams the winner or Jefferson the contender we are left to wonder. Andrew Michael lived to see the dawn of the nineteenth century, dying at age eighty sometime before March 3, 1800, when his will was probated. He and Barbara were buried in the family cemetery at Cooling Springs. The couple had thirteen children who would have many of their own leading to a large Michael clan in the county and nearby.

Andrew's oldest brother Christopher operated his The Sun Is Down and the Moon Is Up tract as a large farm. Given the size of his tract, he may have had tenant farmers as his ancestors had had at Ralligen for centuries. He and his wife Anna had seven children. At least one child died young, and others may have as in 1771 Christopher deeded the family property to his youngest son Petter who took over management of the property in his parents' old age. Christopher Michael, died August 14, 1783, at seventy-five. He is buried in the graveyard of the Old Reformed Cemetery in Sharpsburg, Maryland.

Not as much biography has survived on William and Nicholas who may have died younger than their brothers did and left no trails. In the northwest corner of Frederick County is a Michael Road where it was thought that either of the two had gone but recently it was learned that it was one of Christopher's descendants who settled there. Not far from Cooling Springs is a large property, which until a few years ago was an Alcoa aluminum smelter, that in the early 1800s was owned by a William Michael who could have been the brother William of interest here.

After the Four Brothers

In Frederick's enormous Mount Olivet Cemetery where since 1854 more than 40,000 souls have been buried, the number interred there with a Michael surname rose to 120 when David Michael, 91, was buried in 2017. Mr. Michael was a fourth-great-grandchild of Francis and Anna Michael and direct descendant of Andrew. As the 120 surnamed Michaels at Mount Olivet don't count women born as Michaels who married, nor descendants with other surnames, Francis and Anna's descendants buried there would number well more than 240. Then there are Francis and Anna's offspring buried elsewhere, usually in old family cemeteries as were the first three generations of the Andrew line at Cooling Springs until 1927 when that line of Michael burials began at Mount Olivet Cemetery. From 1893 to 1907, Daniel Jerome Michael chaired the board of directors and served as the administrator of the cemetery. Daniel was a great-grandson of Andrew Michael.

Since the first American generation of Michaels was prolific as was the second, it isn't surprising that after ten American generations there would have been so many of Francis and Anna's progeny. Genealogist Margaret Myers in 2009 published an extensively researched, three-volume genealogy of Francis and Anna's descendants in which she identified more than 1,500 of them. Mathematically, it isn't surprising that a fertile family new to a county with a population at the time of a few thousand would make its mark in census rolls. Of the two brothers whose genealogies are well recorded, Christopher had at least seven children and Andrew fathered thirteen, who themselves were parents of dozens more. And on it went with large Michael families into the twentieth century before urbanized Michaels benefitted from smaller families rather than larger ones helpful on farms.

Several times the author has happened to meet Michaels who turned out to be his sixth cousins whose closest blood relative to the author was our explorer, Frantz Ludwig Michel. In those cases, the individuals descended from Christopher, eldest of the four brothers. Many times the author has received email inquiries from people who wanted to know if they were descendants of "Andrew Michael at Cooling Springs." Just the month before *First Explorer* was completed, two couples from Missouri who visiting Cooling Springs for the first time turned out to be fourth cousins of the author and had recently learned of their Michael family history on the Internet. Michael is one of the most frequent surnames in the county where the brothers settled along with several other old Swiss and German family names of early settlers including Brunner, Zimmerman, Crum, Stup, Ramsburg/Remsburg, Bussard, and Cline/Kline and to name a few.

In examining how a family evolves over several generations, many influences come into play. Because they can be analyzed, occupations and what is called regression toward the mean are especially useful. In the case of the Michel/Michael line, we are fortunate to have twenty-one generations to work from beginning with Itel Michel von Schwertschwendi at Ralligen in the 1300s coming down to the generation of the author's grandchildren today. Beginning with Itel Michel, six generations of the family down to Frantz Ludwig Michel were born in Switzerland. With their noble titles, ranking civic positions, and castles, each of these generations was highly privileged. Following the medieval feudal practices of the era, the privilege was not based on individual merit or earned achievement but virtually entirely on heredity.

When a noble or royal family had its miscreant, imbecile, drunkard, lazy one or just an odd ball as eldest son, he (it was always a male) could be enthroned anyway. Or if the heir were too questionable, he could be skipped over for his younger brother or uncle or cousin as happened once in the Michel von Schwertschwendi line when the title of Lord shifted sideways in the family during the 1400s. However, whomever inherited the title, even if it did pass to someone other than the eldest son, the candidates were small in number, all drawn from the same tight gene pool, and may or may not have had talent.

This skirting of ability in designating a new leader is certainly evident in hereditary leadership around the world even today, from Papa Doc to Baby Doc in Haiti, to the Kims of North Korea, to the British Royal family, to America's Harrison and Bush presidents. What these dynasties have sometimes successfully done to try to maintain status is to marry intelligent women, though this has not been universal. Primogeniture subverts, even masks, the abilities of a younger family member, especially a daughter who may be the most capable one to assume family leadership.

Coming down through Michel generations to Frantz Ludwig, his was the last to be able to coast on titled privilege. His sons became the transition generation that relied on the Michel family wealth that their father had brought with him to America to afford their large land purchases, the foundry, and generous church philanthropy, but they knew that their American offspring would have to get by on their own wits and talents without the crutch of inherited noble status. With the protective cloak of nobility left behind in Switzerland, natural inter-generational evolution would now take its course.

Since the discoveries by the cousin scientists Charles Darwin and Francis Galton in the 1800s, it has been understood that particular traits of living things will vary from one generation to the next according to the principle that extreme outcomes tend to be followed by more moderate ones. An exceptionally good or poor athletic performance is more likely to be followed by an average one than another exceptionally good or bad one. This is because, by definition, exceptional examples of anything are less prevalent than more numerous average ones. Having an especially "bad day" is more likely to be followed by a typical day, and likewise for an especially good day. The child of tall or short parents is more likely to be closer to average in height. These are examples of the principle of regression toward the mean, the average.

In human evolution over several generations, the descendants of wealthy, adventurous, continent-hopping, high-dopamine adventurers such as Francis and Anna would be expected in their life outcomes to become more typical, and, as a group, more varied. Generation by generation, from eighteenth-century to twenty-first–century Michaels, that is inexorably what happened.

The extensive Michael family land holdings of the eighteenth century became divided among sons until after five generations into the twentieth century they could be divided no further if the now smaller farms were to sustain a family. Depending on the management skill of the descendant, some of the farms prospered while others got by.

As urbanization accelerated after the Civil War, each Michael generation became more urban and fewer descendants farmed. By 1922, the United States was half urban, half rural, and today five of six Americans are urban. One result of urbanization has been a much broader variety of occupations in families in addition to farming. Looking at one representative line of Frantz Ludwig Michel's descendants, its recent occupations have broadly spanned the possibilities: clergy (ten!), teaching at all levels, civil service, the trades, the military, florists, musician, land developer, film producer, park ranger, physician, bank founder, magistrate, United Nations officer, geographer, gerontologist, plumber, two last farm owners, and certainly more career paths that the author is not aware of. Occupational levels have run the gamut from Ivy League professor to maid, from founder of a drug store chain to manual laborer, and pretty much everything in between.

Beginning in the 1960s, the family became multiracial and international with marriages blending the world into Michael genes. Thailand, Spain, The Philippines, Mexico, China, Lithuania, Korea, Hong Kong, Sweden, Finland, and Celtic lands have all been absorbed into Michaeldom, and those are just the strains that the author happens to be aware of. At a large family reunion of Andrew's descendants in 2005, all four of the tenth-generation children present had a Mexican grandparent, and these children were from two far distant lines of the family. Two other tenth-generation descendants, college students today, are each a union of Black, White and Asian, a recipe for attractive people.

As in any extended family, there have been hardship cases, mental illnesses, incapacitations, and just sheer bad luck. There have also been Michael prize winners, star athletes, deanships, doctorates, music albums, civic awards, a double-valedictorian, a Fulbright Scholar, and—no one should be surprised—a long-distance trekker with a map-maker son.

So just as Darwin and Galton would have predicted, when the Michel silver spoon was left behind in Switzerland as propped up nobility crutch, Francis and Anna Michael's issue evolved into an unsurprisingly varied mix. Francis and Anna had spawned a typical American family.

That is all good but it does not appear that any descendant of Francis Michael has come close to matching his "old curiosity" and history-bending feats of humanitarianism and exploration. Several of his descendants, mainly but not exclusively clergy, did choose humanitarianism as their lives' work but in 300 years no descendant is known to have come close to matching the scale of accomplishment and exemplary humanitarianism of the Swiss immigrant Frantz Ludwig Michel who made himself into American citizen Francis Michael

Coming down to today through nine generations of his offspring, his life remains one of unequaled, extraordinarily visionary accomplishment. As the philosopher Arthur Schopenhauer once noted, talent hits a target no one else can hit, but genius hits a target no one else can see. What Francis Michael accomplished he was first to see.

May the world now know better this extraordinary American immigrant success story and that of the thousands he saved.

Epilogue

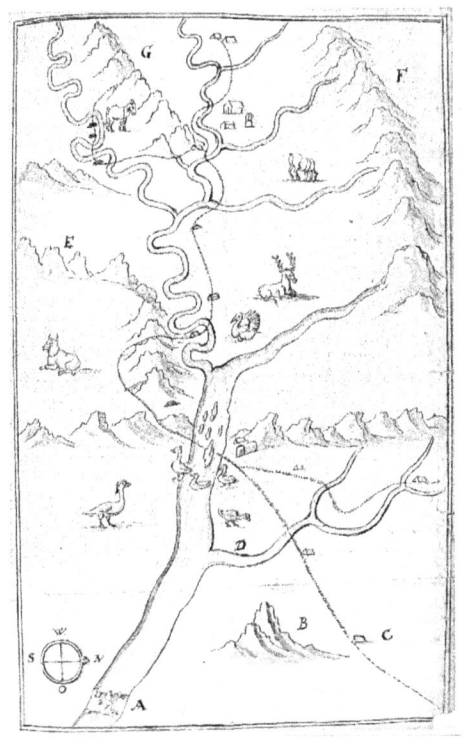

Fates of People

Frantz Ludwig Michel/Francis Michael

One would hope that there will be more to round out the story of our man if it is ever discovered. Perhaps most wanted among what is left to be found would be to locate his and Anna's grave sites, a find that would go far in answering the mysteries that surround the two. There is also the lingering question of who their children were and where they were born.

Anna Barbara von Lerber Michel/Michael

As with her husband, Anna's gravesite is unknown. Ordinarily we would expect to find it beside her husband's.

Christopher Michael, Eldest Son of Francis and Anna Michael

Christopher was also the only one of the four children who did not settle in Frederick. Christopher lived out his life at The Sun Is Down and the Moon Is Up, the large tract that he purchased in the Catoctin Valley west of Frederick soon after his arrival. He lived there with his family until he died in 1783 at age seventy-five. Christopher lived long enough to see the successful conclusion of the Revolutionary War and the creation of the United States in 1781 when the nation's first government was created, and Frederick's John Hanson was elected president. Christopher may have known President Hanson. The author knows several of Christopher's Michael-surname descendants.

William Michael, Second Son of Francis and Anna Michael

This son purchased multiple properties in Frederick soon after arriving. That and his large donation to the building fund of his church show that, like Christopher, William had arrived in America well financed. Genealogical data provided by Michael descendant Evelyn M. Shaver show William descending from Frantz Ludwig Michel and before him from the same Ralligen noble line as did his brother Christopher. One source shows William's occupation as stone mason but, given his noble lineage, wealth, and property purchases, he was more likely what today would be called a property developer. One genealogical website shows William dying in 1773. William drops from the available record before this, but others named William Michael appear at about the same time including one large landowner who may be this William having Anglicized his name. A William Michael living in southern Frederick County near Cooling Springs appears in the 1800 census, though this is likely to have been Andrew Michael's eldest son of this name.[100]

Andrew Michael, Youngest Son of Francis and Anna Michael

Almost all that is known to the author about Andrew Michael has been included in *First Explorer*. What can be emphasized is that he lived a very full life as bred humanitarian rescuing 500 European refugees, industrialist who built his region's first foundry, major donor to his church, lord of his own American manor at Cooling Springs, father of thirteen, and grandfather of thirty-six. Andrew was witness to the American Revolution, the birth of his adopted nation, the launching of its government in 1781 and then another in 1789. He experienced the historical miracle of the successful demonstration of a democratic republic born around him. A special satisfaction to Andrew must have been when in July of 1776 the future first president of the United States bought his Frederick foundry and used it to manufacture munitions that helped win the Revolutionary War. In 1796 at the age of seventy-six, Andrew Michael voted in that year's presidential election.

Nicholas Michael, purported Son of Francis and Anna Michael

Mildred Michael Crewe's research in the mid-twentieth century showing Nicholas Michael as one of the sons of Francis and Anna provides nothing more than this except the single notation of his purchasing forty-six acres of Stony Hall from Ulrich and Margaret Erb in 1758. Some online sources show Nicholas as the child of Francis and Anna while other sources omit him. There are no known clues as to how Crewe concluded that Nicholas was the child of Francis and Anna, leaving a mystery and cause for doubt as to whether Nicholas was, in fact, their child. The same website that provides the year of death for William shows Nicholas dying in 1783. However, this same list shows Nicholas having been born in 1701, four years before 1705, which nearly all other sources show as the year that Francis and Anna married. This anomaly casts further doubt on their parentage of Nicholas

Refugee Settlements

The six colonies which Frantz Ludwig Michel founded—King William, Shenandoah Valley, Pequea, New Berne and the South Carolina two—became North America's magnets for the religious and other refugees who Michel, Ritter and Ochs rescued and sent to America. Every other region where Michel explored—western Maryland, Virginia's Germanna, and especially Lancaster County, Pennsylvania—received refugees sent by the three and those who on their own went there. A large Mennonite community in Lancaster County, Pennsylvania, spawned by the Pequea colony thrives today.

Mennonites in America

Most Mennonite immigrants to North America in the seventeenth and eighteenth centuries were religious refugees but it is difficult to estimate how many arrived during that period. One source claims 3,000[101] but this seems slight given the number sent from Switzerland alone. There are about 672,000 Mennonites in the United States and Canada today, comprising slightly less than half of the worldwide Mennonite population. At present, only four percent—63,000—of Mennonites live in Europe. In 1989, Donald Kraybill counted thirty-seven distinct religious bodies or organizations with 289 congregations and 41,600 baptized members among the living descendants of Mennonite immigrants to Lancaster County, Pennsylvania, the site of Francis Michael's Pequea colony.[102] As of 2000, there were about 3,000 Old Order Mennonites who drive buggies plus a smaller number of Lancaster County buggy-users among two Old Order Mennonite subgroups.

There are about 4,000 members of the car-driving Weaverland Old Order Mennonite Conference.

The Mattaponi People of Virginia

The Mattaponi Tribe is one of only two original Virginia tribes to survive intact enough today to be recognized by the federal government as a tribe. The Mattaponi live in an exceedingly small portion of their ancestral lands in King William County, Virginia, along the Mattaponi River, with another band a few miles west of there. As they always have, the Mattaponi rely on the river for much of their diet. Most enrolled members of the Mattaponi have been absorbed into the general population and live outside the Mattaponi Reservation but many of those retain close ties with their homeland.

The Pamunkey People of Virginia

The Pamunkey Tribe is the only other original Virginia tribe to survive intact enough today to be recognized by the federal government as a tribe. The situation of the Mattaponi described above fits the Pamunkey closely. The Pamunkey live in an even smaller portion of their ancestral lands in King William County, Virginia, along the Pamunkey River. The Pamonkey and Mattaponi reservations are nine miles apart.

The Conoy People of Maryland

The Conoy are a branch of the larger Piscataway Tribe. In recent times, the tribe is usually referred to as the Piscataway-Conoy. In the twenty-first century, Conoy tribal elders Chief Billy Redwing Tayac and Mervin Savoy, using social media, genealogy websites, and DNA analysis, began successfully locating members of the Conoy diaspora and regathering the Piscataway-Conoy who now flourish, celebrate their culture with traditional events, and are trying to reignite their language. Identified Piscataway-Conoy now number over 4,000, with more being identified by DNA and genealogical records. Says Maryland state archeologist Dennis Curry, "The restoration of their culture and history is a tremendous point of pride for tribal members who, for so long, were marginalized and forgotten in their own ancestral home." In January of 2012, Governor Martin O'Malley and the State of Maryland officially recognized the Piscataway-Conoy Tribe of Maryland, opening the door for public assistance and economic development programs that have taken hold and are benefitting tribal members. The Piscataway-Conoy are the only tribe in Maryland officially recognized by the State of Maryland. There is no recognition yet by the federal government.

Chief Billy Redwing Tayac of Port Tobacco, Maryland, architect if the Conoy renaissance, passed away on September 6, 2021 at age eighty-five. "Tayac" is Algonquian for chief.

In the fall of 2022, the University of Maryland recognized the Piscataway–Conoy People by naming a new student service building after the tribe.

Underway as of the publication of *First Explorer*, the St. Clement's Island Museum in the southern Maryland heart of Piscataway country has planned a major renovation for 2023 to include new exhibits that will tell history from the Piscataway perspective. Local Native American leaders are involved in designing the materials and exhibits for the new museum to tell the story and accurate history of the Piscataways.[103]

The Shawnee People of Virginia and Pennsylvania

By 1754, the Shawnee and other tribes had left the Shenandoah Valley and most of Pennsylvania as they fled west avoiding European incursion. Into the eighteenth century, other bands of the Shawnee did the same with most resettling west of the Mississippi River. The last of the eastern Shawnee were force-marched to Oklahoma along Andrew Jackson's Trail of Tears in the winter of 1831. The mortality rate of the march was one-third, mostly the elderly and children. As of 2008, there were 7,584 enrolled Shawnee, most living in Oklahoma.

The Conestoga People of Pennsylvania

After a half century of adopting European customs and living peacefully among Mennonite communities following the Mennonite arrival in 1710, in 1763 a gang of drunken Whites—the Paxton Boys from Harrisburg—wantonly and without reason slaughtered every last man, woman and child of the remaining Conestogas. The atrocity occurred seven miles from Pequea.

The Tuscarora People of North Carolina

After the last Tuscarora War of 1723, most of the surviving North Carolina Tuscarora migrated north to New York state where they joined other Iroquoian-speaking peoples as the sixth nation of the Iroquois Federation. The migration was dense at the beginning but went on for ninety years. Some of the migrants made temporary stops along the way including one in Frederick County, Maryland, a few miles from Conoy and the Great Trading Place at Point of Rocks. The village where the Tuscarora stopped and some settled, called Licksville, was then renamed Tuscarora, its name today. The Tuscarora tribal population has rebounded from near extinction, numbering 5,600 today compared to an estimated 5,000 before the Carolina Tuscarora War and a few hundred after that.

Georg Ritter

The founder and main investor in the Michel-Ritter-Ochs colonization enterprise, Ritter lost patience when the Carolina project went awry, resigned himself and his firm, Ritter & Company, from the resettlement venture, and cut off his funding to the Carolina experiment including Christoph's Graffenried's salary. Ritter then appears to have completely extricated himself from Graffenried. Georg Ritter continued his pharmaceutical production enterprise and resettling of religious and war refugees until he died in Bern in 1723 at fifty-six. He had no descendants.

Johann Rudolph Ochs

Described as master artisan crafter of precious metals,

gems, and cameos, and as "the best engraver of his time," so proficient was Ochs that he spent the last twenty years of his career as Engraver at the Royal Mint in London. Ochs experienced a bad rough spot on the way to this comfortable sinecure when the Mint, then under the direction of the elderly Sir Isaac Newton, did not pay Ochs for several years of contract work, causing his bankruptcy in 1721. In the midst of this turmoil, Ochs became a widower. A year after Newton died in 1727, Ochs secured a lifetime appointment as Engraver at the Mint and thereafter was able to lead a comfortable life again. In the 1730s, his petition to the British Lords of Trade and Plantations for permission to found a second refugee colony in Virginia's Shenandoah Valley languished in the bureaucracy neither approved nor disapproved. The old widower died in 1749 at the age of seventy-six, after continuing to resettle refugees for the rest of his life.

Petter Isoth

Nothing encountered in researching *First Explorer* sheds further light on Petter Isoth, Georg Ritter's brother-in-law.

William Penn

Due to Penn's difficulty in managing money, his proprietorship of Pennsylvania faltered to the degree that he tried to sell the colony back to the British Crown, which had granted it to him. During his second attempt to sell Pennsylvania in 1712, Penn suffered a stroke. A second stroke several months later left him unable to speak or care for himself. After losing his memory, Penn died penniless in 1718 at home in Berkshire, England. He lived his incapacitated years in the care of one of his sons. William Penn deserves to be venerated as the innovator of mass international refugee rescue, recognition that has escaped him.

Christoph von Graffenried

Originally laid to rest at the family chapel at Worb, Christoph von Graffenried was disinterred in 1983 and since then his final resting place has been a storage locker at the University of Bern.[104] How this happened was that developers wanted the graveyard to build on and got it. Despite everything about Graffenried, he did not deserve a fate like this.

Maryland Governor William Stone

In 1648 William Stone was appointed as Governor of Maryland by Cecilius Calvert, Proprietor of the province. Governor Stone founded the Maryland colonial capital of Annapolis in 1649 and the same year led the enactment of the colonial government's Religious Toleration Act guaranteeing freedom of religion. William Stone served as governor until 1656. In 1660, Stone was granted "as much land as he could ride, by horseback, in a day" as reward for faithful service. After building his manor house, William Stone died at his 5,000-acre Poynton Manor in Charles County, Maryland, that year. Governor Stone's great-great-grandsons included Thomas Stone as Signer the Declaration of Independence, Michael Jenifer Stone who represented Maryland in the First United States Congress, John Hoskins Stone as Governor of Maryland 1794–97, and William Murray Stone, the Episcopal Bishop of Baltimore. Governor William Stone was the ninth-great-grandfather of the author on his mother's (Hanson) side.

Martin Chartier

The French-Canadian trapper and woodsman who lived among Indians with his Shawnee wife continued serving as a backwoods guide, translator and effective intermediary between Indian tribes and the European colonial powers, especially in Pennsylvania and Maryland, until late in life when he settled down on a farm. He died on his farm near Francis Michael's Pequea colony in Pennsylvania in 1718 at the age of sixty-seven.

Fates of Places

King William Colony, Virginia

The colony became the town of King William and Frantz

Ludwig Michel's land grant, a large part of King William County, Virginia. The Pamunkey and Mattaponi reservations are in King William County. With its 16,000 inhabitants today, the county is one of the state's least populous and is virtually entirely agricultural. Its beauty makes it easy to see why Michel chose this as the place for his grant. Built in 1725, the small stately King William County Courthouse is the oldest in continuous use in the United States.

Conoy Indian Village and Conoy Island, Maryland

The island is at peace. After the Conoy abandoned Conoy Island in the early 1700s as Europeans began to arrive, the Conoys' fort, longhouse, homes and all else deteriorated and went back to nature. Intermittently afterward, Europeans would live on the island and try farming it but high spring waters of the Potomac River would eventually discourage them as at flood stage the island in under water. One of the families who lived there lent its name to what is now called Heater's Island. In 1970, the University of Maryland conducted an archeological dig on the island unearthing hundreds of Conoy artifacts and the outline of the Conoys' fort. No one has lived on the island for many years though canoers and hikers sometimes still visit.

Point of Rocks, Maryland

The town of 1,900 is located just inland from the Potomac River directly across from Conoy Island. In 1835, Charles Johnson, owner of the land on which the town of Point of Rocks was built, had lots surveyed and streets laid out for a new town that has been there ever since. The town was built to provide housing and services for construction of the Chesapeake & Ohio Canal and the Baltimore and Ohio Railroad, both of which run through Point of Rocks. The rail line, dating from 1831, is the nation's oldest and is still in daily use. Today, Point of Rocks is a placid place from which a number of residents commute on the one-hour train ride to Washington, DC. The 185-mile Chesapeake and Ohio Canal National Park runs beside Point of Rocks on its way from Washington, DC, to Cumberland,

Maryland, the canal's terminus. The busy rail route is a main trans-Appalachian trunk line.

Great Falls, Maryland

Popular for their scenic virtues, the Great Falls today draw thousands of mostly local visitors per year. The Great Falls area is popular for kayaking, whitewater rafting, rock climbing, and hiking, and is accessible from the adjacent Chesapeake and Ohio Canal National Park.

Western Maryland

What hadn't been explored or chartered as a county when Frantz Ludwig Michel explored it in 1704 and 1708 became a single huge county in 1748 encompassing the entire western third of the Maryland colony. As pioneers slowly settled farther west into the Maryland Appalachians, the region became divided into six counties by 1872. Since its inception, Frederick County has been the largest and most agricultural of Maryland's twenty-three counties. Today the county does too little to fight suburban encroachment as the Washington metropolitan area metastasizes ever closer. Beyond Frederick County, western Maryland lies entirely in the Appalachian Range and remains sparsely populated, very rural, rugged, and quite scenic.

Michel's Sidetrip

The sidetrip ended at two creeks which are at the center of today's Frederick, Maryland, the seat of Frederick County. Frederick is a town of 80,000 with a downtown that is one of the nation's best preserved with its largely unmolested collections of eighteenth and nineteenth century architecture. A large area surrounding Michel's route from Conoy to the future Frederick is now designated by the State of Maryland as a Priority Preservation Area in which land must remain in agricultural and natural uses. The area is the most rural and least densely populated part of Frederick County. Andrew Michael's Cooling Springs lies in this part of the county. The ancient path that Michel followed on his sidetrip has remained continuously travelled since and today is the pretty country road Ballenger Creek Pike. Running parallel to Michel's sidetrip route a mile away are the Catoctin Mountain Scenic Byway, Journey Through Hallowed Ground National Scenic Byway, and Journey Through Hallowed Ground National Heritage Area.

Cooling Springs

In the vicinity traversed by Michel on the sidetrip and later settled by his son Andrew, Cooling Springs has now been in the Michael family for seven generations. Cooling Springs is a historic landmark listed on the Maryland Inventory of Historic Places and separately as a Frederick County Landmark. In 2006, a conservation easement donated by the Michael family to the Maryland Environmental Trust endowed Cooling Springs with perpetual protection against development or any major alteration to the home. The original Cooling Springs home lasted until the early twentieth century. The present home was built in 1879 by Francis Michael's great-grandson, Ezra Michael, a county Magistrate, and his wife Margaret. As of this writing, Cooling Springs' pastures are leased to a young farmer who raises cattle. The farm's *circa* 1760s stone spring house, which might predate the founding of Cooling Springs, was fully restored in 2004. Cooling Springs is powered entirely by sun and wind.

The Sun Is Down and the Moon Is Up

Settled by Andrew's oldest brother Christopher Michael shortly after his arrival, the tract stayed in the family well into the nineteenth century. As was the custom, the property became divided among sons. Today it is a series of smaller contiguous farms. It is not known if any present owner is a Michael or Michael descendant.

Shenandoah Valley, Virginia

Long regarded as one of the nation's most beautiful places, the valley's future turned out far better for its settlers than for the natives who got pushed out who by 1754 were gone. The main thoroughfare along the valley began as an ancient aboriginal path which was turned into the Great

Wagon Road by early eighteenth century settlers and then US Route 11 in 1926. Only one town in the valley exceeds 25,000 people and the economy remains mainly agricultural. The beautiful Shenandoah National Park founded in 1935 encompasses much of the highlands above the valley. Michael's 1709 Shenandoah Valley colony permission reached fruition in 1731 when the valley received its first settlers, a group of Mennonite refugees. The colony was located at the southern foot of Massanutten Mountain, the end point of Michel's 1704 expedition. These Mennonites' descendants are found in the Valley today.

The German Settlement, Virginia

In 1828, the German Settlement had its name changed to Lovettsville after David Lovett, a descendant of one of the early families, sold off his farm in small lots creating a commercial center to the old village. After dwindling down to ninety-two people in 1880, Lovettsville slowly grew to over 300 after World War II before losing half of its population by 1970. The village then exploded to over 2,000 as several developments of commuter tract homes went up next to the village. Lovettsville today is a pleasant languid town whose quaint old town center has nicely survived. The Lovettsville Historical Society does an excellent job of portraying the German Settlement era of Lovettsville's history through its museum, research, and monthly lectures.

Pequea, Pennsylvania

Michel's and William Penn's wilderness colony of Pequea proved to be the seed for extensive refugee settlement in what in 1729 became Lancaster County, Pennsylvania, the heart of today's Pennsylvania Dutch Country. ("Dutch" became a misnomer from "*Deitsch*," meaning German, referring to the mainly German-speaking refugees who came flocking in). The oldest surviving dwelling in the county is the home of Mennonite Bishop Hans Herr (1639-1725), built in 1719. Pequea today is a tiny community of perhaps a few dozen people on the east bank of the Susquehanna River eleven miles north of Maryland. By 1729, thousands of refugees and other newcomers had spread out from Pequea to the extent requiring the chartering of Lancaster County, Pennsylvania. One of the county's townships is named Conoy.

Germanna, Virginia

The Germanna mining operation through which Governor Alexander Spotswood hoped to find silver faltered when none was found and the operation was unsuccessfully repurposed as his iron foundry. This discouraged the German miners who the trio had recruited who in a few years moved elsewhere. Spotswood's turnaround attempt by hiring Francis Michael in 1728 was too late to resurrect the operation, costing Germanna its county seat designation, which ultimately led to the complete demise and depopulation of the settlement. Today the deserted site is a state and federal historic landmark. The Germanna Foundation keeps the history of Germanna alive through its research, publications and programs.

New Berne/New Bern, North Carolina

North Carolina's second colony struggled just to survive in its early years but took root and grew when its residents were able to govern themselves and control their destiny after Graffenried deserted them. In a complete reversal of fortune, New Berne served as the capital of North Carolina from 1770 to 1792 and by 1800 had grown to 2,500 people. Today New Bern (modern spelling) is a charming county seat of 30,000 with a remarkable 164 of its homes and other buildings listed on the National Register. There is a bust of Christoph von Graffenried in a town park celebrating him incorrectly as the town's sole founder with no mention of Michel. The author had the pleasure of spending the night in New Bern several years ago.

Ralligen, Switzerland

The Ralligen place name refers to the area covered by the original extended Ralligen estate previously owned for several centuries by the Michel family. The estate is now a state-owned registered national landmark. The beautifully maintained castle and grounds are operated by a brotherhood of monks as a guesthouse and retreat. Ralligen is accessed by a signed entrance along Seestrasse about ten kilometers (six miles) southeast of Thun.

Ralligen Castle

The Ralligen Castle and its appurtenances, cared for by the monks, are included in the registered national landmark. The castle retreat may be reached by telephone at 41 33 252 20 30, email at christustraegerbruderschaft.org or post at Schlossweg 3 3658, Merligen, Switzerland.

Berne/Bern, Switzerland

This beautiful medieval city of 144,000 is the capital of both Bern Canton and Switzerland. Bern is home to 114 Swiss heritage sites of national significance including the entire Old Town, which is also a UNESCO World Heritage Site. The mayor of the city of Bern as of 2022 was Alec Graffenried.

Acknowledgements

I am first indebted to Andreas Mielke and Sandra Yelton, authors of twelve superbly researched articles on the explorer years Frantz Ludwig Michel that comprise an entire eighty-page issue of the *Pennsylvania Mennonite Heritage* quarterly (2011). There is no compendium on the explorer comparable in depth or usefulness to theirs.

Robert Selig's fine article on Frantz Ludwig Michel in *Colonial Williamsburg* (1998) proved to be a key in getting *First Explorer* started. Dr. Selig very generously provided several slides and other materials used in his article, some of which made their way into the pictorial pages of this book.

I thank retired *National Geographic* cartographer Eugene Scheel, for his excellent article cited here on the German Settlement in his area of northern Virginia where Michel explored in 1704.

What has made *First Explorer* much more than it otherwise would have been was the outstanding work done by a group of genealogical researchers hired to help fill the gaps on Francis and Anna. Each was found through the Association of Professional Genealogists, an international organization requiring highest professional qualifications for member genealogists.

Swiss genealogist Teresa Metzger was the key in researching Swiss church and civil records, allowing the conclusion that Frantz and Anna Michel were not present in Switzerland beyond a certain date.

British genealogist and researcher Carolyn Alderson of Cambridge did a superb job of scouring British sources, many of them obscure, looking for evidence of Frantz and Anna's presence in London during the middle years of their lives, allowing the elimination of London residency of Frantz or Anna after 1710.

Genealogist Bridget Sunderlin did an exceptionally deep search in Maryland, eliminating the possibility of the couple's settling in Annapolis or the rest of Maryland after a certain date, and uncovering several Michel and Michael property records on the couple's sons.

Genealogist Brendan Burns's exceptionally productive deep data dives continually hit the jackpot when he uncovered the theretofore unknown Francis Michael and his trail in Virginia after it had appeared to run out, showing that this was Michel, thus adding fifteen years to the biography. This discovery also dispelled the widely held Internet account that Michel had died in 1720.

Before Burns's work, Clelia Walters and Frankie Liles offered helpful suggestions on where research should and shouldn't be directed in Virginia records.

Likewise, Bobbi McMullen identified promising avenues of research and known blind alleys in researching the German refugee communities of Lancaster County, Pennsylvania, where she lives.

I didn't realize it at the time but historian Michael High's lecture to the Point of Rocks Historical Society in 2005 on Frantz Ludwig Michel planted the seed for *First Explorer*. Dr. High also provided me with the first bibliographic suggestions which got me started on researching Frantz Ludwig Michel. Look what you started here, Mike!

Mary Mannix, manager of the wonderful Maryland Room collection of the Frederick County Public Library in Frederick, Maryland, was unfailingly helpful in my research there, often producing particularly useful finds beyond my requests.

Ed Spannaus of the Lovettsville Historical Society and Museum of Lovettsville, Virginia, was helpful in guiding my research on his area of northern Virginia and the German Settlement where Frantz Ludwig Michel explored.

Frederick, Maryland, historian Chris Haugh was helpful in discussing his work and video presentation on Christoph von Graffenried.

Michael Fox of the Office of the President at the College of William and Mary and Larry Smith, docent at the College's

1702 Wren Hall that Frantz Ludwig Michel drew, were very informative during my visit there.

The tours that Debi Moren of the King William County Historical Museum gave my wife and me through the museum and the 1725 county courthouse provided much insight into Michel's first land grant and refugee colony in 1702. This felt like a homecoming.

I am also deeply indebted to the following authors and researchers who are no longer living.

First among these is Frantz Ludwig Michel's younger brother, Hans Ludwig Michel, who meticulously transcribed his brother's 1702 journal and had it placed in the Bern Public Library where it resides today. More than any other source, the journal gives the closest impression of the personality and outlook of Frantz Ludwig Michel. It is a treasure that it has been preserved thanks to Hans.

Margaret Myers's career-long work on the Michael and other family genealogies in Frederick County, Maryland, is a tribute to lay genealogists and the value of their work. Her remarkably extensive genealogy of Frantz Ludwig Michel's American descendants accounting for more than 1,500 of them was invaluable in researching the Michel/Michael family in America. It was the extensiveness of her work that permitted the exploration of how the evolutionary principle of regression toward the mean can be used to examine the dispersion of outcomes when a family of high privilege no longer has it as a prop.

Also of key value was the long 1916 article by William Hinke on Frantz Ludwig Michel's 1701-02 Virginia exploration in *The Virginia Magazine of History and Biography*. *First Explorer* may not have been gotten started without Hinke's curiosity about Michel and his translation of Michel's journal that triggered interest in Michel which reverberated down to the present and to the author.

Charles Kemper's 1921 article on Frantz Ludwig Michel in the *Virginia Magazine of History and Biography* and Klaus Wust's 1969 book, *The Virginia Germans*, proved valuable.

FIRST EXPLORER

The written remembrances of several Michael family members were the indispensable basis of being able to supplement demographic analysis with fact and flavor in tracing Frantz Ludwig Michel's American descendants.

The first of these was Samuel Michael (1820-1891), one of the sons of Frantz Ludwig Michel's grandson, Andrew Michael II. In 1890 Samuel wrote his 15,000-word chronicle to my great-grandfather Marion Michael I and Marion's sister Anna Albertine Michael Cline recounting Samuel's life and times. Aside from Samuel's remembrances, his letter recorded most of the early genealogy of the American Michael family that led to precision in later Michael genealogies.

By her own account, Samuel's remembrances kindled a spark in my father's cousin Margaret Hickman (1902-1995), a fifth-generation American Michael who in 1987, well into her eighties, wrote her *Memory Lane* and distributed it within the Michael and Hickman families. The very bright Miss Hickman was the definitive memorialist of her time of the Hickman and Michael families. All generations following are in her debt for the thorough loving work which she did in her retirement years researching the family, locating old records, donating records to the Daughters of the American Revolution, Carrollton Manor Chapter, for collection and safekeeping, and her devotion to keeping family history alive. All of that worked very nicely, Margaret.

There is the key record compiled by Mildred Michael Crewe (1907-1989) sometime before 1952 entitled *The Michael Family*, which was not circulated widely. Fragments of it existing today contain invaluable research on ship landings of the four purported Michel brothers in the American colonies, their points of embarkation, and their destinations. Crewe is also to be thanked. As of the printing of *First Explorer*, a search is still underway to locate a full copy of her work. A long, surviving extract of unknown origin used in writing *First Explorer* was very revealing in knowing how the brothers fared once reaching their destination of Frederick County, Maryland.

Sometime after Margaret Hickman wrote *Memory Lane,* my father, Pierce B. Michael, Sr. (1913-1997) in an act of foresight commandeered a Xerox machine as they were then called, produced copies of Samuel Michael's *Chronicle* and Margaret Hickman's *Memory Lane* for his children, siblings, and local libraries, and mailed them out. Deep thanks are made to Pierce for his devotion to keeping alive family history.

Several living Michael descendants have taken active roles in doing the same. Nancy Michael Wachter was the first, perhaps anywhere, to verify the blood link between today's Michael family and the Michel von Schwertschwendi dynasty of Switzerland. About the year 2000 Nancy found on the RootsWeb Internet site Michel family genealogy showing the family back to Heinzmann Michel in Bern, Switzerland, in 1419.

Soon afterward, the author's cousin Jean Lagrave extracted from the main genealogical website maintained by the Mormon Church Michael family records from the first American generation of the family on. With this and other sources, she updated the work of Samuel Michael, Mildred Michael Crewe, and Margaret Hickman, and posted the especially useful update online.

My cousin D'Nise Hefner provided useful information on John Lawson, the North Carolina surveyor and very early North Carolina historian, who had a role in founding Frantz Ludwig Michel's New Berne colony and was executed for offending the Tuscarora tribe.

Researching a book became infinitely easier after Sir Tim Berners-Lee developed the World Wide Web in 1989 and a torrent of facts soon ended up at any author's fingertips, making researching and writing more pleasurable than ever. Every modern author should thank him, so thanks, Sir Tim.

Publicizing and selling a book became far more expedient with Amazon's CreateSpace and its successor, Kindle Direct Publishing, a blessing to small e-publishers such as Underground Railroad Free Press, publisher of *First Explorer*. Thanks, Amazon and KDP, for serving as *First Explorer*'s fulfillment vendor.

To more than anyone, I am grateful to my wife Vicki Michael, as her husband once again became absorbed at all hours while he worked on his eighth book for over a year. Vicki is a painter who, as I am fond of saying, is prone to trances when her creative instinct takes hold, and so understands, even sympathizes, with her lost-in-thought writer husband. I revel in this perfect match. Vicki also owns Word Spectrum, a book editing practice, and personally edited *First Explorer* making is a far better product. She wouldn't let me pay her but I have called on other means of reward.

Last, I am grateful to you, reader, for your interest in *First Explorer*. If you like the book, I hope you will spread the word. Please consider leaving a review on the book's Amazon book page.

With best regards,

Peter H. Michael

November 22, 2022

First Explorer

Appendices

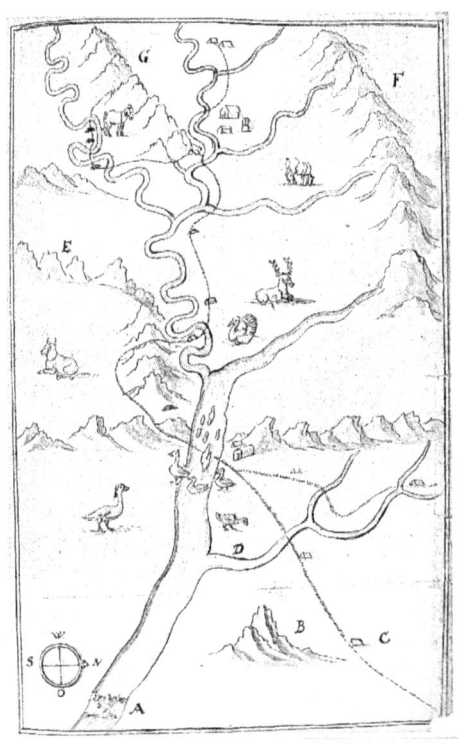

Lords of Ralligen to Frantz Ludwig Michel

Names are formally [first] Michel von Schwertschwendi. Generations through David III held the nobility title Lord of Ralligen and Frantz Ludwig Michel appears to have.

The known Michel/Michael male line extends through 21 generations from Lord Itel Michel below to Hayden Michael, the author's grandson who was born in 2013.

Generation	Born	Died	Age
Itel Michel	1300s		
Berthold Michel I	1409?	1495?	86?
Ludwig Michel	1436?	1519?	83?
Berthold Michel II	1455?		
Lord title line shifted laterally in this generation, retaining surname.			
Heinzmann Michel	1419		
Beat Ludwig Michel I	1440-69	1519	50-79
Jacob Michel	1517	1576	59
David Michel I	1550	1599	49
Beat Ludwig Michel II	September 18, 1580	1630	50
David Michel II	December 2, 1604	1648	44
David Michel III	August 17, 1634	1696	68
Frantz Ludwig Michel	July 29, 1675	≥1746	≥70

Frantz Ludwig Michel's direct bloodline begins with Heinzman Michel in 1419 and goes through Beat I, Jacob, David I, Beat II, David II, and David III to Frantz. The Lord title line begins no later than with Itel Michel von Schwertschwendi and goes through to David III and presumably to Frantz. The title line through Berthold II is a family collateral line of near but uncertain relation to Frantz Ludwig Michel's bloodline. The title shift from one line of the family to the other is most likely from uncle to nephew or between first cousins. Reasons for the shift could be a generation without a male heir, unacceptable heirs, an exceptionally qualified collateral heir, or a collateral line more able to afford and preserve the Lordship.

Swiss Social Ranks in the 1600s and 1700s

Social Rank	Number of Swiss Families	In *First Explorer*
Royalty	None	Switzerland was never a monarchy
Wohledelvest *"Wealthy, noble, dependable"*	6	None in *First Explorer*
Edelvest *"Noble, dependable"*	13	Michel family
Vest *"Dependable"*	16	Graffenried family
Liebe und Getreuwe *"Dear and Loyal"*	9	Lerber family (FLM in-laws)
Commoners	All others	Some FLM associates

Timeline 1291–2022

1291	Swiss fiefdoms of the Holy Roman Empire coalesce into a loose confederation that calls itself Helvetia
1300s	Michel von Schwertschwendi nobility line extends at least this far back
1517	Martin Luther ignites the Protestant Reformation
January 21, 1525	Mennonite denomination established in Zurich by Conrad Grebel, Felix Manz, and George Blaurock
Rest of 1500s	Persecution of Mennonites accelerates in Europe
1590	English colonists of Roanoke along Carolina coast vanish
May 13, 1607	Colony of Virginia established at Jamestown
February 27, 1634	Colony of Maryland established as the *Ark* and the *Dove* land 118 passengers at Point Comfort, Maryland
August 17, 1634	David Michel von Schwertschwendi, Frantz Ludwig Michel's father, born at Ralligen, Berne Canton, Switzerland
1640	Official persecution of European Mennonites intensifies
Before 1643	Shawnee Indians dig lead ore at future site of Pequea colony in Pennsylvania
1643	Roger Williams mentions Indian ore mining at Pequea in his *A Key to the Language of America*
1648	David Michel, father of explorer Frantz Ludwig Michel, becomes Lord of Ralligen upon the death of his father, also Lord David Michel
1649	Maryland Governor William Stone founds settlement of Providence as capital of the colony. Town renamed

FIRST EXPLORER

	Annapolis in 1694.
April 21, 1649	Under Governor Stone, Maryland colony passes Religious Toleration Acts granting freedom of religion to all
1660	Dutch writer Thieleman van Braght documents 4,000 Anabaptist executions by burning, stoning, live burials
November 15, 1661	Christoph von Graffenried born at Worb Castle, Berne Canton
February 6, 1665	Anne, future Queen of England, born
1671	Official persecution of European Mennonites again intensifies
September 2, 1673	Johann Rudolph Ochs baptized. Born shortly before this.
1667	Georg Ritter born
May 17, 1675	**Anna Barbara von Lerber, Frantz Ludwig Michel's wife, born in Bumbach, Berne Canton, Switzerland**
July 24, 1675	**Frantz Ludwig Michel von Schwertschwendi born at Ralligen, Berne Canton, Switzerland**
July 29, 1675	Frantz Ludwig Michel is baptized
December 12, 1676	Future Virginia Governor Alexander Spotswood born in Tangier, Morocco
1681	Colony of Pennsylvania established by William Penn who declares freedom of religion throughout
1683	Germantown, Pennsylvania, founded by German-speaking religious refugees including Mennonites
1688	Germantown becomes birthplace of American anti-slavery movement when it publishes condemnation of slavery
February 8, 1693	College of William and Mary chartered in Virginia
About 1695	Frantz Ludwig Michel completes his formal education
1696	At 21, he appears to have become Lord of Ralligen upon the death of his father

FIRST EXPLORER

1700	College of William and Mary graduates its first class
By 1701	Michel completes military service
About 1701	Michel, Georg Ritter and Johann Rudolph Ochs discuss plight of Swiss Mennonites
1701 or before	Madlain von Lerber and four of her six daughters flee Mennonite religious persecution in Berne, Switzerland, to resettle along the Mattaponi River in Virginia
During 1701	Act passed authorizing creation of King William County, Virginia, in 1702
July, 1701	War of Spanish Succession begins with worst of it along Rhine River
October 8, 1701	Frantz Ludwig Michel departs Berne Canton for London
February 18, 1702	Michel sails for Virginia aboard *HMS Nassau*
March 8, 1702	King William III of England dies. Queen Anne becomes English Monarch.
April 11, 1702	King William County, Virginia, formed
May 2, 1702	Georg Ritter's wife Elisabetha sponsors marriage of Johann Rudolph Ochs and widow Anna Katherina von Lerber
May 8, 1702	Michel disembarks at Yorktown, Virginia
May 23, 1702	Michel begins exploring large Virginia tract granted him by Governor Francis Nicholson, names it King William.
During his 55-day stay in Virginia	Michel explores Tidewater Virginia up to Maryland border, visits Lerber sisters and other Swiss along Mattaponi River, pens oldest surviving drawings of College of William and Mary and other Williamsburg buildings
July 2, 1702	Michel sails for England
Same date	Anna Barbara von Lerber sails in the same convoy of ships

FIRST EXPLORER

During passage	Michel nearly perishes in hurricane and then from leaking ship
October 8, 1702	Frantz Ludwig Michel begins dangerous overland walk home during war
December 1, 1702	He reaches Switzerland
After this	Tells Ritter, Ochs, brother Hans and Michel family of his Virginia experiences
After this	Brother Hans Ludwig Michel transcribes Frantz's 1702 Virginia journal, enters it into Berne public library
February 14, 1703	Michel departs Berne for London with Ochs-cut gems to show William Penn
May 6-16, 1703	Meets Penn in London, writes letter to Ochs on North American possibilities
August 29, 1703	Begins second voyage to America, arrives on unknown date
January 16, 1704	Michel is at Annapolis, Maryland
May 20-30, 1704	Writes letter to Ochs on feasibility of establishing North American colonies. Mentions home he has had built for himself in or near Annapolis.
Summer, 1704	Undertakes epic exploration of western Maryland and Virginia's Shenandoah Valley, draws the first map of these areas
In 1704 exploration	Takes sidetrip exploration up the Monocacy Plain to exact places where his sons would settle in the 1760s and first western Maryland county seat would be situated
In 1704 exploration	Explores Virginia area near Canoy where refugees would found the German Settlement in 1732
In 1704 exploration	Explores Virginia's Shenandoah Valley where he would found his third colony in 1709 and refugees would begin settling in 1731
Late 1704	Visits Philadelphia and Germantown refugee communities, scouts 70 miles into Pennsylvania frontier to Pequea

	region. Probably witnesses Shawnee Indians mining lead and silver there.
1705	Michel marries Mennonite refugee Anna Barbara von Lerber, relative of Ochs wife Anna Katherina von Lerber
1705	Co-founds Swiss refugee resettlement partnership with Georg Ritter and Johann Rudolph Ochs
1705	Ritter visits Shenandoah Valley
1705	Michel, Ritter, and Ochs submit first proposal for colonies in America to English Lords of Trade and Plantations
August 25, 1706	Great Council of Berne petitions England to permit Michel, Ritter and Ochs to create a colony in America to receive Swiss settlers, especially Mennonites
Early 1707	Michel's western Maryland exploration aborted by Maryland-Pennsylvania border dispute. Michel is called to account by Pennsylvania.
February 25, 1707	Michel exonerated by Pennsylvania, ceases 1707 expedition
"A considerable time before June, 1707"[105]	Michel "Travels with Governor Evans in Pennsylvania."[106] During this time, explores around Pequea Creek as possible refugee colony locale.
May 1, 1707	Great Britain comes into being as England and Scotland unite
May 25, 1707	Georg Ritter writes to Christoph von Graffenried informing him of trio's plans for American refugee colonies
April 4, 1708	First Michel son Christopher born
By September 24, 1708	Frantz Ludwig Michel is in Annapolis
Same date	Writes "Virginia letter" to Ritter
December 25, 1708	Writes "America letter" to Ritter urging Ritter to hire a London representative for trio's resettlement project
January 6, 1709	Michel sails from Virginia for London
Unknown date 1709	Ritter hires Christoph von Graffenried to represent Michel-Ritter-Ochs colo-

	nization proposal in London
Spring, 1709	London begins receiving thousands of Palatine religious and war refugees
May, 1709	Graffenried departs Berne, abandoning wife and 13 children, and stiffing his creditors
June 5, 1709	Michel in London takes British citizenship making him a dual national
June 28, 1709	Queen Anne refers trio's colonization proposal to Lords of Trade and Plantations for consideration
July 11, 1709	Shenandoah Valley colony proposal to Lords of Trade and Plantations includes Michel 1704 map for first time
July 13, 1709	Michel and Graffenried submit modified Shenandoah Valley proposal
July 15, 1709	Michel and Graffenried submit further modified Shenandoah Valley proposal
About this time	Graffenried takes British citizenship making him a dual national
August, 1709	Graffenried's wife Regina applies to Great Council of Berne for assistance to pay husband's creditors
August 4, 1709	Graffenried buys 5,000 acres in North Carolina. In exchange, Carolina proprietors give him titles as Baron and Landgrave of "Bernberg."
August 22, 1709	Reversing earlier decision, Lords of Trade and Plantations approve Michel-Ritter-Ochs colony in Shenandoah Valley
September 10, 1709	Queen Anne grants permission to proceed with Shenandoah Valley colony
Soon after this	Lords of Trade and Plantations switch colony approval to Graffenried-Lawson North Carolina proposal
October 10, 1709	Michel, Ochs, Graffenried and John Lawson granted permission to settle Palatine refugees in North Carolina
Soon after this	Two shiploads of 900 Palatine refugees depart London for North Carolina

Late 1709	Palatines arrive at Bath, North Carolina after one-third die in transit
1710-1711	Official Swiss persecution of Mennonites intensifies again
January 6, 1710	Ochs takes British citizenship making him a dual national
Before the following date	Michel proposes to William Penn a refugee colony in the Pequea region of Pennsylvania. Penn donates the land for the colony.
March 31, 1710	Michel meets with Swiss Mennonites in Berne
April 1710	William Penn alerts British ambassador in Holland to expect 50-60 Swiss Mennonite refugees from Berne
At this time	Georg Ritter escorts the group from Berne to Holland
Shortly after this	Michel meets Ritter in Holland, diplomat Pesme de Saphorin in The Hague
May 18, 1710	Michel, Ritter, Graffenried, Petter Isoth and four others form stock company as investment in colonies in Virginia and North Carolina
June 3, 1710	Michel appointed by William Penn as Pennsylvania Director of Mines
June 23, 1710	Alexander Spotswood appointed Governor of Virginia
Shortly before June 27, 1710	Six Mennonite families are first to settle at Pequea colony[107]
September 23, 1710	Michel sails aboard *Maria Hope* escorting 40 to 50 Mennonite refugees to Philadelphia who go on to Pequea
October 23, 1710	These Swiss Mennonite refugees arrive at Pequea refugee colony
October, 1710	Carolina proprietors designate Michel and Graffenried as co-founders of New Berne colony.
1711	Johann Rudolph Ochs publishes *America Guide* emigrant handbook
Early in 1711	Graffenried begins referring to himself

FIRST EXPLORER

	as Landgrave of all of North Carolina
Early in 1711	Only 300 of original 900 refugees to New Berne still alive
Immediately following this	Michel goes to New Berne to turn around dire situation but Carolina proprietors back Graffenried
Soon after this	Ritter & Cie. dissolves, ceases North Carolina operations. Ritter terminates Graffenried's employment and salary.
At this time	Michel departs New Berne colony
March 21, 1711	From London, Ochs begins facilitating Swiss Mennonite relocation to Pequea
May 6, 1711	Graffenried acknowledges to Ritter end of contract between the two, writes "Little Old Englishman" letter, begins lifelong invective against Michel
July 17, 1711	North Carolina colonial official John Urmston reports Graffenried as "having no money anywhere"
September 1711	After trial, John Lawson executed by Indians for crimes against them. Graffenried avoids same by posing as Governor of North Carolina.
Spring of 1712	To no avail, Graffenried retraces Michel's 1704 Maryland exploration route trying to find Michel's nonexistent "Shenandoah Valley mines"
Soon after this	New Berne settlers refuse Graffenried's order to relocate to Virginia
March 2, 1712	Michel acquires 2,500 acres in South Carolina, his fifth refugee colony
March 12, 1712	Michel peace treaty averts slaughter of Tuscarora Indians in South Carolina
March 12-23, 1712	Michel praised by South Carolina commander John Barnwell
May 12, 1712	Georg Ritter confers with German mining engineer Johann Justus Albrecht about possible Virginia mining venture
June 7, 1712	Pennsylvania bans importation of slaves

Fall 1713	Johann Justus Albrecht and his hired German miners arrive in London
October 19, 1713	Michel names South Carolinian William Brice as his power of attorney, leaves South Carolina
Same date	Record on Michel goes blank until 1715
April 1714	Arriving German miners met by Virginia Governor Alexander Spotswood and are settled on part of his estate
At this time	Spotswood names the new settlement Germanna, puts miners to work digging for precious metals.
Soon after this	Miners discover only iron ore. Spotswood builds an iron foundry which at first is modestly successful.
August 1, 1714	Queen Anne dies, is succeeded by George I
September 11, 1714	War of Spanish Succession ends
Fall 1714	With tumultuous escape through America and Europe, Christoph von Graffenried abandons New Berne, flees American and European creditors
November 11, 1714	Graffenried reaches home in Worb, Switzerland, is scorned by family and community
By 1715	Conoy Indians have vacated village at Canoy and resettled in Pennsylvania near Pequea
1715	Michel's son William born
August 3, 1716	Michel reappears in South Carolina, proposes that colonial government resettle more refugees on new land grant
August, 1716	Inspects approved settlement site, his sixth refugee colony
Soon after this	Leaves South Carolina, "returns northward," seems to go home to King William for good
At this time	Record on Michel goes blank again, but he appears to have continued resettling refugees. His and Anna's resi-

	dence almost certainly America.
August 20, 1716 to September 17, 1716	Via Germanna, Virginia Governor Alexander Spotswood leads "Knights of the Golden Horseshoe" expedition into the Shenandoah Valley
February 1717	European Mennonite leaders initiate mass migration of Mennonites from Europe to Pennsylvania
August 24, 1717	Three ships carrying 363 Mennonites arrive in Philadelphia, destined for new settlements around Pequea
1717	Graffenried publishes his memoirs
1717	Johann Rudolph Ochs moves to London, begins contract engraving for Royal Mint of Great Britain reporting to Sir Isaac Newton, accelerates relocation of refugees to America
1717-18	Ship's Captain Tarbett hijacks German passengers to Virginia where they become indentured servants of Governor Spotswood at Germanna foundry
1718	Indian-English intermediary and peace maker Martin Chartier dies at Pequea
April 12, 1718	**Michel's King William County land patent mentioned in official records shows him now as "Francis Michael"**
July 30, 1718	William Penn dies
1720	Francis and Anna Michael youngest son Andrew born
1720	**Internet genealogies show Anna Michael dying at 44 or 45 but no found source shows documentation**
1720	Internet genealogies show Frantz Ludwig Michel dying at 44 or 45 without documentation. This proven wrong through *First Explorer* research.
After April 29, 1720	Virginia Governor Alexander Spotswood awarded 86,000 acres including Germanna
December 19, 1720	Frantz Ludwig von Lerber, father of Anna Barbara von Lerber Michel, dies

About this time	in Berne at age 72 Christoph von Graffenried writes in margin of his memoir that Michel "died among the Indians"
1720 and after	After near wipe-out, North Carolina Tuscarora tribe begins migrating to Iroquois Six Nations in New York state
1721	Unpaid by Isaac Newton for Mint work, Ochs declares bankruptcy
May 1721	Spotsylvania County, Virginia formed in honor of Alexander Spotswood. Created in part from King William County.
March 19, 1722	Frantz Ludwig Michel again shown as Francis Michael in 1722 sale of parcel by Robert Farish to Edward Herndon adjoining Michael's King William land grant
August 20, 1722	Ochs wife Catherina dies
September 27, 1722	Alexander Spotswood retires as Virginia Governor, moves to Germanna
At this time	Spotsylvania County formed in honor of Alexander Spotswood
1723	Georg Ritter continues resettling Swiss Mennonite refugees until he dies in Berne at fifty-six, first of trio to die
1725-30	German-speaking settlers including refugees begin filtering into western Maryland from Pequea, Pennsylvania colony and nearby
March 20, 1726	Royal Mint director Sir Isaac Newton dies mentally debilitated at 84
September 6, 1727	Johann Rudolph Ochs officially appointed Engraver of the Royal Mint
1727	German Mennonite Adam Mueller migrates from near Pequea to become first settler in Shenandoah Valley
September 28, 1728	Francis Michael awarded tract of 400 acres at Germanna directly adjacent to Governor Spotswood's estate in Spotsylvania County
1728-1731	Francis Michael appears in Spotsylva-

	nia County official records 26 times, usually as a Court appointee
1729	With 50,000 acres, Robert Carter receives second Shenandoah Valley land grant after the trio's in 1709
May 10, 1729	Lancaster County, Pennsylvania, is chartered after Michel/Penn colony of Pequea spreads outward
1730-1736	More than 500,000 acres in Shenandoah Valley awarded in 11 grants
June 17, 1730	Swiss immigrant Jacob Stover awarded 5,000-acre grant at Massanutten Mountain
1731	First group of Mennonite settlers reaches Shenandoah Valley, settle at Michel colony site at furthest point of his 1704 exploration
September 5, 1731	Francis Michael sells his 400 Germanna acres to Samuel Wright for £15. He vanishes from the record again until 1734.
1732	Virginia's German Settlement near Canoy founded by migrants from Pennsylvania
July 19, 1732	Lords of Trade and Plantations grant Ochs and three associates permission to found a second Shenandoah Valley colony
August 1734	Orange County, Virginia formed by severing northern part of Spotsylvania County. Germanna is first seat of Orange County.
May 1735	Francis Michael appears in Orange County, Virginia records performing in similar court-appointed roles as he had in Spotsylvania County
February 27, 1736	Ochs and an associate propose resettlement of 6,000 Swiss refugees to North Carolina
1740	His family has Christoph von Graffenried declared as a ward of the state

June 7, 1740	Alexander Spotswood dies while visiting Annapolis. Burial site unknown.
1743	Graffenried dies at Worb at 82, is buried in family cemetery there
1744	Annual Swiss emigration to America reaches 12,000, with 3,000 from Berne Canton alone
1745	Daniel Dulaney the Elder plats Fredericktowne, Maryland, begins selling lots
February 26, 1746	**Orange County, Virginia official record is last known mention anywhere of Francis Michael, now 70**
June 10, 1748	Frederick County, Maryland, chartered
October, 1749	Johann Rudolph Ochs dies in London at 76 after resettling refugees for nearly 50 years
By 1754	Shawnee and other tribes have vacated the Shenandoah Valley
1756	French and Indian War begins, European settlement of western Maryland reverses tide as Appalachian settlers retreat to Fredericktown
1757	Andrew Michael, youngest of four Frantz Ludwig and Anna Michel's sons, first appears in colonial records
December 1, 1757	In father's footsteps, John Ralph Ochs, Jr., appointed Royal Mint Engraver
By 1760	64,800 German-speaking immigrants have arrived in America since 1700, 40 percent of total immigration, with most settling at Michael's six colonies
By 1762	Four Michael brothers now living in or near Frederick, Maryland
1762	Andrew Michael constructs and begins operating Michael Foundry in Frederick, first foundry in western Maryland
By 1763	All four Michael brothers become naturalized as British citizens
February 10, 1763	Britain, Spain, France sign Treaty of Paris, ending French and Indian War

December 27, 1763	Last of Pennsylvania's peaceful Conestoga Indians slaughtered and scalped near Pequea by Paxton Boys gang
1767	Mason-Dixon Line surveyed, finally settling territorial disputes between Pennsylvania and Maryland
November 23, 1767	Andrew Michael delivers 500 European religious refugees and other settlers to his father's Michel's Pennsylvania refugee communities around Pequea
March 1768	Andrew sells Michael Foundry to Samuel Barrance
July 12, 1768	Andrew purchases 340-acre tract near his father's 1704 sidetrip campsite, naming it Cooling Springs
1773	Francis Michael second son William dies probably in Frederick
July 1776	Samuel Barrance sells Michael Foundry to John Hanson, future first president of the United States. Hanson begins using foundry to produce Revolutionary War munitions.
July 4, 1776	United States Declaration of Independence published
August 2, 1776	Declaration of Independence ratified, creating thirteen independent nation-states
1778	Andrew Michael swears oath of allegiance to the United States
1779	Citing age, John Ralph Ochs, Jr. declines Royal Mint Chief Engraver offer
March 1, 1781	With John Hanson's signature the last, Articles of Confederation ratified authorizing creation of United States as single nation on first Monday of November
November 5, 1781	United States of America comes into being with first meeting of its original government, the United States in Congress Assembled
Same day	Frederick, Maryland's John Hanson elected by original government as first

	President of the United States
November 4, 1782	President John Hanson completes his one-year term of office after successfully launching the first United States nation, government and cabinet
November 15, 1783	John Hanson dies at 68
1783	Francis and Anna Michael's eldest son Christopher dies at home.
1783	Nicholas Michael, possible son of Frantz Ludwig and Anna Michel, dies
1786	Andrew Michael, 66, adds 107-acre Flag Pond tract to Cooling Springs
January 25, 1787	John Ralph Ochs, Jr. retires on pension
July 1788	John Ralph Ochs, Jr. obituary appears
November 9-12, 1796	Andrew Michael votes in 1796 presidential election
Early 1800	Andrew Michael, youngest son of Francis and Anna Michael, dies at Cooling Springs at 80, is buried there
1825-1833	In Andrew Jackson's Trail of Tears, Shawnee Tribe forcibly resettled to newly designated Oklahoma Indian Territory
1831	The nation's first long distance rail line is laid down by the Baltimore and Ohio Railroad Company from Baltimore to Conoy, transecting Cooling Springs lands
About the same time	Construction of the Chesapeake and Ohio Canal reaches Conoy
1835	Landowner Charles Johnson has lots surveyed, streets laid out for new town near site of Conoy that he names Point of Rocks
September 12, 1848	Confederation of Helvetia (Switzerland) founded, unifying Switzerland's 26 theretofore independent cantons into a single nation. Berne is named capital.
Following this	Swiss persecution of Mennonites and

	other Anabaptists begins to abate
1879	Magistrate Ezra Michael, great-grandson of Francis Michael, builds second Cooling Springs home in use today
January 17, 1885	Most official records of King William County, Virginia, destroyed in a courthouse fire
1890	Samuel Michael writes 15,000-word chronicle to his niece and nephew detailing genealogy of the first four American generations of Andrew Michael descendants
1916	William Hinke translates and publishes Frantz Ludwig Michel's 1701-02 Virginia journal
1921	Charles Kemper article on Michel appears in same journal
About this time	Scholars debunk Graffenried scrawl that Michael "died among the Indians"
June 2, 1924	American Indians, inhabitants of the Americas for 18,500 years or more, are finally reclassified by the United States government as United States citizens
1948	Congress passes law for resettlement of 650,000 World War II refugees
Not later than 1952	Mildred Michael Crewe writes *The Michael Family* with extensive primary source data on four ostensible Michael brothers
1969	Klaus Wust book *The Virginia Germans* discusses Frantz Ludwig Michel
May 5, 1974	Cooling Springs sold outside Michael family after 206 years. Next two owners do much to renovate home while preserving its look and character.
1980	United States establishes permanent Federal Refugee Resettlement Program in State Department's Office of Refugee Resettlement
1983	Christoph von Graffenried disinterred, his remains transferred to locker at

	University of Bern
July 6, 1987	Margaret Hickman, 85, publishes *Memory Lane* chronicling 20th century lives of Andrew Michael's branch of Michael family
1999	Robert Selig authors article on Frantz Ludwig Michel's early official work in Virginia and his drawings of and comments on Williamsburg
February 22, 2001	Peter and Vicki Michael purchase Cooling Springs, bringing it back into the Michael family after 27 years
From then until now	Cooling Springs home, outbuildings, lands renovated, keeping original look
Early 21st century	Genealogists reveal Michel/Michael family line twenty-one generations back, tying Swiss Michel von Schwertschwendi nobility line directly to Frantz Ludwig Michel and his Michael descendants
2009	Genealogist Margaret Myers's three-volume publication documents more than 1,500 American descendants of Francis and Anna Michael including many still residing in western Maryland where he explored
April, 2011	Andreas Mielke and Sandra Yelton's deeply researched compendium of 12 articles on Frantz Ludwig Michel published
June, 2012	Their translation of Johann Rudolph Ochs's *American Guide* is published
Early 21st century	In a modern miracle, social media, genealogy and DNA analysis allow Chief Billy Redwing Tayac and Mervin Savoy to re-gather 4,000 of the Piscataway-Conoy tribe
January 9, 2012	Maryland Governor Martin O'Malley and the Maryland General Assembly officially recognize the Piscataway-Conoy Tribe
July 12, 2018	Cooling Springs observes 250th anniversary of its founding and of

	Michel/Michel family ownership
Christmas Day, 2021	In reprisal of the public-private partnership that the Michel-Ritter-Ochs trio pioneered, United States announces expansion of its refugee resettlement program now to include non-profit humanitarian organizations relocating refugees to America[108]
Fall 2022	In honor of the state's Piscataway-Conoy People, the University of Maryland dedicates a large new student center in the College Park campus's new Heritage Community
November 22, 2022	*First Explorer*, only known biography of Frantz Ludwig Michel, is published
1702-present	Without interruption, Mattaponi and Pamunkey tribes retain ancestral homelands within Frantz Ludwig Michel 1702 King William land grant
Present	Federal government continues to deny recognition to mixed-race North Carolina Lumbee Tribe as "not Indian enough"
Present	The Tuscarora Tribe of about 2,200 members occupies nine-square-mile reservation near Niagara Falls, New York. After the State granted a developer 600 acres of the reservation that he flooded to create a reservoir, the tribe has experienced water shortages and contaminated water.
Present	Afghan, Ukrainian and other refugees arriving to the United States are assisted by United States Office of Refugee Resettlement.

Michel's 1704 Expedition Camps

The sites are listed in the order that Michel stayed at them as shown by the "pup tent" symbols on his map. Letters refer to places on the annotated map shown in the center pictorial pages here.

1. At a spring's rising point (C) at Sugarloaf Mountain (B)
2. On the east bank of the Monocacy River (D)
3. At Conoy Indian village (J) on the Potomac River (L)
4. On Michel's sidetrip near the future Cooling Springs
5. Just east of the confluence of the Monocacy River (D) and Carroll Creek (I)

    Probably at 4 again going back to Conoy

6. Near the future site of the German Settlement (M)
7. On Shenandoah River south bank near today's West Virginia Route 115 bridge crossing
8. Upstream on Shenandoah River north bank
9. At confluence of Shenandoah River north and south branches (Q)
10. At Indian village along the north branch
11. Along the north branch at a prospective settlement site
12. Close by camp 11
13. Along south bank of south fork of Shenandoah River
14. Along the south fork at prospective settlement site
15. Near camp 14 at Massanutten Mountain trailhead

There is no indication that Michel did not trace this same route back to Annapolis. He may have used these same campsites on his way back.

Ritter & Company New Berne Operating Contract

CONTRACT OF RITTER & CIE.
AS TO THE FOUNDING OF A COLONY

May our help and beginning be in the might of the Lord who created Heaven and Earth. Amen.

Know herewith that between the hereafter subscribed gentlemen and friends, Mr. Frantz Ludwig Michel and Christoph von Graffenried on the one part, and Mr. Georg Ritter and Mr. Peter Isoth in their own and Mr. Albrecht von Graffenried's, Mr. Johann Anthoni Jarsing's, Mr. Samuel Hopf's and Mr. Emanuel Kilchberger's names on the other part, there has been made and concluded with another present, true, and bona fide society, a contract consisting of the following points.

1. There shall serve as the foundation the one hundred seventeen thousand five hundred acres of land lying in North Carolina, between the Neuse River and Cape Fear, which in the name of this society have been purchased from the Proprietors of Carolina according to the patents obtained for that purpose, with all the privileges and rights thereto pertaining, whatever name they may have, and with all those that shall or can be obtained in the future. And there also belong to this the twelve hundred and fifty acres of land which were purchased from Mr. Lawson, situated in the angle, between the Rivers Neuse and Trent.

2. There is also placed as foundations the concession in Virginia obtained from the Queen of Great Britain; also, whatever further liberties, rights, mines, or other concessions, whatever name they may bear, which shall be obtained from the same queen or her successors, so that all shall be for the good of this society.

3. We under the blessing of God shall constitute the board of directors.

4. Mr. Frantz L. Michel promises that of all minerals which he has already found and shall yet find, he will put in all the portion coming to him therefrom to the good of the society.

5. This society shall be conducted under the name, Georg Ritter and Company. All the papers, writings, letters, and obligations shall be signed by this name; and the Society shall have its own seal; also, no member, except the one or the ones whom the Society shall empower so to do, shall have power to sign or to seal any document or writing in the name of the society.

6. The capital of this society shall consist of seven thousand two hundred pounds sterling which shall be employed for the payment of the above-described lands, to the support of the Palatine and Swiss colonies already sent there and those following after, and also for the conduct of proposed trade and mining operations.

7. To the formation of this capital there are set twenty-four shares, each at three hundred pounds sterling, which shall be made over to the gentleman here at London appointed therefor, who shall also send a receipt for it, and credit shall also be given him in the books.

8. No one shall be able to possess more than one share for himself, but two or at most three can combine for one share; but if, after the lapse of three years, these twenty-four shares are not complete, it shall be free to those who already have a share to take another.

9. In the transaction of matters of importance which may occur, such as the election of a director, one or more deputies to the Royal Court, to negotiate with the Lords Proprietors or elsewhere, at the nomination of the society's salaried servants and officers, as also the acceptance of one or more new associates, the building and the purchasing of the ships useful for trade, and the opening of mines, everything shall be done and election made according to the majority of votes, with this in explanation, that where there are more than one to a whole share they shall count as one vote only and also, no one who has not a whole

share shall be elected director.

10. It is free to each to go to Carolina or Virginia, or to remain in his Fatherland; and then his deputy shall enjoy similar privileges in his stead, except that he cannot be elected director.

11. It is free to everyone to sell his share to another, to trade it off or to give it away, to use and control it just as his other goods and property; and if he dies intestate the same shall fall to his nearest heir, just as his other goods. But the Society reserves to itself, at the sale of it, to have the preference, and ordains that it shall not fall into mortmain and be sold or given to Papists.

12. To every participant there shall be designated a piece of land in an acceptable place at the building up of the city, as well as a free estate of five hundred acres in Virginia; but as much as he shall desire shall be free from interest and tithes, with the exception of what is due to the Lords Proprietors.

13. Mr. Michel reserves this to himself, because he contributes the mines in Pennsylvania to the good of the Society, that the first three years, when these mines shall be open and begin to produce the profits, shall come to him in advance. In the fourth year Mr. Ritter and Mr. von Graffenried, since they have more of the expenses, shall take out according to the amount of their shares contributed before the beginning of this same mine. What is left (for that year), as well as the whole profits on the other portion belonging to the Society, shall go to the Society for the remaining seventeen years. He hereby promises, with good success of the above-mentioned mine, to repay Mr. Ritter's principal from these first years of the Society.

14. So there is put to the credit of Mr. Michel, for his labor and for the mine contributed to the benefit of the company, an entire share; but he shall, as soon as possible, pay back all that the Society to date has advanced and may still advance.

15. Mr. Christoph von Graffenried's money laid out for five

thousand acres of land in Carolina, as well as the expenses incurred through the Palatines and others, according to the enclosed specifications, shall be credited to him for a share; but anything more than that he shall, according to the thirteenth article, take from the Pennsylvania mines.

16. In like manner an entire share shall be given and credited to Mr. Georg Ritter for the expenses he has incurred; but anything more than that he shall, according to the thirteenth article, take from the Pennsylvania mines.

17. It is not allowed to anyone to take up land in North Carolina on his own account, except the named free lands; but all land shall be taken up on the account of the Society.

18. No member shall be allowed to carry on private trade, either in North Carolina or Virginia, but everything shall be done there for the benefit of the society; and yet it is free to every one to associate himself with others not trading in this province, and to carry on a trade on his own account, always understood that it shall not be to the detriment of this Society.

19. The other above named gentlemen, associates, who have not entirely paid in their capital, shall pay it in before the next approaching September and make it over to the gentleman in England, already named.

20. There shall be no definite end set for the Society, because each one who does not wish to remain longer in the Society has liberty to sell his share. But in view of the fact that nothing in this world can be made fixed or immutable, it is agreed and resolved that this Society shall exist twenty years, and that in this time, neither shall or can there be talk of any separation. But after the lapse of these twenty years the Society can, at the discretion of three-fourths of the associates, be abolished; when they can make their division of the effects then existing, according to the majority of the votes.

21. Before the expiration of four years shall no separation be made, but a report shall be made yearly of the state of

things, a reckoning of the balance shall be made, and for each share-holder a copy be prepared; but after the expiration of the four years each stock-holder shall draw ten per cent of his invested capital, according to the judgment of the whole Society. But whatever, by the blessing of God, is gained in the mines, that shall be divided yearly.

22. It is free to the Society to elucidate this contract by the majority of votes, to explain, to diminish, to increase, according as the advantage of the Society demands it.

23. The associates promise each other love, faith, and true friendship, and that they will help to further, to best of their ability, whatever may serve and promote the good of this Society; and, as much as in them lies ward off injury and do everything which is in any way within the meaning of this contract, two copies of which, uniform and of the same tenor, shall be prepared. And may the Lord our God give his blessing to it, to whom alone belongs the praise, honor, and glory, from eternity to eternity, Amen.

Done in London, the 18th of May, 1710.

Witnesses

William Edwards	Fr. Ludwig Michel
Edward Woods	Chr. Von Graffenried
	Georg Ritter
	Petter Isoth

This contract may be found in *Swiss American Historical Society Review*, Vol. 45, No. 3, Article 6. scholarchive.byu.edu/sahs_review/vol45/iss3/6.

Michael's Six Colonies and Maryland Refuge

LOCALE	PERMITTED BY	IN YEAR
1. King William, Virginia	Provincial grant	1702
2. Western Maryland	Proprietor consent	1704
3. Shenandoah Valley, Virginia	Crown grant	1709
4. New Berne, North Carolina	Crown grant	1709
5. Pequea, Pennsylvania	Proprietor consent	1710
6. South Carolina I	Michael purchase	1713
7. South Carolina II	Provincial grant	1716

The four officially granted colonies were the two permitted by Crown grants for the Shenandoah Valley and New Berne in 1709 by the Lords of Trade and Plantations, the King William grant by the Virginia colonial government in 1702, and the grant by the colonial government of South Carolina in 1716. The two others founded by Michel were the Pequea, Pennsylvania, colony in 1710 with William Penn; and the colony for which Michel purchased land in 1713 in South Carolina.

As for the Maryland refuge, though Michel explored western Maryland in 1704 and 1708, he never founded a colony in Maryland because the Maryland proprietors, the Calvert family, had approved of Michel settling refugees anywhere in Maryland from the start. Refugees and other settlers first began arriving in western Maryland around 1725-30, coming mainly from the Pequea area.

While Maryland and Pennsylvania were never petitioned by Michel and his partners to grant them colonies, these two provinces consented to and encouraged resettlement of refugees and resulted in Michel's two largest concentrations of immigrant refugees.

Sorting Out Michel/Michael Genealogy

Despite the revealing in-depth research completed by Andreas Mielke, Sandra Yelton, Mildred Michael Crewe, Nancy Michael Wachter, Margaret Myers, and the contemporary genealogists mentioned in the acknowledgements, a key gap remains for which deeper answers would go far in adding to any biography of Frantz Ludwig Michel/Francis Michael. The cloudy area is better verification of the parenthood of the four sons attributed to Francis and Anna. Solving the relationship question could go far in addressing parenthood.

The mystery of where Michel spent his years beginning with 1713 has been analyzed in depth as far as possible in the body of *First Explorer* by examining the relative likelihoods of feasible scenarios and how actual circumstances support each or not, concluding that from 1713 on Frantz and Anna resided in King William or nearby.

Graffenried's jab that Francis Michael improbably deserted all he knew to live out his life with an Indian tribe has been readily debunked here and elsewhere. However, if Graffenried was speaking derogatorily of Michael living at his King William lands because they included the native Mattaponi and Pamonkey peoples who Michael welcomed, then Graffenried's margin scrawl may be seen in the different light of insulting half-truth.

The question of where Anna von Lerber Michael lived during her marriage has been examined according to her circumstances and the relative likelihoods of the three European possibilities—Switzerland, London or travelling with her very mobile husband—coming to the confirmed conclusion that none of these was her home rather than America. Also, the custom of the time was that the wife would not be traveling with her husband on business but be tending the home and children. If Anna lived in America when Francis was elsewhere, did she reside with her sisters in the small Swiss settlement at Mattaponi, nearby at King William, at the Annapolis home, or elsewhere? All signs point to Anna remaining at King William except perhaps when her husband's work took him to Annapolis, Philadelphia and London for extended periods.

A rational and likely life course is that Anna returned to Mattaponi and her sisters after buying provisions for them in London in 1702 and then remained in America for the rest of her life. After all, she had uprooted her entire life to be free of religious discrimination and had succeeded in gaining freedom from it in Virginia. There wasn't much reason she would want to abandon this newfound equanimity.

We don't know when the spark was first lit between Frantz and Anna but do know that by 1705 they married.[109] The two could have been childhood or young adult sweethearts in Switzerland or have fallen for each other on Frantz's 1702 Virginia visit to her home, or in London at the end of their perilous voyage, or during Frantz's second stay in America. After marriage in this scenario, the couple had choices of where to live: near the Lerber sisters at Mattaponi, a few miles away at Frantz's King William, or at the home Frantz had built in Annapolis the year before they married.

What confounds this logical life course is that the four sons attributed to Frantz and Anna are said to have emigrated from Europe. This leads to the unsolved puzzle in sorting our Frantz Ludwig Michel's life, which is the question of the identities of the couple's children and whether the four men who found their way to Frederick, Maryland, in the 1760s were in fact each the progeny of Frantz and Anna. Multiple modern sources are consistent with each another that they were, but nothing found offers conclusive sourcing.

Certainly, what is most convincing toward Francis and Anna's parentage is the unmistakably conspicuous string of associations between Francis and youngest son Andrew. Andrew may have first settled in the Pequea area that Frantz had established as a refugee colony. He then moves to Frederick, the precise destination of Francis's 1704 sidetrip. With family wealth, of which his parents had plenty, he arrives with enough money to construct what may have been the largest building in western Maryland at the time. Five years later, he travels to Europe and returns with 500 refugees who he delivers to the Pequea area precisely as Francis had done. A year later, he purchases a large tract near or perhaps directly where Francis had camped on his sidetrip. He lives on his large expanse in landed gentry style as his Michel von Schwertschwendi ancestors had for the past 600 years. His grandson Ezra (1813-1886) is appointed as the local Magistrate for twenty-eight years, in effect as a Swiss-style *landvogt* of that part of the county.

Further pointing to Francis and Anna's parentage of the sons is that the first daughter of son Christopher was named Anna Barbara. Naming children after grandparents was a common practice in 1741 when grand-daughter Anna Barbara Michael was born. Francis was still alive when the child was named.

The earliest detailed narrative reference to the family in America is the 15,000-word missive written in 1890 by Samuel Michael to his niece and nephew, Anna Michael Cline and Marion S. Michael, describing Samuel's life and times. Marion was the author's great-grandfather and this Anna was Marion's sister. (Here is an Anna descendant again.) Samuel's letter was written as he was going blind a year before his passing at age seventy-one in 1891. Samuel was born at Cooling Springs in 1820 and raised there. After the Civil War, Samuel migrated to Illinois then Indiana where he lived out his life. He was a was a great-grandson of Francis and Anna, who Samuel doesn't mention in his remembrances, probably because most people don't know who their great-grandparents were.

His account, referred to today as *Samuel Michael's Chronicle*, has become an invaluable resource in Michael family research. Samuel began his long missive by reciting the names, wives' names, and children's names of the descendants of his grandfather, Andrew Michael, and telling what he knew about where they resided and what they did for a living. To the extent that he could, Samuel thus carried the list up through the grandchildren of his own generation, these grandchildren being the fifth generation of the family in America. *Samuel's Chronicle* covers the first 133 years of American Michaels from the time of Andrew's immigration in 1757.

Samuel writes that his grandfather Andrew, Francis Michael's youngest son, had embarked from Alsace along the Rhine River when emigrating to America. This oral tradition passed down by Samuel to today seems to conform with reliable primary documentation in the form of ship passenger lists. But is this Andreas Michel the same Andrew Michael who shows up in Frederick in the 1760s? Alsace in the 1700s was a largely German-speaking area bordering Switzerland and France. Today it is part of France but went back and forth between French and German occupation during war and peace up through World War II after which it was awarded to France. In 2017, the author and his wife visited Alsace. Samuel does not mention his great-uncles, Christopher, William, and Nicholas Michel—Franz and Anna's other sons—probably because most people are unaware of who their great-uncles were.

In his chronicle, Samuel conspicuously does not mention the major event of his lifetime, the Civil War. What he does mention as most notable to him is not the harnessing of electricity, transcontinental rail travel, or the advent of compulsory public education but the convenience of manufactured shoes in all sizes and how he no longer had to make his own. As his occupation, Samuel worked as a railroad stationmaster in Illinois and Indiana, a coveted position in that era.

The earliest known written reference to Frantz Ludwig Michel's four sons collectively is Mildred Michael Crewe's *The Michael Family* that she compiled sometime before 1952[110] and distributed privately within one branch of the family. Mrs. Crewe chaired the board of directors of J.J. Crewe & Sons, a manufacturer of gas compression and industrial refrigeration systems, until she died in 1989. She hired James Parker, shown in online references as her coauthor, as a researcher to ferret out data from the Library of Congress and from county and state archives on ship logs, immigration records, tax rolls, and church and civil records on births, deaths, baptisms, inheritances, and land purchases among other primary data. Based on what she and her researcher found, what survives of Crewe's publication presents detailed information on the four sons she attributes to Frantz and Anna Michel and includes some passed-down oral tradition and family lore of which she was aware. She is unequivocal in presenting the four found in Frederick as brothers but the blood link between parents and sons isn't conclusive from what is available in the remnants of her work. In particular, there appears to be only Crewe's assumption that the four Michel-surnamed men found in the Library of Congress's collection of ship manifests are the same four who are found in Frederick, Maryland civil and church records several years later.

A half century or more went by until around 2000 when Nancy Michael Wachter, an Andrew descendant, found posted on genealogybank.com the full Michel von Schwertschwendi genealogy from Heinzmann Michel von Schwertschwendi in 1419 down to David Michel von Schwertschwendi, Lord of Ralligen, in the late 1600s, to David's children including Frantz Ludwig Michel. This genealogy website is regarded as having one of the more comprehensive and reliable genealogical data collections.

Wachter's unearthing of this trove introduced today's Michel/Michael descendants to their interesting family history back another 325 years before the first American generation in the eighteenth century. Her findings and other online sources show the four men Crewe found as Frantz Ludwig and Anna Michel's sons but again without sourcing stated. At this juncture, it isn't apparent whether web posters came to the parent-son relationships independently or inferred them from Crewe's unpublished work, but the latter source is doubtful because of its limited distribution long before the advent of the Internet.

In the early 2000s another Michel/Michael descendant and then another saw the same long Michel genealogy posted on multiple genealogy websites. By this time, the extended genealogy had become relatively easy to find in Internet searches. In recent years, websites began to show a Michel collateral line back to Itel Michel in the early 1400s and the Lordship line down from him.

An Internet search in October of 2021 turned up multiple mentions on Anna von Lerber's marriage to Frantz Ludwig Michel. However, none was found in this or later searches with a sourced wedding date for the 1705 shown. Postings from multiple families' genealogical records at myheritage.com showing the couple's marriage list their children's names. For example, a posting by Berndt Ehrhardt of Germany lists Christoph, Wilhelm and Andreas in that birth order, but no Nicholas. This birth order conforms to some other observed birth orders for these children. The posting also shows Anna's birth and death as occurring in Berne Canton but again without sourcing. Another website's entry on Anna shows "Christopher and 3 other children," in this case presumably including Nicholas.

One genealogical website shows Frantz and Anna also having a daughter, Jacobine Anna Margaretha Michel, but without birth year. This is feasible but is almost certainly a posting error confused with a person of this name who lived in the nineteenth century.[111]

All of this is convincing regarding the couple's marriage and Frantz Ludwig and Anna Michel's family but what would be more definitive are birth or baptismal records of the children ascribed to them. These might be available if the children were born in Switzerland or London but not if born at unknown places elsewhere. This also brings us back to the question of whether Anna travelled with Frantz after 1713 if he was roaming the Rhineland making arrangements for refugees, or if the couple may have been living in London then.

In the attempt to uncover civil or church records that could shed light on the couple's whereabouts after 1713 and on confirming their parentage of as many of the four boys as possible, the author contracted with well credentialed genealogists in Switzerland, Great Britain, Maryland and Virginia to research records from 1705 onward. Searched were birth, baptismal, marriage, death, burial, immigration, ship log, naturalization, and other records. Several other genealogists contacted contributed usefully. All performed most commendably and are thanked in the acknowledgments above.

What their worked confirmed convincingly if not always absolutely was that Frantz became Francis in the 1710s, that he, Anna and their family did not settle in Switzerland or London but at King William, that Francis did not die in 1720, that Anna did die sometime before 1738, that Francis lived at or near King William until at least 1746, and that he was busy working in official capacities up to that time. These researchers' findings completely upended the widely held Internet narrative that the couple both died in 1720 leaving four orphans in Switzerland. The findings also put the lie to Graffenried's claim that Francis had "died among the Indians." When Christoph von Graffenried died in 1743, Francis Michael was still very much alive.

There is more work to do in trying to further explore the question of the parent-child relationships if the very old records necessary can ever be found to provide answers. Readers are encouraged to get in touch with the author with anything that might shed light on the Michael couple or their children.

Misconceptions Corrected

As addressed in the body of *First Explorer*, misrepresentations of Michel propagated by Christoph von Graffenried in his memoirs have been exposed and dissected here and earlier by others. Nevertheless, it is too easy for the unsuspecting researcher to come across seepage from the Graffenried memoirs and unwittingly take away falsehoods. For the same reason, this is even easier with modern-day Internet postings that unintentionally (or deliberately) spread falsehoods. This last appendix of *First Explorer* addresses several probably unintentionally misleading assertions regarding Francis or Anna Michel. Claims, summarized from their original postings for clarity, are presented in *italics*.

Michel spent so much time exploring America that it is unlikely that he fathered four children in Switzerland.

Here we contend with Internet misinformation again. The children were almost certainly not fathered in Switzerland as research turned up no Swiss civil or church records on any children by the couple. We do know that from 1711 on, when the last three of the couple's children were born, the parents were living at King William. When Christopher was born in 1708, his parents were living in Annapolis.

Christopher and Andrew lived miles apart in their county, belonged to different churches, and weren't brothers.

They worshipped at different churches *because* they lived in different parts of a frontier county separated by Catoctin Mountain, still a major barrier back then. The brothers were likely raised in the Swiss Reformed faith. Andrew worshipped at the Evangelical Lutheran Church in the county seat, still a village at the time. Christopher would worship at the Reformed Church in Sharpsburg after the church was founded in 1764. At the time, the Reformed Church was in full communion with the Evangelical Lutheran Church. The brothers appear to have belonged to the related denominations because those were all that were available where they lived. Christopher's tract was in what was still wilderness when he and his family settled there. He and Andreas show up as brothers in multiple online sources cited here and arrived in Frederick, purchased large properties, and were naturalized on dates close to each other at each step. Christopher's oldest daughter was named Anna Barbara apparently after her grandmother, Anna Barbara Michael. Absent a birth or baptismal record for Andrew as proof positive, all of this taken together is strong circumstantial evidence that the two were brothers. This is bolstered further by independent oral traditions of Christopher's and Andrew's related lines of descendants, which are in touch with each other to this day.

Anna Barbara Lerber lived in Virginia when Francis Louis arrived in 1702. He did sail to England on the same ship with her, but she would not have returned to Bern where she had been exiled for being Anabaptist.

This is almost correct. Here with the "Francis Louis" we have the occasionally seen mistake that Michel was French. The error stems from an incorrect translation in 1916 as addressed earlier. Frantz Ludwig Michel was German-speaking Swiss, not French. Anna and Frantz sailed in the same convoy in 1702, but not on the same ship. Anna very likely did not return to Berne where her father was a high Swiss government official in good position to shelter her from persecution. Genealogical data show Anna dying in Bern Canton but, based on everything gathered here, this is now certain to be incorrect. A careful professional search in 2022 turned up no evidence of Anna ever returning to Switzerland.

Christopher Michel was the son of another immigrant couple from Morzheim, Germany because Frederick was popular in Morzheim and the two towns became sister cities.

Though there could have been some other Christopher Michael who came from Morzheim to Frederick County, nothing in the record shows that the Christopher in question emigrated from there. Only one Christopher Michael appears in official county records of the time.

Christopher Michael's farm, "Sun is Down, Moon is Up," is called a plantation. Western Maryland farms were humble, not big tobacco plantations found elsewhere in Maryland.

"Plantation" as used in Michel's era had a broader meaning than today. One definition then and still means "a settlement in a new country or region" as when in 1709 the British Lords of Trade and Plantations gave the trio permission to establish new settlements—"plantations"— in the Shenandoah Valley and North Carolina. In the American English lexicon, "plantation" took on a separate, narrower, strictly American meaning in the slavery era as a term peculiar to the South and to tobacco and cotton cultivation.

First Explorer

Bibliography

Print

1. Alderson, Carolyn, Certified Genealogist. Various reports of commissioned research on Frantz Ludwig and Anna Michel in Britain. Private communications (email), March 18, 2022. *et seq.*

2. Allred, Fred J. and Alonzo T. Dill. "The Founding of New Bern: A Footnote," *North Carolina Historical Review*, No. 3, July, 1963

3. American Psychiatric Association. *Diagnostic and Statistical Manual of Mental Disorders, DSM-5*, 5th edition, 2022

4. Barnwell, Joseph W. "The Second Tuscarora Expedition," *South Carolina Historical and Genealogical Magazine*, Vol. 10, January, 1909

5. Blankenbaker, John. "The Second Germanna Colony and Other Pioneers," *The Germanna Record*, no. 18, Memorial Foundation of the Germanna Colonies of Virginia, 2008

6. Brackbill, Martin. "John (Hans, Jr.) Herr (Died 1756) at Pequea," unpublished essay, Lancaster Mennonite Historical Society, (undated)

7. Brown, Kathryn, editor. "Germanna Studies: Essays Honoring John V. Blankenbaker," *The Germanna Record*, no. 20, Memorial Foundation of the Germanna Colonies of Virginia, 2013

8. Burgerbibliothek Bern. *Neues Berner Taschenbuch auf das Jahr 1898, (New Berne Pocket Book for the Year 1898)*

9. Burns, Brendan, Certified Genealogist. Various reports of commissioned research on Frantz Ludwig and Anna Michel in Virginia. Private communications (email), May 31, 2022. *et seq.*

10. Crewe, Mildred Michael and James Parker, *The Michael Family*, before 1952. Private manuscript

11. Curry, Dennis. "A Closer Look at the 'Last Appearance' of the Conoy Indians," *Maryland Historical Magazine*, vol. 106, no. 3, pp. 344-353, 2011

12. Davis, Richard. "Swiss and German Mennonite Immigrants from the Palatine, 1704-1717, *Mennonite Family History*, January, 1994, pp. 9-16

13. Faust, Albert. "Swiss Emigration to the American Colonies in the Eighteenth Century," *The American Historical Review*, vol. 22, no. 1, October, 1916, pp. 21- 44

14. Fogelman, Aaron. *Hopeful Journeys: German Immigration, Settlement, and Political Culture in Colonial America, 1717-1775* (Illustrated edition), University of Pennsylvania Press, 1996

15. Guyer, Alan R. "The History and Mystery of the Pequea Silver Mines," *Pennsylvania Geology*, pp. 2-5, April 1976

16. Graffenried, Christoph von. His journal written in French held in the Bibliothèque Publique d'Yverdon-les-Bains at Yverdon, Switzerland. An English version is available in *Colonial Records of North Carolina*, vol. 1, pp. 905-992, 1886. He also wrote a German version.

17. Green, Fletcher. "Gold Mining in Ante-Bellum Virginia, *The Virginia Magazine of History and Biography*, Vol. 45, No. 4, October 1937, pp. 363, 366

18. Harrison, Fairfax. "Project for the Establishment of a Colony along the Potomak River in Virginia and Maryland," (Christoph von Graffenried's 1712 report), in *Landmarks of Old Prince William*, Old Dominion Press, Richmond, Virginia, 1924

19. Hickman, Margaret. *Memory Lane*, June 6, 1987. The memoir of a Michel/Michael descendant, private manuscript in possession of family members including the *First Explorer* author

20. Hinke, William J. "Report of the Journey of Francis Louis Michel from Berne, Switzerland, to Virginia, October 2, 1701-December 1, 1702" (translation of the original), T*he Virginia Magazine of History and Biography,* Vol. XXIV, No. 1, January, 1916

21. Huber, Joseph. "The British Queen Responsible for the U.S.A.," *Torch*, Vol. 95, Issue 3, Spring 2011

22. Kemp, Dear and Peter. *Oxford Companion to Ships and the Sea* (2nd edition), Oxford University Press, 2008

23. Kemper, Charles E., editor. "Documents Relating to Early Projected Swiss Colonies in the Valley of Virginia, 1706–1709," *Virginia Magazine of History and Biography*, Vol. XXIX, January, 1921

24. Kraybill, Donald. *Anabaptist World USA*, (with C. Nelson Hostetter), Herald Press, 2001

25. Kraybill, Donald. *Concise Encyclopedia of Amish, Brethren, Hutterites, and Mennonites*, Johns Hopkins University Press, 2010

26. Lavery, Brian. *The Ship of the Line - Volume 1: The development of the battlefleet 1650-1850*, Conway Maritime Press, 2003

27. Metzger, Teresa, Certified Genealogist. Various reports of commissioned research on Frantz Ludwig and Anna Michel in Switzerland. Private communications (email), April 8, 2022, *et seq.*

28. Michael, Peter H. *Remembering John Hanson: A Biography of the First President of the Original United States Government*, Underground Railroad Free Press, 2011

29. Michael, Peter H. *Running on Empty: Along an Epic 12,000-Mile Road Trip America Has Its Say on Economic Inequality*, Underground Railroad Free Press, 2015

30. Michael, Peter H. *Sixteen Michael Generations*, private manuscript in possession of the author

31. Michael, Samuel. *Samuel Michael's Chronicle.* The document is an untitled 15,032-word letter, as he describes it, written by Samuel Michael to his niece and nephew, Anna Michael Cline and Marion S. Michael I, in 1870, the year before Samuel's death at seventy-one. The "letter" was composed in what at the time was commonly used as a student's composition notebook. In the 1970s, Samuel's great-grand-nephew, Pierce B. Michael, Sr., had the letter typed and distributed widely among the Michael family. The typed rendition preserves all of Samuel's original spellings and English usages. The notebook had been handed down through two generations to Pierce. The author has worked from his own copy handed down from Pierce, his father. The original was donated to the central library of the Daughters of the American Revolution in Washington,

D.C., which now is unable to locate it. A donated copy of the typed version of *Samuel's Chronicle* is available at the Maryland Room of the Frederick County Public Library, Frederick, Maryland.

32. Michel, Frantz Ludwig. "Michel's German Letter to Ochs: From London, May 6/16, 1703," *Swiss American Historical Society Review*, vol. 48, no. 2, Article 3, 2012. Available at https://scholarsarchive.byu.edu/sahs_review/vol48/iss2/3.

33. Michel, Frantz Ludwig. "Michel's German letter to Ochs: From Arundel Conti, Maryland, May 20/30, 1704", *Swiss American Historical Society Review*, vol. 48, no. 2, Article 3, 2012. The article is available at https://scholarsarchive.byu.edu/sahs_review/vol48/iss2/3.

34. Michel, Frantz Ludwig. *Report of the Journey of Frantz Ludwig Michel from Berne, Switzerland, to Virginia, October 2, 1701-December 1, 1702*. The original is not known to exist. A strict transcription by Frantz Ludwig Michel's brother, Hans Ludwig Michel, is in the Bern, Switzerland public library, Burgerbibliothek Bern.

35. Michel, Hans Ludwig. *Meines Bruders Frantz Ludwig Michels Kurze Americanische Reißbeschreibung (My Brother Frantz Ludwig Michel's Short Account of his American Travels)*, Bern, Switzerland public library, Burgerbibliothek Bern

36. Mielke, Andreas and Sandra Yelton. "America Guide" by Johann Rudolf Ochs, 1711 (translation), *Swiss American Historical Society Review*, Vol. 48, No. 2, June 2012

37. Mielke, Andreas and Sandra Yelton. "Johann Rudolf Ochs (1673-1749) and his Social Network," *Swiss American Historical Society Review*, vol. 48, no. 2, art. 3, 2020

38. Mielke, Andreas and Sandra Yelton. "Towards a Swiss American Colony," *Swiss American Historical Society Review*, Vol. 48, No. 2, Article 3. 2012

39. Mielke, Andreas and Sandra Yelton. "Michel's Mysterious Mines," *Pennsylvania Mennonite Heritage*, Vol. 24, No. 2, April, 2011. The entire issue, all eighty pages of

it, is devoted to twelve articles by these authors on the life of Frantz Ludwig Michel up through 1716 but not the remainder of his life after that year. These authors' work is an outstanding collection of research and scholarship and at the time of its publication comprised by far the most complete compendium on Frantz Ludwig Michel. However, the articles make no mention of Anna of the couple's children.

40. Myers, Margaret E., *Frantz Ludwig Michel (1675-1720) and Descendants*, Heritage Books, Inc., three volumes, 1,071 pages, 2009. The publication is hard to find. A copy resides in the Maryland Room of the C. Burr Artz Public Library in Frederick, Maryland.

41. Ochs, Johann Rudolph. *America Guide*, 1711. Translation by Andreas Mielke and Sandra Yelton in *Swiss American Historical Society Review*, Vol. 48, No. 2, June 2021

42. Pannabecker, Samuel, *Open Doors: A History of the General Conference Mennonite Church*, Faith and Life Press, 1975

43. Rice, James. *Nature and History in the Potomac Country*, Johns Hopkins University Press, 2009

44. Ritter, Georg. "Ritter's Letter to NN: [From Bern to Christoph von Graffenried in Yverdon], May 25, 1707, *Swiss American Historical Society Review*, vol. 48, no. 2, Article 3, 2012. Available at https://scholarsarchive.byu.edu/cgi/viewcontent.cgi?article=1199&context=sahs_review

45. Schildknecht, C. E., editor, *Monocacy and Catoctin*, Family Line Publications, 1952, pp. 110-111

46. Selig, Robert A. "Wilhelmsburg in the Year 1702: The Account of Franz Ludwig Michel," *Colonial Williamsburg: The Journal of the Colonial Williamsburg Foundation*, Vol. 20, No. 4, Summer 1998, pp. 23-31

47. Selig, Robert A. "Swiss Anabaptists to Virginia? Franz Ludwig Michel's Journey to Williamsburg," *German Life*, Vol. 6, No. 1, June/July, 1999, pp. 42-45

48. Stegall, Joel. "From Roanoke to Pembroke: Lumbee and Smilings of Robeson County, North Carolina,"

Torch, Vol. 95, No. 2, winter 2022, pp. 13-17

49. Todd, Vincent H. and Julius Goebel, editors. "Christoph Graffenried's Account of the Founding of New Bern, *North Carolina Historical Commission,*" 1920

50. "Toward a Swiss American Colony," *Swiss American Historical Society Review,* vol. 48, no. 2, Article 3, 2012. Available at https://scholarsarchive.byu.edu/sahs_review/vol48/iss2/3. Oddly, authorship of this article is unattributed. However, its style, date and topical focus suggest that it was probably written by Andreas Mielke (see above).

51. Tracy, Grace and John Dern, *Pioneers of Old Monocacy: The Early Settlement of Frederick County, Maryland, 1721-1743,* Clearfield, 2001

52. Vann, Elizabeth and Margaret Dixon. *Virginia's First German Colony,* Literary Licensing, LLC, 1961

53. Vest, Jay. "Crossing Paths: Intersections between Louis Michel and Monacan Oral Traditions." *Native South,* Vol. 2, 2009 pp. 163-174. Also available at http://muse.jhu.edu/journals

54. Wallace, P. A. "Indians in Pennsylvania," The *Pennsylvania Historical and Museum Commission,* 1981

55. Wenger, Samuel. "1710 Pequea Settlement Tour Resource Information Booklet," Mennonite Historical Society, pp. 1-6, 1999. This report contains historical maps of the area and genealogical data of families who settled within each tract of the Pequea Settlement.

56. Wise, D. U., "The Pequea Silver Mine of Lancaster County, Pennsylvania," *Pennsylvania Geology,* Vol. 36, No. 1, Spring, 2006

57. Wise, D. U., "The Pequea Silver Mine, "*25th Annual Field Conference of Pennsylvania Geologists Guidebook,* Lancaster, Pennsylvania, pp. 53–59, 1960

58. Wust, Klaus. *The Virginia Germans,* University Press of Virginia, 1969

Digital

59. Curry, Dennis. *The Piscataway Indians in the Colonial*

Period, Maryland Historical Trust, https://www.academia.edu/6444318/_We_have_been e_with_the_Empeour_of_Pifcattaway_att_his_forte_The_ Piscataway_Indians_on_Heaters_Island

60. Goodhart, Briscoe. *The German Settlement*, publisher unknown,1900 http://www.lovettsvillehistoricalsociety.org/index.php/the-german-settlement-by-briscoe-goodhart-1900/

61. Graffenried, Christoph von. *Relation of My American Project*, 1716. https://books.xmediafile.com.

62. Haugh, Chris. *Monocacy* (video cassette), GS Communications, 1999

63. Haugh, Chris. *Sugarloaf* (video cassette), GS Communications, 2000

64. *North Carolina Colonial Records*, docsouth.unc.edu/csr/index/index.html/volumes/volume_01

65. Spannaus, Edward. "So you think your log house is old?," http://www.lovettsvillehistoricalsociety.org/index.php/a-most-excellent-barn-a-pennsylvania-german-barn-in-lovettsville/

66. Thornton, Richard. *Eyewitness Accounts to Early Indian Settlements in Shenandoah Valley,* accessed at https://accessgenealogy.com/virginia/eyewitness-accounts-to-early-indian-settlements-in-shenandoah-valley.htm

67. http://docsouth.unc.edu/csr/index/index.html/volumes/volume_01http://firstsettlersshenandoahvalley.com/index.html

68. https://en.wikipedia.org/wiki/Huguenots#North_America

69. http://firstsettlersshenandoahvalley.com/index.html

70. http://www.lovettsvillehistoricalsociety.org/?p=4776&preview=true

71. http://www.us-mining.com/virginia/front-royal/silver-mines

72. https://en.wikipedia.org/wiki/Exploration_of_North_America

73. https://mht.maryland.gov/documents/pdf/archeology/currentresearch/heatersisland.pdfhttps://military.wikia.org/wiki/HMS_Nassau_ (1699) June 19, 2021

74. https://mht.maryland.gov/documents/pdf/archeology/currentresearch/conoy-last-appearance.pdf

75. https://scholarsarchive.byu.edu/sahs_reviewscholarsarchive@byu.edu, ellen_amatangelo@byu.edu

76. https://threedecks.org/index.php?display_type=show_ship&id=178 June 19, 2021

77. https://unchartedlancaster.com/2020/03/20/sidequest-explore-the-300-year-old-pequea-silver-mine/

78. https://www.ancestry.com/genealogy/records/anna-barbara-vonlerber-24-121shbj

79. https://www.axios.com/afghan-refugee-private-sponsorship-biden-ed9a2793-4482-42c0-8b73-aedf4cd9ce45.html?utm_source=newsletter&utm_medium=email&utm_campaign=newsletter_axiosam&stream=top

80. https://www.cbsnews.com/news/north-america-has-lost-nearly-3-billion-birds-since-1970-study-released-today-2019-09-19/

81. https://www.dmme.virginia.gov/DGMR/silver.shtml

82. https://www.familysearch.org/wiki/en/Sigriswil_Parish,_Bern,_Switzerland_Genealogy#Marriages

83. https://www.geni.com/people/AnnaMichael/6000000013176503585

84. https://www.myheritage.com/names/anna_lerber

85. https://www.nap.edu/read/5355/chapter/7

86. La Grave, Jean. *Michael Family- From Switzerland to the United States: Information about Andrew (Andreas) Michael I,* https://www.genealogy.com/ftm/l/a/g/Jean-Lagrave/ website-0001/UHP-0001.html

87. Scheel, Eugene. Lovettsville, a German Settlement, lovettsvillehistoricalsociety.org/index.php /664

88. Spannaus, Edward, "Looking for our Palatine German

ancestors: A short trip to New York's Mohawk Valley"
http://www.lovettsvillehistoricalsociety.org/?p=4776&preview=true

89. Zipp, Nanne van der. "Ritter, George" (17th/18th centuries). *Global Anabaptist Mennonite Encyclopedia Online*, 1959. Retrieved 23 January 2022, from https://gameo.org/index.php?title=Ritter,_George_(17th/18th_centuries)&oldid=146178

FIRST EXPLORER

Index

Years 1291-1999

1291 · 6
1419 · 274, 278, 309
1614 · 229
1634 · 7, 83, 278, 280
1649 · 18, 84, 119, 281
1670 · 100
1670 map · 13
1675 · 9, 281, 320
1683 · 118, 281
1688 · 118, 281
1699 · 11, 38, 93, 94, 234, 323
1700 · 5, 12, 17, 26, 32, 34, 39, 65, 224, 234, 282, 292
1701 · 11, 17, 22, 69, 94, 117, 216, 272, 282, 317, 319
1701-04 journal, Michel's · 11, 69, 216
1702 · 9, 4, 12, 15, 17, 19, 23, 25, 26, 32, 33, 36, 41, 43, 45, 66, 67, 72, 75, 76, 85, 106, 107, 110, 111, 112, 120, 226, 231, 272, 282, 283, 295, 297, 313, 317, 319, 320, 341
1703 · 26, 33, 72, 74, 83, 115, 117, 283, 319
1704 · 9, 4, 6, 7, 10, 13, 15, 17, 19, 32, 44, 72, 75, 76, 79, 83, 84, 85, 86, 88, 90, 95, 97, 99, 101, 107, 110, 112, 117, 124, 125, 131, 132, 135, 170, 174, 226, 229, 231, 242, 247, 265, 270, 283, 285, 293, 298, 304, 319
1704 map, Michel's · 4, 7, 10, 14, 72, 229, 247, 285
1705 · 16, 17, 19, 73, 75, 94, 112, 117, 119, 284
1707 · 15, 87, 94, 107, 124, 129, 132, 179, 284, 320
1708 · 125, 126, 128, 211, 228, 265, 284, 287
1709 · 121, 132, 134, 164, 166, 167, 168, 180, 284, 285, 314, 318
1710 · 15, 20, 39, 84, 85, 94, 100, 107, 112, 116, 118, 119, 129, 130, 134, 135, 158, 159, 161, 162, 163, 174, 188, 189, 192, 194, 199, 200, 217, 225, 229, 235, 261, 270, 286, 303, 304, 321
1711 · 19, 166, 176, 177, 180, 286, 287, 319, 320, 341
1712 · 15, 94, 174, 180, 181, 210, 262, 287, 317
1713 · 182, 183, 186, 187, 189, 191, 214, 240, 288, 304, 305, 310
1714 · 66, 174, 178, 179, 187, 189, 210, 288
1715 · 72, 183, 211, 212, 240, 288
1716 · 15, 183, 210, 288, 304, 322
1717 · 216, 240, 289, 317

325

1719 · 210
1720 · 9, 47, 115, 177, 178,
    201, 211, 212, 216, 234,
    235, 236, 240, 271, 289,
    311, 320
1722 · 195, 196, 200, 235,
    290
1723 · 16, 19, 209, 227,
    261, 290
1725 · 35, 84, 264, 290,
    304
1728 · 72, 183, 197, 198,
    199, 203, 238, 268, 290
1729 · 84, 135, 206, 267,
    290
1730 · 84, 97, 99, 215, 230
1731 · 103, 132, 197, 199,
    201, 202, 203, 212, 267,
    283, 290, 291
1732 · 224, 225, 230, 291
1734 · 203, 227, 291
1736 · 84, 243, 291
1737 · 215
1738 · 206, 311
1740 · 215, 221, 291
1741 · 84, 100, 230
1743 · 215, 221, 243, 291,
    321
1745 · 84, 99, 243, 291
1746 · 9, 103, 178, 204,
    206, 207, 208, 212, 227,
    234, 235, 236, 238, 245,
    278, 291, 311
1748 · 84, 265, 292
1749 · 16, 206, 209, 211,
    262, 292, 319
1754 · 266
1758 · 243
1761 · 242, 243
1762 · 242, 243, 244, 292

1763 · 241, 242, 261, 292
1764 · 242, 244, 312
1767 · 127, 246, 292
1768 · 46, 293
1769 · 47, 224, 231
1776 · 118, 242, 246, 293
1780 · 118
1781 · 43, 137, 242, 256,
    257, 293
1783 · 248, 256, 258, 293,
    294
1786 · 247, 294
1787 · 183, 294
1796 · 248, 294
1800 · 294
1803 · 244
1828 · 267
1835 · 264
1854 · 243, 249
1880 · 25, 267
1883 · 228
1885 · 126, 196, 203, 208,
    294
1890 · 47, 48, 273, 295,
    307
1916 · 8, 216, 221, 272,
    295, 313, 317, 341
1926 · 267
1927 · 249
1935 · 267
1952 · 236, 273, 295, 308,
    316, 320
1970 · 264, 267, 323
1980s · 50
1983 · 262, 295
1989 · 273, 274, 309

FIRST EXPLORER

Twentieth Century

2000 · 46, 274, 309
2012 · 49, 90, 247, 260, 296, 319, 320, 321, 341
2017 · 249
2021 · 52, 243, 260, 296, 310, 320, 323
2022 · 7, 9, 3, 38, 112, 189, 234, 243, 260, 269, 275, 280, 297, 313, 316, 318, 321, 324

A

Aarau, Switzerland · 8
Aboriginal path · 247, 266
African immigrants · 224
Alaska · 51
Albany, New York · 229
Aldermanbury, London · 190
Alderson, Carolyn · 270, 316
Algonquian languages · 92, 101
Allegheny Front of Appalachian Range · 231
Alsace, France · 5, 67, 225, 308
Alsatians · 225, 226
American Revolution · 94, 273, 318
Amish · 18, 116, 135
Amsterdam, The Netherlands · 19, 67
Anabaptists · 4, 119, 313, 320

Anne, Queen of Englamd· 53, 75, 121, 164, 225, 285
Anglicizing Michel's name · 196, 232
Annapolis, Maryland · 10, 75, 76, 83, 84, 86, 87, 88, 90, 102, 105, 106, 107, 117, 119, 183, 191, 229, 245, 283, 298
Appalachian Range· 9, 13, 22, 43, 80, 83, 84, 91, 93, 100, 102, 104, 105, 229, 265
Arcata Bay, California · 48
Archeological dig at Canoy· 264
Ark and *Dove* settler ships· 83
Articles of Confederation.,· 246
Atlantic coast · 7, 9, 6, 1, 12, 17, 18, 43, 78, 80, 229, 230
Atlantic Ocean · 15, 24, 56, 66, 229
Atlantic seaboard · 9, 6, 83, 216, 228

B

Ballenger Creek · 9, 95, 248, 266
Ballenger Creek Pike · 9, 95, 248, 266
Baltimore, Maryland · 84, 93, 127, 247, 264
Bankrolling foreign expeditions, Georg Ritter's

· 17
Baptism · 4, 72
Barnwell, John · 181, 287
Baron as Graffenried's
  purchased title · 180,
  214, 219, 221, 285
Basel, Switzerland · 11, 22,
  66
Bath, England · 229
Beatty-Cramer House · 230
Bending history · 82
Bern Public Library · 72
Bern, Switzerland
  (contemporary) · 274
Berne, Switzerland
  (historical) · 7, 5, 6, 8, 9,
  17, 18, 19, 23, 33, 36, 42,
  65, 66, 68, 73, 74, 75, 76,
  83, 107, 110, 111, 115,
  119, 120, 129, 133, 134,
  158, 163, 166, 167, 168,
  172, 174, 176, 177, 178,
  179, 180, 183, 187, 188,
  191, 209, 214, 218, 220,
  221, 227, 229, 258, 268,
  269, 274, 282, 283, 285,
  287, 288, 291, 310, 313,
  316, 317, 319
Berne Canton, Switzerland ·
  8, 108, 110, 129, 176,
  313
Berners-Lee, Sir Tim · 274
Bison · 50, 51, 52
**Blankenbaker, John ·
175**
Block to exploration,
  Appalachians as · 229
Blue Ridge Mountains,
  Virginia· 12, 43, 85, 87,
  100, 103, 104, 131, 200,

231
Bogus title, Graffenried's ·
  214
Bordewich, Fergus · 48
Born explorer, Frantz
  Ludwig Michel as · 17,
  106
Botanicals importer, George
  Ritter as · 16
Both parents died, myth
  that · 234
Braght, Thieleman van · 4,
  281
Britain · 6, 8, 12, 19, 36,
  43, 45, 65, 66, 87, 115,
  118, 121, 130, 132, 133,
  165, 170, 189, 226, 284,
  289, 292
British citizen,
  naturalization as · 168,
  242
British citizenship · 9, 112,
  129, 168, 181, 192, 196,
  232, 285, 286
British Crown · 17, 262
British Lords of Trade and
  Plantations · 119, 132,
  262, 314
Buffalo · 48, 51
Buffalo County, South
  Dakota · 49
Bunhill Fields Cemetery,
  London · 190
Burgerbibliothek Bern · 69,
  316, 319
Burns, Brendon · 271, 316

C

California · 48
Calvert, Cecil · 13
Camp David presidential retreat · 92
Carolina Trail. · 95
Carolinas · 41, 85, 86, 94, 95, 132, 165, 168, 186, 188, 218, 228, 240
Carroll, Charles of Carrollton · 247
Carroll Creek · 96
Carrollton Manor · 247, 273
Catoctin Mountain · 9, 91, 92, 105, 229, 243, 247, 312
Catoctin Valley · 243, 256
Centrentua, Michel's rendition of Shenandoah as· 101
CEOs as most psychopathic occupation · 219
Charles County, Maryland · 93
· 251, 253
Chartier, Martin · 174, 263
Chattoka Indian village · 176
Chesapeake and Ohio Canal · 93, 264, 265
Chesapeake Bay · 45, 56, 83, 93, 229
Chief Hancock · 181
Christustraegern Bruderschaft · 8
Cline, Anna Michael · 307, 318
"Coast on titled privilege" · 251
Colonel Louis Mitchell· 228
Commissioner of Mines, Michel as Pennsylvania's · 20, 107, 116, 117, 118, 158
Competing lines of reasoning on Michel sons' parentage · 234
Conestoga Indians · 126, 128, 135, 261, 292
Confiscation of Mennonite property, Swiss · 5
Conoy Indians and village· 10, 88, 92, 93, 94, 95, 96, 97, 99, 100, 101, 105, 121, 124, 131, 132, 228, 229, 230, 242, 247, 259, 260, 261, 264, 265, 268, 288, 294, 296, 297, 298, 316
Conoy Island · 94, 264
Constitutional Convention · 183
Continuing enmity, Graffenried'a. · 214
Contraband, Graffenried's · 179, 218
Cooling Springs · 238, 244, 247, 248, 249, 250, 257, 265, 266, 293, 294, 295, 296, 298, 307
Courthouse fire, King William County's· 196, 208, 295
Cresap, Thomas · 84
Crewe, Mildred Michael · 234, 236, 257, 273, 274,

295, 305, 308
Crow Creek Indian
   Reservation · 49
Crutch of title · 251

D

Darwin, Charles · 251, 253
Declaration of Independence
   · 247
Declared mentally
   incompetent, Graffenried ·
   215
Delaware · 127
Detroit · 94
Diaspora of Indians · 50, 52
"Died among the Indians" ·
   178, 289, 295
Director of Mines, Michel as
   Pennsylvania · 129, 134,
   171, 189, 199, 286
Divided among sons,
   Cooling Springs · 252,
   266
Dixon, Jeremiah · 127
Dulaney, Daniel · 243, 291
Dutton, Kevin · 219

E

Earliest American
   exploration · 6
Eastern seaboard of the
   United States. · 91, 229
Economic opportunity in
   nature, Michel's 1707
   search for · 124
Embarrassed father,
   Graffenried's · 214, 218

England · 17, 18, 19, 22,
   26, 27, 31, 33, 36, 39, 40,
   47, 53, 59, 64, 75, 80, 83,
   99, 108, 117, 176, 224,
   227, 228, 230, 262, 282,
   313
England's Atlantic coast
   colonies · 80
Europe · 6, 4, 16, 25, 32,
   43, 44, 45, 47, 58, 59, 65,
   66, 67, 79, 81, 99, 107,
   116, 117, 125, 133, 164,
   167, 173, 186, 187, 214,
   230, 240, 241, 258, 313
European diseases · 94
European nobility · 7, 166
European royalty · 7
European settlement of
   America · 85, 86, 95, 105,
   182, 229
European Union, today's · 6
Evangelical Lutheran
   Church of Frederick · 84,
   242, 243, 312

F

Fall line of America's east
   coast tivers · 43, 66, 87,
   91, 229
Father for the first time,
   Michel as · 128
Fauna and flora, American ·
   51, 58
Faust, A.B. · 227
Federation of the Rhine · 5,
   67
Fels, Ursula · 8
Fever, Michel's 1702

Virginia · 29, 58, 59, 60, 80
First head of state, John Hanson as United States · 246
Flag Pond tract addition to Cooking Springs · 247, 294
Florida · 65
Fogelman, Aaron · 224, 225, 317
Food stamps · 49
Fort Hancock, North Carolina · 228
Foundry, the Michael · 244, 246, 247, 251
Four sons not orphaned · 236
Franklin, Benjamin · 183, 201
Frederick, Maryland · 4, 44, 47, 84, 85, 95, 96, 241, 242, 243, 244, 246, 247, 248, 249, 261, 265, 266, 271, 272, 274, 292, 293, 306, 313, 319, 320, 321
Frederick County, Maryland · 4
Fredericktowne, Maryland · 84, 96, 99, 241, 242, 244, 291
Freedom of religion · 106, 116, 118, 136, 228, 281
French and Indian War · 136, 237, 241, 292
French privateers · 163
Furnace Mountain · 91, 97

G

Galley, *HMS Nassau*'s · 28, 29, 60, 220
Gann Valley, South Dakota · 49
Geneva, Switzerland · 11
Galton, Francis · 251, 253
George I, King of England · 247
Georg Ritter & Co. · 129
German miners, Germanna's · 174, 200, 268, 287, 288
German Settlement, The · 98, 99, 225, 226, 230, 258, 267, 291, 298, 322, 323
Germanna, Virginia · 175, 197, 198, 199, 200, 201, 202, 203, 204, 205, 206, 245, 268, 288, 289, 290, 291, 316
Germantown, Pennsylvania · 77, 117, 118, 133, 225, 281, 283
Germantown Quaker Petition Against Slavery · 118
Gibraltar · 26, 66
Gottstatt, Switzerland · 8
Graffenried, Christoph von or family · 4, 10, 102, 107, 125, 129, 130, 131, 132, 134, 158, 159, 164, 165, 166, 167, 168, 169, 170, 171, 172, 173, 175,

176, 177, 178, 179, 180, 181, 188, 191, 211, 214, 215, 216, 217, 218, 220, 221, 222, 261, 262, 268, 269, 279, 284, 285, 286, 287, 288, 289, 291, 295, 305, 312, 317, 320, 321, 322
Graffenried's memoir · 216, 217
Grand vision, the Michel-Ritter-Ochs · 78, 79, 232
Grasslands · 51
Grave sites unknown · 256
Gravesend, England · 65
Great Council of Berne · 5, 18, 167
Great Falls, Maryland · 87, 88, 91, 121, 131, 265
Great Law of Peace, Iriquoian · 183
Great Plains · 49, 50, 51, 52
Great Trading Place · 93, 94, 97, 131, 261

H

Half urban, half rural, US in 1922 · 252
Hanson, United States President John · 43, 246, 293, 318
Harper's Ferry, West Virginia · 101, 125
Harrison, Burr · 93
Heater's Island (Conoy), Maryland · 94, 264
Hefner, D'Nise · 274
Heredity · 24, 250

Herman, Augustine · 13, 14, 15, 100, 102
Hickman, Margaret · 273, 274, 295, 317
High Alps · 8
High dopamine, adventurers' endowment of · 24, 252
Hinke, William · 8, 10, 216, 221, 272, 295
History-bending · 6
Hite, Jost · 230
HMS Nassau · 59
Hole in the ship · 63
Holy Roman Empire · 6
Homestead Act of 1862 · 51
Huguenot refugees · 40, 116
Humane instincts of the Trio · 17, 56, 74
Humanitarian actions of Trio · 9, 13, 6, 1, 6, 16, 17, 19, 20, 36, 54, 70, 73, 74, 75, 79, 81, 104, 110, 133, 135, 158, 182, 187, 209, 210, 222, 226, 227, 228, 231, 232, 246, 296
Humanitarian triumph · 226
Hurricane, 1702 Atlantic · 62, 64, 69, 80, 110, 283
Hutterites · 4, 18

I

Imaginary baroncy, Graffenried's · 215
Indian Island, California · 48
Indian populations · 48, 49, 50, 224

Indian reservations · 48, 50
Indians, American · 4, 6, 37, 47, 48, 49, 50, 51, 52, 53, 54, 58, 78, 89, 94, 124, 131, 176, 178, 182, 220, 228, 229, 263, 287, 289, 295, 316, 322
Inherited iron implements, Michael Foundry · 245
Involuntary expulsion of Mennonites, Swiss · 5
Iroquois Indians · 182, 261, 289
Iroquois Six Nations Confederation · 182
Isoth, Petter · 129, 262, 286

J

Juan Carlos, Michel descendant King of Spain · 7

K

Kansas · 49
Killing the White Man's Indian · 48
King Charles III, United Kingdom's · 7
King William County Courthouse · 264
Knights of the Golden Horseshoe expedition, Alexander Spotwood's · 200

L

Lack of curiosity · 229
Lagrave, Jean · 274
Lake Thun, Switzerland · 8, 212
Landgrave title, Graffenried's · 166, 218, 221, 286
Lausanne, Switzerland · 11
Lawson, John · 165, 177, 274, 285, 287
Lederer, John · 100
Lerber, Anna Barbara von · 59, 73, 104, 110, 256, 284
Lerber family · 59, 114
Lerber, Frantz Ludwig von · 42, 110, 114 · 110
Lerber, Madlain von · 11
Lerber sisters · 36, 59, 110, 282
Licksville, Maryland · 261
"Like none before him" · 226
Limit of navigability, east coast rivers' · 91
"Little Old Englishman," Graffenried letter · 172
London, England · 6, 8, 22, 27, 60, 65, 66, 72, 74, 76, 83, 87, 107, 110, 111, 115, 117, 119, 121, 130, 131, 132, 134, 164, 165, 166, 168, 174, 179, 180, 186, 227, 240, 262, 282, 283, 284, 292, 319
Long Acre tract · 244

Long distance hiker, Michel
as · 6, 10, 89, 253
Longhouses, Indian · 102,
183, 264
Lord Fairfax, Virginia
proprietor · 230
Lords of Ralligen · 6, 7, 8,
23, 68, 166, 208, 309
Lord of Worb · 129, 169,
180
Lords of Trade and
Plantations, British · 119,
121, 134, 158, 164, 189,
284, 285, 291, 304
Lorraine, France · 67
Louis XIV, King of France ·
11, 132
Love of long-distance hiking
· 9
Lovettsville, Virginia · 99,
230, 267, 271, 323
Lovettsville Historical
Society · 267
Luxembourg · 67

M

Make-believe baroncy,
Graffenried's · 218
Mannix, Mary · 271
Map-maker son · 253
Mason, Charles · 127
Massacre · 48, 182, 183
Massanutten Range · 9, 87,
91, 102, 103, 174
Master engraver, Ochs as ·
16
Mattaponi Indians· 36, 42,
53, 55, 56, 110, 111, 112,
228, 240, 259, 264, 297
Mattaponi, Virginia · 59
Medieval feudal practices ·
250
Mediterranean Sea · 26, 65,
66
Mennonism · 114
Mennonite religion· 5, 9, 19,
40, 42, 72, 73, 74, 75, 79,
112, 114, 118, 120, 188,
209, 212, 221, 258, 270,
284, 319, 320, 341
Mennonite beliefs · 40, 238
Mennonites · 4, 5, 18, 19,
33, 42, 73, 74, 75, 114,
115, 116, 119, 258, 281,
282, 286
Metzger, Teresa · 270, 305
Michael, Andreas/Andrew ·
13, 8, 11, 74, 102, 211,
221, 234, 242, 243, 246,
247, 248, 266, 270, 289,
292, 293, 294, 296, 305,
310, 313, 319, 320, 321,
323, 341
Michael, Christopher · 248,
314
Michael, David, · 249
Michael Foundry · 245, 292,
293
Michael, Francis · 190, 195,
196, 197, 198, 199, 201,
202, 203, 204, 205, 206,
207, 208, 209, 212, 223,
227, 232, 235, 239, 248,
266, 268, 271, 289, 290,
291, 292, 293, 305, 308,
311
Michael, Hayden · 278
Michael, Marion S. · 307,

318
Michael, Nicholas · 211, 242, 243, 248, 310
Michael, Pierce B., Sr. · 274, 318
Michael Road · 248
Michael, Samuel · 273, 274, 295, 307, 31
Michael, Vicki · 275, 296
Michael, William· 211, 212, 241, 242, 244, 248, 288, 310
Michael's Branch of Rapidan River · 197
Michel, Andrew · 4, 201, 227, 238, 241, 242, 243, 244, 245, 246, 247, 248, 249, 250, 253, 257, 260, 265, 266, 273, 293, 294, 295, 306, 308, 309, 312, 323
Michel, Christopher · 243, 266, 313
Michel, Hans Ludwig · 86, 272, 283, 319
Michel, Heinzmann · 274, 278, 309
Michel, Johann Ludwig · 8
Michel's finest moment · 182
Michel's legacy · 226
Michel's outpost · 128
Michel's tone toward Indians · 94
Michel von Schwertschwendi, Berthold · 7
Michel von Schwertschwendi, David · 7, 9, 309

Michel von Schwertschwendi, Itel · 6, 250, 278
Michel Virginia 1718 land record · 183
Michel Virginia 1722 land record · 183
Middle Ages · 7
Mielke, Andreas · 13, 8, 11, 74, 102, 221, 270, 296, 305, 321
Militzary service, Michel's · 17, 42, 227, 282
Misrepresentations, Graffenried's of Michel · 312
Monocacy River · 84, 87, 91, 174, 242, 298
Monocacy River Valley · 91, 97, 131, 136
Moren, Debi · 272
"Most important American traveller of his time" · 13, 11
Mount Olivet Cemetery · 249
Mr. Clark · 90, 102
Myers, Margaret · 249, 272, 296

N

Nassau, the *HMS*· 23, 25, 26, 27, 28, 29, 30, 31, 32, 60, 62, 64, 65, 66, 81, 282, 323
Nation's oldest courthouse · 207
National Archives · 87, 132

National Register of Historic
  Places · 35, 199
National Road · 244
Native Americans · 48, 49,
  52
Natural philosophy · 11
Naturalist, Michel as · 11,
  28, 32, 45, 62, 81
Nemesis of Michel,
  Graffenried as · 102
Netherlands, The · 18, 19,
  22, 65, 66, 67, 75, 189,
  209
Never-satisfied curiosity · 17
New Bern, North Carolina
  (contemporary) · 4, 10,
  216, 217, 220, 268, 316,
  321
New Berne, North Carolina
  (historical) · 3, 122, 129,
  158, 161, 162, 163, 166,
  169, 172, 174, 176, 177,
  178, 180, 186, 191, 206,
  207, 208, 215, 217, 221,
  229, 268, 286, 287, 299,
  304
New World · 6, 17, 18, 44,
  58, 69, 78, 83, 86, 90, 94,
  106, 175, 208, 212
New York city and state ·
  94, 179, 182, 225, 226,
  229, 261, 289, 324
Newton, Sir Isaac · 210,
  262, 289, 290
Nicholson, Virginia
  Governor Francis· 33, 34,
  173
No known images of Francis
  or Anna Michael · 232
No known memoir of
  Francis Michael · 216
Nobility crutch · 253
North Carolina · 10, 15, 36,
  37, 132, 134, 158, 164,
  167, 168, 175, 176, 178,
  180, 181, 182, 214, 217,
  220, 229, 261, 268, 274,
  285, 286, 287, 289, 316,
  317, 321, 322
November 5, 1781, founding
  date of the United States ·
  246, 293
Number of refugees · 227

O

Ochs home · 73
Ochs, Eva · 72
Ochs, Johann Rudolph · 4,
  16, 33, 72, 73, 115, 209,
  232, 261, 282, 284, 292
Ochs, Judith. · 129
Ohio River · 84, 131
Oldtown, Maryland · 84
Oligarchy of Bernese
  nobility · 18
Oneida Indians · 101, 182
Opening a new continent ·
  231
Orange County, Virginia ·
  204, 205, 206, 291
Original Americans · 52
Oxford University · 219, 317

P

Palatinate, the · 165
Palatine · 132, 165, 217,
  285, 323

Palatine refugees · 132, 285
Pamunkey Indians · 53, 55, 56, 228, 259, 264, 297
Patawomeck (Potomac River) · 92
Paupers, Swiss · 11
Peace treaties · 181, 228, 287
Pelts · 53, 125
Penn, William · 4, 18, 74 77, 79, 115, 117, 118, 127, 130, 133, 134, 135, 189, 199, 210, 262, 281, 286, 289
Penn, William, Jr. · 117
Penn's Quaker philosophy of religious tolerance · 115
Pequea Colony, Pennsylvania · 84, 85, 94, 97, 100, 118, 119, 122, 126, 129, 134, 135, 136, 137, 158, 159, 161, 170, 171, 180, 183, 191, 199, 206, 207, 226, 229, 230, 234, 237, 238, 246, 258, 261, 263, 267, 280, 283, 284, 286, 287, 289, 290, 292, 304, 306, 316, 317, 321
Persecution, religious · 4, 5, 18, 36, 42, 73, 110, 118, 244
Pharmaceuticals manufacturer, Georg Ritter as · 16
Philadelphia, Pennsylvania · 76, 77, 116, 117, 118, 119, 127, 128, 135, 173, 183, 191, 225, 229, 230, 283
Pirates · 30, 31, 60, 61, 75, 80, 163
Piscataway Indians · 93, 259, 296, 321
Piscataway-Conoy Tribe · 259
Point of Rocks, Maryland · 91, 92, 95, 261, 264, 271, 294
Point of Rocks Road · 95
Poorest United States county · 49
Port Tobacco, Maryland · 119, 260
Postmaster General of North America, Alexander Spotswood as · 201
Potomac River · 4, 41, 43, 84, 87, 91, 92, 93, 95, 96, 121, 124, 131, 136, 177, 228, 230, 264, 298
Poverty line, United States · 49
Prairie, North American · 51
Price, William · 183
Privileged comforts · 17
Probate record, Frantz Ludwig Michel's absence of · 208
Protect his reputation · 188
Protective cloak of nobility · 251
Protestant Reformation · 4
Psychopaths · 219, 220
Psychopathy · 219
Public Record Office, British · 87, 132
Public-private partnership between Michel-Ritter-

Ochs trio and British government · 5, 78, 108, 226

Q

Quaker refuge, Pennsylvania as · 115
Quaker religious tolerance · 117
Quakers · 4, 18, 116

R

Ralligen, Switzerland · 4, 7, 9, 66, 80, 107, 115, 124, 129, 208, 248, 250, 268, 269, 278, 280, 281, 341
Ralligen castle · 8
Rapidan River · 197, 212
Rappahannock River · 197, 204
Real estate purchases, Michael sons' · 237
Reconnaissance of opportunities, Michel 1702 Virginia exploration as · 17
Re-entering Switzerland after expulsion · 5
Refugee livelihood · 124
Regression toward the mean · 250, 252, 272
Relation of My American Project, Graffenried's memoir · 215, 218, 322
Religious freedom · 231
Religious refugees · 16, 19, 22, 33, 34, 75, 79, 104, 108, 135, 187, 210, 212, 227, 258, 281, 285
Rafugee resettlement · 6, 17, 19, 33, 36, 78, 118, 120, 130, 133, 134, 135, 136, 158, 186, 187, 209, 211, 224, 226, 241, 261, 295
Revolutionary War, American · 3, 45, 137, 224, 246, 256, 257
Rhine River · 5, 15, 22, 66, 67, 120, 134, 187, 209, 282
Ritter, Elisabetha · 72, 282
Ritter, Georg · 16, 19, 33, 75, 107, 115, 119, 129, 135, 164, 169, 174, 179, 209, 232, 261, 262, 282, 284, 290
Roman Catholic Church · 4
Route that their father had walked · 247

S

Sanctuaries · 16
Sandy Hook, Maryland · 125
Savoy, Mervin · 259, 296
Schaffhausen, Switzerland · 67, 69
Scheel, Eugene · 98, 270
Schmid, Ship's Captain · 59
Selig, Robert · 270, 295
Self-rehabilitation · 217
Seven Years War · 241
Sharpsburg, Maryland · 248
Shawnee Indians · 102, 117, 119, 126, 170, 260, 263, 280, 284, 292, 294

FIRST EXPLORER

Shenandoah National Park, · 267
Shenandoah River · 10, 91, 97, 103, 124, 131, 164, 228, 298
Shenandoah Valley · 9, 10, 12, 14, 15, 78, 85, 100, 101, 103, 104, 105, 120, 121, 122, 124, 125, 126, 132, 134, 158, 164, 165, 170, 183, 199, 200, 207, 226, 230, 258, 260, 262, 266, 267, 283, 285, 287, 289, 290, 291, 292, 304, 314, 322, 341
Ship logs · 237, 238, 239, 309
Side trip, Michel's 1704· 10, 91, 95, 96, 99, 228, 242, 247, 265, 266, 298
Silver · 46, 102, 103, 116, 117, 125, 126, 169, 170, 171, 173, 174, 177, 253, 322, 323
Sinn, Maria Barbel "Barbara" · 243
Sioux Nation · 50
Sky Stage, Michael Foundry's modern use as· 245
Smallpox · 94, 100
Smallwood, Colonel James · 94
Smuggling · 179, 218
Social elite · 18
Society for the Swiss Colony of Virginia · 132, 164
Society of Friends, Quaker faith's · 118
Sons as orphans, myth of Michel's · 234
Sons as Virginians, Michel's · 234
South Carolina · 9, 10, 15, 107, 174, 181, 182, 183, 193, 196, 209, 210, 211, 220, 227, 240, 258, 287, 288, 304, 316
Spanish Empire · 65, 66
Spannaus, Edward · 99, 271, 322, 323
Speaking trumpet · 31, 61, 64
Spirit of the adventurer · 64
Spotswood, Virginia Governor Alexander · 72, 174, 197, 198, 199, 200, 201, 203, 205, 230, 245, 268, 281, 286, 288, 289, 290, 291
Spotswood Mansion · 199
Spotswood's mismanagement of Germanna · 198
Spotsylvania County, Virginia · 197, 198, 199, 200, 201, 202, 203, 204, 205, 290
St. Clement's Island, Maryland · 260
St. Martin's Day · 179, 180
Stepsons, Michel's · 205, 239
Stone, Maryland Governor William · 18, 84, 106, 263, 280, 281
Sugarloaf Mountain · 87, 91, 298
Sun Is Down and the Moon Is Up tract· 243, 248, 266

Sunderlin, Bridget · 270
Superior execution, Michel's
  · 232
Susquehanna Path · 84, 95,
  97, 230
Susquehanna River · 94, 97,
  126, 230, 267
Swiss Colonization Society ·
  172, 175, 287
Swiss Confederation · 6, 8
Swiss federal state · 6
Swiss Federation · 18, 228
Swiss fiefdoms · 6
Swiss national capital · 8
Swiss national historic
  landmark, Ralligen Castle
  as · 8
Swiss nobility · 6, 130, 218
Swiss religious refugees ·
  16, 35, 115

T

Tasker's Chance · 243, 244
Tayac, Conoy Chief Billy
  Redwing · 259, 260, 296
Terra incognita · 101
Thames River, England · 22,
  24, 65, 67
"The Baron had no credit" ·
  176
The Michael Family, Mildred
  Michael Crewe's · 273,
  295, 308, 316
The Wisdom of Psychopaths
  · 219
Thirteen colonies · 36, 106,
  137, 224, 242
Thunersee, Switzerland, the

· 8
Tidewater Virginia · 17
Tobacco · 45, 46, 53, 59,
  63, 314
Trapping · 125, 126
Treaty of Paris, first (1763) ·
  241, 292
Treaty of Utrecht · 187
Tuscarora Indians · 176,
  177, 181, 182, 228, 261,
  274, 287, 289, 316
Tuscarora War · 177, 261
Twentieth century · 51
Twenty-one generations of
  Michel/Michael family ·
  250

U

UNESCO World Heritage
  Site · 269
Unexplored territory · 89,
  101
Unfinished business · 198
United States Federal
  Refugee Resettlement
  Program · 5
University of Bern · 262
Unwanted religions,
  Switzerland's · 17
Urmston, John · 176
Utopia of personal
  freedoms, Penn's
  Pennsylvania as · 116

V

Vandercastle, Giles · 93
Virginia piedmont · 85, 231

W

Wachter, Nancy Michael · 274, 305, 309
War of the League of Augsburg · 11
War of the Spanish Succession · 65, 75, 107, 120, 187, 189, 210
Ward of the state, Graffenried committed as · 215, 219, 221, 291
West Virginia Route 115 · 101
Western Maryland · 15, 84, 85, 265, 284
Widowerhood, Francis Michael's · 201
Wild continent, North America as · 17
Williamsburg, Virginia · 34, 38, 39, 40, 41, 53, 85, 231, 270, 296, 320, 341
William, King of England · 35, 36, 39, 53, 54, 55, 131, 180, 183, 191, 226, 228, 240, 258, 259, 263, 264, 304
Wiyot Indians · 48
Worb, Switzerland and castle · 179, 214, 215, 262, 288, 291
World's largest private landowner, William Penn as · 116
Wurttemberg, Confederation of the Rhine · 67, 69
Wust, Klaus · 272, 295

Y

Yelton, Sandra · 8, 221, 270, 296, 319, 320, 341
York River · 32, 34, 41, 56
Yorktown, Virginia · 32, 41, 43, 58, 59, 85, 110, 282
Yverdon, Switzerland · 8, 317, 320

Z

Zekiah Swamp · 93

First Explorer

Endnotes

[1] Mielke, Andreas & Sandra Yelton. "Meanwhile in Bern," *Pennsylvania Mennonite Heritage*, Vol. 24, No. 2, April, 2011, pp. 54-55.

[2] Mielke and Yelton, who have researched Frantz Ludwig Michel more deeply than anyone, show Frantz Ludwig Michel as the son of an unnamed governor of Burgdorf, a district in northwest Bern Canton. They cite no sources for their claim, which is at odds with the multiple sources used here that all show Michel as the son of David Michel von Schwertschwendi, the Lord of Ralligen, 27 miles (43 kilometers) south of Burgdorf. For the Burgdorf claim, see Mielke, Andreas and Sandra Yelton. "America Guide" by Johann Rudolf Ochs, 1711 (translation), *Swiss American Historical Society Review*, Vol. 48, No. 2, June 2012, p. 14.

[3] The author is a fourteenth-great-grandson of Berthold. https://gw.geneanet.org/cvpolier?lang=en&n=michel+von+schwertschwendi&oc=1&p=berthold

[4] https://www.christustraeger-bruderschaft.org

[5] Frantz was David Michel's third son, Beat and Sigissmund being older. If it was Frantz who inherited the title of Lord, this would indicate that Beat and Sigismund were not alive when their father died, or that they survived but were incapable of fulfilling the duties of the title, or perhaps had fallen out of favor.

[6] Frantz Ludwig Michel's digitized baptismal record is filed in a historical database of the Bern Public Library.

[7] Hinke, William J., *The Virginia Magazine of History and Biography*, Vol. XXIV, No. 1, January, 1916, p. 2

[8] Selig, Robert A. "Wilhelmsburg in the Year 1702: The Account of Franz Ludwig Michel," *Colonial Williamsburg: The Journal of the Colonial Williamsburg Foundation*, Vol. 20, No.4, Summer 1998, pp. 23-31

[9] Mielke, op. cit., p. 2

[10] Thornton, Richard. Eyewitness Accounts to Early Indian Settlements in Shenandoah Valley, accessed at https://accessgenealogy.com/virginia/eyewitness-

accounts-to-early-indian-settlements-in-shenandoah-valley.htm

[11] https://en.wikipedia.org/wiki/Exploration_of_North_America

[12] One sees both Georg and George in references to Ritter. George is sometimes found in documents translated into English and Georg in their Swiss German originals. His name was Georg.

[13] Kemper, Charles E. "Documents Relating to Early Projected Swiss Colonies in the Valley of Virginia, 1706-1709," *Virginia Magazine of History and Biography*, Vol. XXIX January, 1921, No. 1, p. 7 footnote

[14] Ibid.

[15] Colonial Maryland Governor William Stone (1603-1660) was the ninth-great-grandfather of the author.

[16] The Kingdom of Great Britain was formed May 1, 1707. Before that the sovereign authority was England.

[17] Selig, op. cit., p. 4

[18] This from the journal that Michel kept covering the period from his departure from Berne to his return there fourteen months later

[19] For an accessible, plain-English discussion of high dopamine individuals, the reader is referred to Freeland, Chrystia. *Plutocrats: The Rise of the New Global Super-Rich and the Fall of Everyone Else.* Penguin Books, 2013. This is a definitive dissection of American and international plutocracy.

[20] For more on American wanderlust, see the author's *Running on Empty: Along an Epic 12,000-Mile Road Trip America Has Its Say on Economic Inequality*, Underground Railroad Free Press, 2015. https://book-runningonempty.com/ROE/Home.html

[21] Quoted entries from Michel's journal are from the 1916 translation of the journal by William Hinke who was liberal in using grammatically correct English in his prod-

uct that could not always correspond to the original German. Hinke, William J. "Report of the Journey of Francis Louis Michel from Berne, Switzerland, to Virginia, October 2, 1701-December 1, 1702" (translation of the original), T*he Virginia Magazine of History and Biography,* Vol. XXIV, No. 1, January, 1916

[22] This paragraph is based on the article on Huguenots at https://en.wikipedia.org/wiki/Huguenots#North_America

[23] Stegall, Joel. "From Roanoke to Pembroke: Lumbee and Smilings of Robeson County, North Carolina, *Torch*, Vol. 95, No. 2, winter 2022

[24] Ibid., pp. 14-15

[25] This, the only known journal that Frantz Ludwig Michel ever kept, contains 124 pages of text on his Virginia stay, eighteen pages on his second journey to America, plans for a settlement in Virginia, and four illustrations with descriptions, the earliest known drawings of several Williamsburg buildings.

[26] The following note is found in the "Berne Year Book," page 83, about these women. "They were probably the daughters of Francis Ludwig Lerber, Secretary to the city treasurer of Berne, who had the following daughters: Anna Barbara, born 1675; Anna Magdalena, born 1676; Catharine, born 1678; Maria, born 1680; Johanna Margaretha, born 1682; and Barbara Elizabeth, born 1685. In the proceedings against the Anabaptists at that time the 'Lerber sisters' are mentioned. It is, therefore, probable, though not certain that they left Switzerland, because of their faith. In Brock's Huguenot Emigration to Virginia, page 33, 'Madame Herbert and her four daughters,' is mentioned as a Swiss settler."

[27] Today it is 8.6 million making Virginia the twelfth most populous state.

[28] https://www.cbsnews.com/news/north-america-has-lost-nearly-3-billion-birds-since-1970-study-released-

today-2019-09-19/

29 Most of what follows on the next few pages comes from the author's previous research for his book *Running on Empty: Along an Epic 12,000-Mile Road Trip America Has Its Say on Economic Inequality*.

30 Passel, Jeffrey, "The Growing American Indian Population, 1960–1990: Beyond Demography," *Changing Numbers, Changing Needs: American Indian Demography and Public Health*, National Academy Press, 1996

31 Michael, Peter, op. cit.

32 King William had died on March 19.

33 For more visit https://mattaponination.com/home.html

34 For more visit https://pamunkey.org.

35 Here he means a farm's outbuildings, not privies.

36 England had been one of the last major European countries to convert from the Julian calendar to the Gregorian calendar, introduced in 1582, which added eleven days to dates. Britain's American colonies did not get around to making the change until 1752.

37 In quite a career turn, Johann Rudolph Ochs would become a naturalized British citizen who ended up reporting to Sir Isaac Newton, the then director of the Royal Mint. See the entry for Ochs in the chapter Fates: People here for more.

38 "Toward a Swiss American Colony," *Swiss American Historical Society Review*, vol. 48, no. 2, Article 3, 2012, p. 11-12 (unattributed)

39 Ritter's father-in-law, Mr. Gaudot, from time to time aided the trio's work as when he would act on their behalf dealing with matters in Britain when requested.

40 Michel, Frantz Ludwig. "Michel's German Letter to Ochs: From London, May 6/16, 1703," *Swiss American Historical Society Review*, vol. 48, no. 2, Article 3, 2012

41 Mielke, op. cit., p. 18.

42 Michel, Frantz Ludwig. "Michel's German letter to Ochs: From Arundel Conti, Maryland, May 20/30, 1704" *Swiss American Historical Society Review*, vol. 48, no. 2, Article 3, 2012

43 Here Michel speaks of the prevalent practice of young Swiss noblemen with military training hiring themselves out as officer mercenaries to the highest bidder among warring European powers.

44 Selig, op. cit.

45 The world's oldest range is the Urals which form the demarcation between Europe and Asia.

46 Scheel, Eugene. "Lovettsville, a German Settlement," lovettsvillehistoricalsociety.org/index.php /664

47 Spannaus, Edward. "So you think your log house is old?,"http://www.lovettsvillehistoricalsociety.org/index. php/a-most-excellent-barn-a-pennsylvania-german-barn-in-lovettsville

48 Mielke, op. cit., p. 38.

49 Colonial Maryland Governor William Stone was the author's ninth-great-grandfather.

50 Thornton, op. cit.

51 Kemper, op. cit., p. 7 footnote

52 What is identified as "Michel's Map, 1707" in the Kemper article is mislabeled. It is Michel's 1704 map from his exploration that year of western Maryland and the Shenandoah Valley. The map was submitted in 1707 as part of the proposal to the British Lords of Trade and Plantations.

53 http://www.us-mining.com/virginia/front-royal/silver-mines

54 https://www.dmme.virginia.gov/DGMR/silver.shtml

55 The Michel family social rank of Edelvest, "noble and dependable," put the Michels among the top nineteen Swiss families. The Graffenried family social rank of

Vest, "dependable," put his family among the next sixteen Swiss families. The Edelvest rank, but not the Vest rank, was formally classified as nobility. This distinction might seem overwrought today but much socially hinged on it then. See the appendices here for a full list of Swiss gentry ranks of the era.

[56] Op. cit., https://gameo.org/index.php?title=Ritter,_George_ (17th/18th_centuries)

[57] Wenger, Samuel. *1710 Pequea Settlement Tour Resource Information Booklet*, Mennonite Historical Society, Lancaster, Pennsylvania, (undated), pp. 1-6

[58] They were Albrecht von Graffenried, Johann Anthoni Jarsing, Samuel Hopf and Emanuel Kilchberger. Albrecht von Graffenried was a cousin of the Christoph Graffenried of interest here. Albrecht died in 1711, the year after he became a New Berne investor.

[59] Guyer, Alan R. "The History and Mystery of the Pequea Silver Mines," *Pennsylvania Geology*, pp. 2-5, April 1976

[60] Op. cit., Mielke and Yelton, *Michel's Mysterious Mines*

[61] As of December 2021, the median asking price per acre of vacant land in and around New Bern North Carolina, was $10,150.

[62] Green, Fletcher. "Gold Mining in Ante-Bellum Virginia, *The Virginia Magazine of History and Biography*, Vol. 45, No. 4, October 1937, pp. 363, 366

[63] Blankenship. John. *Germanna History*, http://homepages.rootsweb.com/~george/johnsgermnotes/germhs21.html

[64] *North Carolina Colonial Records*, vol. 1, pp. 773-775.

[65] Graffenried, Christoph von. His journal written in French is held in the Bibliothèque Publique d'Yverdon-les-Bains at Yverdon, Switzerland.

[66] Mielke, op. cit., p. 73. Graffenried's marginal note did not state a date for his alleged disappearance of Frantz Ludwig Michel. The year 1720 was much later assigned

by scholars from their sequencing Graffenried's manuscripts.

[67] https://de.wikipedia.org/wiki/Schultheiss_von_Bern

[68] Christof and Emanuel's father Anton von Graffenried had served as Schultheiss (Mayor) of Berne from 1651 to 1674, and Anton's father, also Anton, from 1623 to 1628. As of January, 2022, the Mayor of Bern was Alec Graffenried.

[69] Mielke op. cit., pp. 60-61

[70] Ibid.

[71] Alderson, Carolyn, Certified Genealogist. Private communication, March 18, 2022

[72] Burns, Brendan, Certified Genealogist. Private communication, June 4, 2022

[73] Burns, Brendon S., Genealogist, *Frantz Ludwig Michel Project*, private research report to the author, August 20, 2022, p. 4

[74] In 1734, Wright then sells the 400 acres to William Hackney of Prince William County for 2,000 pounds of tobacco.

[75] The expedition takes its name from the souvenir miniature horseshoes that Spotswood gave to members of his party.

[76] Several historical accounts mistakenly refer to this expedition as the first by any Europeans into the valley. Spotswood himself would have known that Frantz Ludwig Michel had been the first in 1704.

[77] Research shows that wanderlust appears to be heritable. For example, the author has moved fifty-seven times.

[78] Orange County, Virginia Deeds 1: 267-269 [FHL 33,011]

[79] American Psychiatric Association. *Diagnostic and Statistical Manual of Mental Disorders, DSM-5*, 5th edition, 2022

80 Next in order are salespeople, surgeons, journalists, police, ministers, chefs and civil servants. As for the latter three, who would have guessed? Dutton found that sociopathy can cut both ways. On the nonsociopathic side—what Dutton calls empathetic—care aides, nurses and therapists are the least sociopathic professions, followed in order by craftsmen, beauticians, charity workers, artists, physicians other than surgeons, and accountants.

81 Late in the twentieth century, scholars parsed the several editions of Graffenried's memoires, determining that Graffenried had entered this notation in the margin while Michel was still alive. While it is possible that Graffenried may not have known that Michel was still alive, that makes the notation no less fabricated.

82 Graffenried, Christoph von, *Relation of My American Project,* op. cit.

83 Michael, Peter. *Running on Empty: Along an Epic 12,000-Mile Road Trip America Has Its Say on Economic Inequality,* op. cit.

84 https://vongraffenried.wordpress.com/2021/02/16/sad-ending-to-the-remarkable-christopher-von-graffenried/

85 Fogelman, Aaron. *Hopeful Journeys: German Immigration, Settlement, and Political Culture in Colonial America, 1717-1775,* University of Pennsylvania Press (illustrated edition), 1996

86 Spannaus, Edward, "Looking for our Palatine German Ancestors: A short trip to New York's Mohawk Valley" http://www.lovettsvillehistoricalsociety.org/?p=4776&preview=true

87 Faust, Albert. "Swiss Emigration to the American Colonies in the Eighteenth Century," *The American Historical Review*, vol. 22, no. 1, October, 1916, pp. 21- 44

88 https://en.wikipedia.org/wiki/Exploration_of_North_America

89 The home still exists as a prized historical site.

90 http://firstsettlersshenandoahvalley.com/index.html

91 Ibid., pp. 60-65

92 Michael family historian Margaret Hickman has Andreas Michel/Andrew Michael arriving in America at Philadelphia from Germany aboard the ship "Hero" on October 27, 1764. This would have been a different Andreas Michel than found by Mildred Michael Crewe on a 1757 ship manifest who landed at Annapolis. This difference only adds to the confusion over the true identity of the person who shows up in Frederick County, Maryland, civil and church records in 1762.

93 Three other Michels or Michaels show in county records of the era but are not indicated in Crewe's research to be related to the brothers. A Daniel Michael appears in Frederick County Court records as of 1759. In 1768 Lodowich (Ludwig) Michel bought a property from Joseph Smith. In 1773 Jacob Michel or Michael bought a property from Ann Dickson.

94 For example, in 1768 when he purchased his 340-acre tract, Andreas Michel paid 17 pounds sterling, 20 pounds per acre.

95 https://www.skystagefrederick.com

96 Crewe, Mildred Michael. *The Michael Family*, unpublished manuscript (undated but not later than 1952)

97 For more on President Hanson, see Michael, Peter, *Remembering John Hanson: A Biography of the First President of the Original United States Government*, Underground Railroad Free Press, 2012.

98 https://www.johnhansonmemorial.org/

99 Michael, Peter H. *Sixteen Michael Generations*, private manuscript in possession of the author

100 Ibid.

101 Pannabecker, Samuel. *Open Doors: A History of the General Conference of the Mennonite Church*, Faith and Life Press, 1975

102 Kraybill, Donald. *Anabaptist World USA,* (with C. Nelson Hostetter), Herald Press, 2001

103 Hedgpeth, Dana, "Unearthing Native American History on an Island in Southern Maryland," *The Washington Post,* November 9, 2022

104 Op. cit., Kraybill

105 Op. cit., Mielke and Yelton, *Michel's Mysterious Mines,* pp. 28-29

106 Ibid., pp. 61

107 On this date, the families wrote from London to Mennonite leaders in Amsterdam thanking them for assistance rendered. The families would have arrived in Philadelphia some time before September 23 when the second group of Mennonite settlers is known to have arrived.

108 https://www.axios.com/afghan-refugee-private-sponsorship-biden-ed9a2793-4482-42c0-8b73-aedf4cd9ce45.html?utm_source=newsletter&utm_medium=email&utm_campaign=newsletter_axiosam&stream=top

109 There is no known civil or church record of Frantz and Anna's marriage. The many Internet genealogy sites on Frantz or Anna show three dates for their marriage. One shows a wedding date of June 26, 1699 and the couple having 13 children, a few show 1695 without a date and the wedding taking place in Bavaria, but most show 1705 without date or place. Given the couple's ages, each of these dates is feasible, though thirteen children and Bavaria are far-fetched. As it is more likely that a couple of that era would have their first child sooner rather than later after marriage, this fits with the 1705 date. Also, if Anna was already living in Virginia when Frantz first arrived there in 1702, it is unlikely that they would have been married already.

110 Mildred Michael Crewe's *The Michael Family* is mentioned in C. E. Schildknecht's *Monocacy and Catoctin,* which was published in 1952, so her work came before this. See the bibliography here.

[111] Found at ancestry.com/genealogy/records/anna-barbara-vonlerber-24-121shbj

Printed in the USA
CPSIA information can be obtained
at www.ICGtesting.com
CBHW022152241024
16383CB00014B/29/J